COMPASSIONATE PRESENCE

Compassionate Presence

The Trinitarian Spirituality
of
ADRIENNE VON SPEYR

MATTHEW LEWIS SUTTON

Angelico Press

First published in the USA
by Angelico Press 2022
Copyright © 2022

All rights reserved:
No part of this book may be reproduced or transmitted,
in any form or by any means, without permission

For information, address:
Angelico Press, Ltd.
169 Monitor St.
Brooklyn, NY 11222
www.angelicopress.com

ppr   978-1-62138-868-5
cloth   978-1-62138-869-2
ebook   978-1-62138-870-8

Book and cover design
by Michael Schrauzer

With thanksgiving to all those who spread the compassion of God's abiding presence, I dedicate this work to my friends in Con-solatio, a Brooklyn-based Catholic non-profit organization, that runs an international volunteer program to almost two dozen different countries to serve those who are lonely, forgotten, disabled, sick, imprisoned, orphaned, or elderly. I especially want to thank Regine Fohrer, Diana Narballo, Mariana Canteros, Katie Kustusch, Fr. Paul Anel, Fr. Alex Morard, Laetitia Palluat de Besset, Natalia Fassano, Melanie Delesalle, Cécile Fourmeaux, Kari Stender, Katie Barrett, Marian West, Amy Koreski, and so many volunteers and friends of the mission.

There is one particular day in Western history
about which neither historical record nor myth
nor Scripture make report. It is a Saturday.
And it has become the longest of days... ours
is the long day's journey of the Saturday.
—George Steiner

I paint on black because painting is not representing
a light that is and that's all, but rather participating
in the light that is becoming out of the darkness.
—William Congdon

Where shall I go from your Spirit?
Or where shall I flee from your presence?
—Psalm 139:7

CONTENTS

PREFACE

THIS BOOK IS ABOUT COMPASSION—TRUE, authentic compassion. The book comes most immediately out of my involvement with a religious movement called Con-solatio which has implemented the spirituality of Adrienne von Speyr (1902–1967) and Catherine Doherty (1896–1985) to serve the poorest of the poor through offering their compassionate presence.[1]

My study of Adrienne von Speyr, who was a twentieth-century Catholic physician and mystic, has led me to think seriously about the meaning of the Christian belief in the descent of Christ into hell. In the ancient Apostle's Creed, the fourth line states that Jesus Christ "suffered under Pontius Pilate, was crucified, died, and was buried; he went down to the dead (*ad inferos—to hell*)."[2] For Speyr, Jesus's descent to hell has plunged his presence into our loneliness. Christ has brought to us his divine, compassionate, saving presence even here in hell.[3] Additionally, the teaching of Hans Urs von Balthasar, an important twentieth-century Catholic theologian who worked with Speyr and was influenced by her mysticism, has also prompted me to think deeply about the Trinitarian revelation accomplished in the descent of Christ into hell. God is always Trinity and always reveals his deepest mystery to us, but, for Balthasar, in the Father's seeming abandonment of the Son on the Cross and the Son's yielding up his Holy Spirit, we see most clearly the distinction of the Divine Persons who enact our redemption by bringing us into their eternal triune love.

Balthasar uses theater in constructive dialogue with theology—an approach that completely informs my theological view—to articulate

---

1 For more information about Con-solatio, see https://con-solatio.org and see Con-solatio Missionaries, *Come Abide: Con-solatio, a Ministry of Presence* (Brooklyn, NY: Angelico Press, 2021).

2 Jacques Dupuis and J. Neuner, eds, *The Christian Faith: In the Doctrinal Documents of the Catholic Church*, 7th ed. (New York: Alba House, 2001), n. 5. This creed becomes standard in the tenth century in Rome, but was used frequently in the Western Church much earlier. The creed of Rufinus (c. 404) contains the phrase and, of course, the pseudo-Athanasian Creed (*Quicumque*) contains the belief of Jesus Christ's descent to the underworld.

3 You can find my thorough engagement with her life and thought in my book, Matthew Lewis Sutton, *Heaven Opens: The Trinitarian Mysticism of Adrienne von Speyr* (Minneapolis, MN: Fortress Press, 2014).

this divine enrapturing of us.[4] On the stage, we see much of the human search for truth, goodness, and beauty, but also, we see the divine quest to answer our suffering, dying, and loneliness. By going to a play or a film, we express a desire to belong to something bigger than ourselves. Man has been touched by being on the stage or watching a narrative unfold. All of these theatrical dynamics, Christianity has in its fullness touched. Certainly, at times Christianity has ignored or condemned drama, but no longer. The theater must once again be adopted by Christians to do theology and once again evangelize the world through culture-making.[5] And Christianity's most dramatic moment is the descent of Jesus into hell. The collapse of the hero so often depicted on the stage is at the heart of Christianity. And this hero's death is not a three-minute interlude, but a three-day despair such that the disciples have given up hope for any redemption (Lk 24:21). They *had* hoped (indicative pluperfect). What drama, indeed, there is in this day of despair! But who do the disciples speak with? Jesus of the Nazareth, whom they will recognize in the breaking of the bread (Lk 24:35), is compassionately present with them even when they have lost their hope.

Whether you have read Adrienne von Speyr or Hans Urs von Balthasar does not matter. You see, what has also brought both of us into this encounter is the desire to make sense of man's loneliness and more specifically our own loneliness. In my life, I have experienced this type of loneliness and feeling of abandonment. Perhaps you have experienced similar loneliness. Maybe you are like me and have felt abandoned by God and others. I, and perhaps you, have experienced a deep, depressing loneliness. Even with those around us valiantly offering help, I, and perhaps you, have felt forsaken, abandoned, and left alone. We *had* hoped for redemption from our loneliness.

In an important article in the *New Yorker* called "Why Are So Many Americans Living by Themselves," Nathan Heller writes about the growing demographic shift toward living alone.[6] He

---

4 Hans Urs von Balthasar, *Theo-Drama: Theological Dramatic Theory*, 5 vols., trans. Graham Harrison (San Francisco: Ignatius Press, 1988–98).
5 Andy Crouch, *Culture Making: Recovering Our Creative Calling* (Downers Grove, IL: InterVarsity Press, 2008).
6 *The New Yorker* (April 16, 2012), accessed January 1, 2014, www.newyorker.

writes that protracted solitude has mostly been pitied throughout history, only chosen by a few spiritual ascetics (Benedict) or the most desperate of writers (Thoreau). However, through the research of Eric Klinenberg, a professor and sociologist at New York University, we can see in American society and other societies that living in solitude is a chosen lifestyle with growing appeal. In his book *Going Solo: The Extraordinary Rise and Surprising Appeal of Living Alone*, he documents this trend toward willed loneliness. Heller comments: "Women's liberation, widespread urbanization, communications technology, and increased longevity—these four trends lend our era its cultural contours, and each gives rise to solo living."[7] Klinenberg sees in these men and women not sad lonely people, but those who choose to live a new life of the "cult of the individual" in which the complications of living with another person can be overcome by not living with another person. Maybe some of us could see in this choice selfish motivations (living alone gives you more control over your own life), but Klinenberg and other scholars see in this trend a liberation from the social mores of previous generations that defined fulfillment in terms of who you were married to or with whom you were living. Additional books, like the classic *Bowling Alone* (2000) and *Alone Together: Why We Expect More from Technology and Less from Each Other* (2011), also make the case that more people are choosing to live alone to be alone.[8]

Because of the COVID-19 pandemic, our societies, governments, and relationships have forced an emergency, social-distancing isolation. The ramifications of almost two years of extensive societal distancing mandated in workplaces, schools, cultural events, and family lives will be long-lasting. From the many who have died alone to the many young people disconnected from their school and social life, this pandemic has only made solitude even more widespread and deeply ingrained in our societies. We should be

com/magazine/2012/04/16/the-disconnect. The article is a review of Eric Klinenberg, *Going Solo: The Extraordinary Rise and Surprising Appeal of Living Alone* (New York: Penguin, 2012).

7 Ibid.

8 R. D. Putnam, *Bowling Alone: The Collapse and Revival of American Community* (New York: Simon & Schuster, 2000) and Sherry Turkle, *Alone Together: Why We Expect More from Technology and Less from Each Other* (New York: Basic Books, 2011).

moved by the heroic actions of health care workers and scientists. We also need to acknowledge the cultural fear of others that was spread through divisive policitial discourse.

A desire to make sense of this arranged or forced isolation brings me to writing this book. Perhaps it has brought you to this book too. If you receive any consolation through this book, please know that it has come to you by the grace of God who alone has descended into your loneliness and offered his compassionate, redeeming presence. I call this a theology of compassion or a theology of Holy Saturday—the liturgical day between Good Friday and Easter Sunday on which is remembered the descent of the Son to the dead.

I believe that God alone has loved us to the utmost extent and God alone can save us from our loneliness by his compassionate presence.

Through these eleven chapters I intend to make a complete sketch of a compassionate theology of Holy Saturday in which one theological moment will be used to interpret the most important aspects of Christianity. I hope that this theology makes Christianity relevant to you. Or, put differently, I hope you will come to know the compassionate presence of Jesus Christ in your life.

When I think about the nodal point of systematizing the dogma of Catholic faith it must be the mystery of Holy Saturday. The point could be summarized clearly:

> *Through his extreme kenosis (self-emptying), the Son's descent into hell has overtaken all that disobeys God and within this disobedience he has given his obediential love to the Father through the Holy Spirit, as their mutual love, in order to bring all into their self-offering triune love.*

When we come to think and pray deeply about the revelation of Jesus Christ's descent to the dead for three days, we see that these days of darkness are the point of his mission. After this nodal point, everything becomes ascent for him, for us, and for the world. The light has gone into the darkness and the darkness has not overcome it (Jn 1:5). The darkness is not just the world, it is also death and hell. The light has gone even there into the dark absence of Godforsakenness and manifested its radiant presence. For me, Christian theology is that simple and profound.

The first chapter will provide a foundational point of reasoning for engaging in a theology of Holy Saturday, especially in reference to the shifting philosophical world of postmodernism and its new importance for Christian thought. The second, third, and fourth chapters will take us through what is revealed about each Person of the Trinity in light of the descent of the Son into hell. In these chapters, we will see the compelling aspects of a Trinitarian theology of compassion. The fifth chapter will consider man in light of the revelation of the Son's descent to the dead. We will think about how the loneliness of man is answered by the God-forsakenness of the Son. The sixth chapter will provide a sketch of an ecclesiology that takes seriously the Trinitarian revelation of God in the event of Holy Saturday and will also apply this theological perspective to the sacraments. The seventh chapter will demonstrate that Mary, the Mother of God, participates uniquely in the descent of the Son through her compassion for her child. She becomes then the model of the compassionate Christian who must sinlessly suffer with humanity, offering presence as the answer. The eighth chapter will propose Beauty as a balm to the alienation of modern and postmodern man. We will then think about how a theology of Holy Saturday is already present in works of art—iconography, sculpture, drama, music—whether they be explicitly Christian or not. The ninth chapter examines time, eternity, and suffering in light of the three days of the Son's Godforsakenness. The tenth chapter will offer a theology of prayer in light of the Holy Saturday mystery as we think about one of the last words of Christ on the Cross, "My God, my God, why have you forsaken me?" (Mk 15:34). The last and final chapter will attempt to consolidate all that has been learned by an intense focus on Psalm 51, "Have mercy on me, O God, according to your compassionate love."

May this book be a sign of compassion in the darkness of loneliness for you as you read it as it has been for me as I wrote it.

I
Compassion

COMPASSION IS THE WORD THAT WILL BE credible in this postmodern age of loneliness. The philosophical school of existentialism confronted the Western world with the strong life-changing statement that there is no intrinsic meaning to life and therefore it is up to us to create meaning. And yet, this hallowed courageous call could not survive the chaotic winds of suffering and it was soon blown apart. In the history of philosophical thought, existentialism will be seen as yet another attempt to construct a meta-narrative. In the present climate of postmodernism, no call for courage can be found because there is no reason (universal or particular) to be courageous. We have seen that Paul Tillich's *Courage to Be* cannot rescue existentialism, even its Christian variations. According to the many strands of postmodernism, yes, there is no meaning in the world and also yes, there is no reason to construct one. All alone is all we are.

What I like about postmodernism is that it follows through to the end of nihilism. The postmodernist deconstructs not in an attempt to reconstruct a new foundation—that would be inconsistently foolish. No, he deconstructs to deconstruct. Any more building must be greeted with irony and maybe a little appetite for the deconstruction that will come later. Everything becomes criticism and any attempt to reconstruct in the face of this criticism will surely be judged as naïve, pointless, shortsighted, unsophisticated, inexperienced, childish, or starry-eyed. The postmodern aim is to have no construction and only long lists of the critique's deconstructed bits of previous buildings. Maybe I'm stating it all oversimply, but postmodernism in its various manifestations cannot stand a building for long.

Undaunted, I begin a new construction with compassion as our first word. Even though postmodernists will deconstruct this from the start, we must remember that postmodernists are humans and humans desire compassion. And so I have another construction— the human person's desire. Yes, there is an anthropology here.

We could observe phenomenologically the desire of man across cultures and see universally that man desires love. It can be seen in the cry of a newborn, the angst of a teenager scorned by her parents, the sorrow of a young widower, and in the eyes of an elderly person about to die alone. Yes, man desires compassion. Therefore, we could begin to think about the word compassion phenomenologically. But there is another path, a better path. The quicker route is the one preferred.

Compassion shall be the first word because God is love. We will begin with God because in the end, God is our beginning and in the beginning we must remember God is our end. God is the Alpha and Omega of our world and of our lives. And the meaning of our lives constructed by God will be found in the word compassion.

When we allow the God of Jesus Christ to reveal who he says he is, we will see that God's eternal beginning (outside creation) is overabundant compassion. God's divine being is always already love. The Father takes his activity, that is, being divine love, and gives that being divine love to the Son, who receives this being divine love, and offers it back to the Father, from which activity proceeds the Holy Spirit, who from the Father through the Son is always already their shared love.

From the Trinity who is love, we begin our path toward understanding compassion—toward understanding why the beginning and the end of man is compassion. In the end, it will be this theology of compassion that will be credible within this postmodern age.

The credibility of God's compassionate presence alone has a double meaning. First, if we think about man in the postmodern context, we will see that there is a strong sense that man is always alone. Our various language games and our society are structured to alleviate this loneliness, but in truth, we are still lonely. Christianity offers this world of loneliness a belief in a God who took within himself this loneliness. When he was lifted on the Cross, God let himself experience Godforsakenness ("My God, my God, why have you forsaken me?" the Son asks the Father). When the Son descends to the dead for three days he experiences the deepest loneliness. In this solitary confinement of hell, the Son is alone. God is alone. The weight of this loneliness has been neglected in

Christian thought, but in this book you will see that God alone will not be forgotten. It may be the surest way to communicate to the postmodern world the love God has for us. God experienced this loneliness and within this experience God offers his compassion. He entered our loneliness to suffer with us. That is the first meaning of God alone.

The second meaning is that our postmodern lives have offered every kind of thing and relationship to fill the hole of our loneliness, but as we will see in the many stories offered in this book, God alone can fill our loneliness. If we are hungry to death, bread alone can feed our hunger. If we are thirsty to death, water alone can quench our thirst. But man does not live by bread and water alone (Deut 8:3; cf. Mt 4:4, Lk 4:4). After one's hunger and thirst are sated, what remains? A desire for a relationship? If one is lonely, a spouse alone can fill that desire. After this desire is filled, what is desired next? Maybe a child? After this child has grown up, what is desired next? Still loneliness continues. It has been postponed when one is in a fruitful relationship, but all of this can disappear, unwind, or collapse. The true hunger for eternal relationship demands some kind of final, definitive relation of love. The compassionate presence of God alone can fill this eternal hunger.

The story of the Samaritan woman can help us understand. In the Gospel of John, a woman of Samaria came to draw water at Jacob's well (Jn 4:7). Jesus was there and asked her to give him a drink. An exchange about the impossibility of this question begins, but ends quickly when Jesus changes the conversation to talking about "living water" (Jn 4:10). This water welling up from Jesus himself satiates eternally. The woman responds, "Sir, give me this water, that I may not thirst" (Jn 10:15). Jesus then turns the conversation to the many men that the woman has used to fill this eternal thirst. Every attempt to fill this thirst with relationships has failed her. Having acknowledged that her real thirst is for the Messiah, the one man that can give her heart what it truly desires, she leaves behind her water jar in her haste to share the joy of experiencing God alone (Jn 4:28–29). She comes to know God alone is her only true love because in Jesus this God has come by himself alone to the well asking for a drink. Everyone else abandoned her, except Jesus, and he has come to the well thirsty to meet this woman who is thirsty. God alone is thirsty for the thirsty. We could put it another way: Jesus who experienced true thirst is the one who is able to offer true water. It is because Jesus is thirsty (alone) that he goes to the well and in this thirst he alone offers what satiates the woman from Samaria. God lets himself experience our loneliness and in this God reveals his compassion. We are then able to recognize that God alone can fill our loneliness. It is he alone that we desire.

In Psalm 62, we sing "For God alone my soul waits in silence" (Ps 62:1a). The soul of postmodern man waits in silence for God alone. In postmodernism we finally have the philosophical acknowledgment that nothing human gives definitive, universal, meta-narrative meaning. Postmodern man waits in silence because all human words have proved vacuous. As you read this book, you will see—and I hope you will come to believe—that it is for God alone that your soul in postmodern silence waits. It is he who will experience this silence to its utmost extent, who will alone speak the words you long to hear—"You are loved." The Psalm continues, "Trust in him at all times, O people" (Ps 62:8a). If God alone is our only meaning, then we will be able to trust in him at all times because "God is a refuge for us" (Ps 62:8b). He alone will compassionately comfort us. No matter one's class (Ps 62:9), no matter one's acquired power (Ps 62:10), to God alone "belongs steadfast love" (Ps 62:12). Everything else will fall short except for the compassion of God.

Compassion shall be our first word because God is love and man desires this love. Our beginning comes out of this Alpha love and our ending comes to conclusion in this Omega love. Because God has descended to our loneliness, we are rescued by his compassion.

Let's consider the postmodern need to see in Christianity not something foreign, but something central to its philosophical thought. Both postmodernism and Christianity believe man is alone; that is where they can meet and speak to each other.

In order to understand postmodernism, let's think about modernism. We could begin with René Descartes (d. 1650). He was a great philosopher reassembling Christian thought based upon a novel authority—human reasoning alone. The Church's foundations rest upon Scripture and Tradition. The formula established by the Council of Trent confirmed what had been the assumptions of the previous Christian ages. How do we come to know God? Through Jesus Christ. How do we come to know Jesus Christ?

Through his Church in its written and oral tradition. The Protestant Reformation, of course, critiqued this double source as one coming from God and the other from man. Martin Luther, preferring the words of God (*sola Scriptura*), narrowed the field of sources for coming to know Jesus Christ. René Descartes wanted to reconstruct Christian thought on neither the written nor the oral tradition, but on the one thing that one can trust—one's own reason. A good mathematician like Descartes doesn't just inherit a previous generation's theorems, he seeks to prove them again. Doubt and test; doubt and test. And so Descartes began Christianity again, not from Scripture, Tradition, or even revelation, which he considered unreliable, but from reason alone.

And now we can talk about Immanuel Kant (1804). A good start for exploring his thought, specifically as it relates to Christianity, is his book *Religion within the Limits of Reason Alone*.[1] Here, rather than reconstructing Christian thought upon one's reason as Descartes had done, Kant critiques Christianity based upon whether it is reasonable or not. Doubting and testing Christianity for Kant means doing away with the unthinkable parts like the miracles, the Resurrection, and the Trinity. For Kant, if it is unreasonable it should be unbelievable. Kant's Christianity becomes a man-made construction consisting mostly of proper morality based upon the categorical imperative (that behavior should be determined by duty) which, we could say, is his version of the golden rule, a golden rule so idealistic it becomes impossible. This Enlightenment view of religion has dominated modern life and it will continue to do so. Much of the New Atheism is just a rehashing of the Kantian critique of religion.

This leads us to postmodernism. If modernism constructed a successful new building of meaning based upon human reason, the postmodernists say, then all would be well. But, the postmodernist asks, what about the conflict between the reasoning of different humans? If human thought should be consistent as a method for arriving at universal truth, then seemingly there should be no major conflicts of thought between philosophical truth systems properly employing human reason. And so the conclusion must be that the method is flawed from the beginning. Friedrich Nietzsche

---

1 Immanuel Kant, *Religion Within the Limits of Reason Alone*, trans. Theodore M. Greene and Hoyt H. Hudson (New York: Harper, 1960).

(d. 1900), a precursor to postmodernism, sees the destruction of the modern age early and clearly. The twilight of the gods and men is at hand. Postmodernism is the darkness after this twilight.

Postmodernism, which has many beginnings and founders, drops the testing and desire for new knowledge. Doubt alone remains. Perpetual doubt (and the irony of that) alone is credible. A person's opinion remains just that, his opinion. Perhaps this opinion is arrived at through consistent application of human reason, but it remains an opinion and not constructible knowledge. For postmodernism, all knowledge already begins with a priori assumptions that destroy the universality of its claim. It may be knowledge for one man or maybe even his parochial community, but no knowledge will ever be universal knowledge.

In this sense, postmodernism and Christianity agree. The Tower of Babel had to be destroyed. It was a man-made construction that could never reach the heavens. Postmodernism will continue to critique every construction and Christianity will continue to say with the Psalmist, "Unless the Lord builds the house, those who build it labor in vain" (Ps 127:1).

Religion, typically understood as a creedal community making universalist claims, cannot survive in a strict postmodern context. For the postmodern, the Nicene Creed, written over seventeen hundred years ago in a Greco-Roman context by political and ecclesial powers, cannot have any current validity. The new heaven and new earth desired by Christianity are just fantasy constructions of the ideal city. Only those non-creedal, highly relativistic forms of religion can continue in a thoroughly postmodern world.

One way to understand postmodernism would be to consider the figure of Pontius Pilate who is *the* postmodern figure sympathetically caught between his worldly governing position and his wife's spiritual dream. This is his question to the savior of the world: "'What is truth?'" (Jn 18:38). According to postmodernism no answer exists to this judgment against meta-narrative truth. As the prominent postmodernist Jacques Derrida (d. 2004) argued, truth can have no universally normative meaning because it is tied up in texts that are constantly shifting and can be interpreted necessarily in any number of ways.

Another thing that postmodernism breeds is radical individualism. If no one can present an idea of truth that can overcome your own, then you are free to construct your own meaning of reality as long as you realize that you cannot impose that on anyone else. And so we are at the dead end of postmodernism: the remnant of philosophy in which no truth is universal, no knowledge can claim meta-narrative status. Modernism aimed to construct something universally valid; for postmodernism, the constructing is over. There is no universal human nature, no universal understanding of sexual difference, and certainly no universal religion. All is relative and even that statement is relative.

Accordingly, you and I can never communicate knowledge that might be valid and grow our community of relationship. We could temporarily agree, but that would be just self-deception for some kind of temporary power game. In the end, we will never be able to agree. We will never be able to see for each other what is truth, what is reality. Even though we may pretend we are speaking about the same reality, there will always be someone else who will never be able to accept that understanding of reality. All is relative.

That being the case, all are alone. We are perpetually alone and strangers to each other, even to ourselves. You and I may pretend that we know each other and agree with each other and love each other. But again we deceive ourselves. It will not take long to deconstruct our relationship into loneliness again. Why seek a relationship founded on universally accepted truth? Why not just accept relationships for what they are—temporary agreements based on temporary truths that are temporarily valid only to the parties involved? How many times have you thought you were in love and you really were not? Even if you think you are in love now, how do you really know? And so continues postmodernism's deconstruction of everything sacred or profane. Postmodernism will collapse us all into what we instinctively already know—we are alone and that's all we are.

Instead of hope, courage, compassion, love, or truth, postmodernism offers perpetual strangeness to each other and even to one's self. But at least it is honest. Without God, you cannot create an Enlightenment Shangri-La or even a Platonic Atlantis. Unless God builds it, it will not last. Postmoderns and Christians can agree here, but postmodernists believe there is no God while Christians believe that the Lord is our God.

Deus ex machina

For postmodernism, religion is one of many man-made constructions that continue to perpetuate a community-constructed false exit from perpetual loneliness. For postmodernism, the Christian God above all is yet another *deus ex machina*. Just at the end, when everything is finally desperate, behold, some divine force from outside the system intervenes in the narrative of humanity saving those who believe. The postmodernist would say this God is pious drivel.

Does Christianity propose a *deus ex machina*? If it does, the implication is that it is just a literary device to create meaning and a happy ending when otherwise there would be none. If Christianity does think of itself like this, well, I could understand the objections. I would object too! A God suddenly intruding in the narrative as if produced by a machine would be a man-made construction.

Is Meaning Possible?

Let me make a case for meaning-making. The idea I want to give to you is an idea from Adrienne von Speyr, "Things have meaning only to the extent that they lead to God, come from him and can be placed at his service."[2]

What is at stake in this statement is the agreement that yes, postmodernism negates the possibility of meaning-making universally. If anything, meaning can be generated for a particular community for a particular time, but not universally so for all humanity across all times. Speyr is in agreement with postmodernism to a point. There is no universally valid human truth at least as it is generated by humans for each other. Man's word will always remain subjective. The only universally objective truth is God's alone in as much as truth comes from him and can be placed at his service.

The response to the suffering of others and to ourselves will be determined decisively by this statement that the origin and end of all meaning is only in God. The process of meaning-making will have no final validity if it does not come from Christ as the finally valid concrete universal.

2 Adrienne von Speyr, *Mystery of Death*, trans. Graham Harrison (San Francisco: Ignatius Press, 1988), 47.

This perspective on meaning-making will be prominent in our approach to suffering so it will be central to our contemplation and discernment concerning how to overcome human loneliness.

For the postmodern, there is no meaning to suffering. The only response is empathy and societal or technological transformation to end suffering. But let's enter into this question of suffering further. What is human suffering? For the Christian, human suffering is destitution of one's personhood (kenosis). Man can withstand much physical, psychic, chronic, and even social suffering, but what is the most difficult suffering for the human person? It is loneliness felt as destitution of one's personhood. The squashing, the removing of the inherent dignity of one's personhood from its development with meaning-making relationships digs into the humanness of being human to such an extent that this destitution of one's self through non-relation compromises everything about being human. Excepting capital punishment, the worst punishment contemporary societies give to prison inmates is solitary confinement. When we want to inflict the severest suffering on a criminal, we cast him into the pit of the solitary. This of course happens outside of prison, too. When as a society we degrade others' dignity we remove them from meaning-making relations. We send them into solitary confinement. We do this when we marginalize the homeless, the drug addict, the mentally handicapped, the deranged, the elderly, and the unborn.

What would be God's relationship to suffering? Does God suffer like this? Of course, the traditional belief about the suffering of God would be that God cannot suffer by definition: his nature is perfectly complete. We will see in the next chapters that a robust Trinitarian theology of the relation of the Divine Persons will help us see through the divine monad philosophical God of the Greeks to a thoroughly Christian view of the triune God who suffers with us and for us.

The Christian view of God is that the Father eternally generates the Son and together they eternally co-spirate the Holy Spirit. Put another way, the Father perpetually divests himself of the divine nature such that he generates another Divine Person, the Son. Together, the Father and the Son perpetually divest themselves of their divine nature such that they co-spirate the Holy Spirit. For divest, we could use the words kenosis, emptying oneself, or making oneself destitute. For the Divine Person to be a Person, analogically speaking, the Person perpetually empties himself in order that the other Divine Persons may exist. This sort of super-kenosis should be the heart of any contemporary orthodox Trinitarian theology.

We must take seriously that the Cross has become the symbol of Christianity because it articulates our Christian view of God. Put another way, the only vantage point for fully accepting the revelation of the Christian God is through the Cross of Jesus Christ who on the Cross as Son was abandoned, if only seemingly, for three days, and who also surrendered the Holy Spirit, if only for three days. If we take seriously that God, the triune God is on the Cross, we can see how kenosis as self-emptying can be a concept for interpretation of our God.

Here on the Cross, the Son of God experiences Godforsakenness, a sort of non-relational abyss, as he cries out "My God, my God, why have you forsaken me?" (Mk 15:34). The relations of the Divine Persons are expressed to their utmost extent and can be more clearly distinguished. It is no mistake that Mark's gospel contains the centurion's act of faith after Jesus died. Now the centurion can believe that "Truly this man was the Son of God" (Mk 15:39).

The death of Jesus Christ continues for three days. The meaning of death is revealed here, but also the confirmation that even in Sheol, God has shared his presence as the Psalm articulates so clearly, "Where shall I go from your Spirit? Or where shall I flee from your presence? If I ascend to heaven, you are there! If I make my bed in Sheol, you are there!" (Ps 139:7–8).

The first observation on the meaning of suffering must be that God suffers on the Cross and in death. Now let's go back to the question: Is there meaning to suffering? Once again, according to Speyr, "Things have meaning only to the extent that they lead to God, come from him and can be placed at his service."[3] In as much as our meaning-making leads to him, comes from him, or can be used in his service, then yes.

Speyr continues to clarify her statement by saying that, "if a person seriously tries to locate all meaning in God, while he will become far more aware of his limitations, he will continually be meeting realities unfamiliar to ordinary life, things that have

3 Ibid.

their life in God and cannot be reached by reasoning but only by prayer."[4] So for Speyr, prayer can discern meaning because in authentic prayer one receives God himself. For Adrienne von Speyr, "All meaning resides in God. Without him everything would literally be meaningless."[5]

One of the aspects of suffering is that it forces us all the way into the pain of our profound limitations. When we suffer we have no other choice but to become dependent. A very little child will not question this dependence but as one grows older, depending on one's culture, the dependence upon others might be viewed as inhuman. However, the reality is that man is entirely dependent. We can never be independent. Acute suffering (immediate and chronic) makes this fact painfully obvious and shatters all attempts at pure individualistic autonomy. The praise of pluralism, collaboration, and communal meaning-making is rightly celebrated by postmodernism as attempts to correct the overly-optimistic enlightenment view of the pure rational individual as the pinnacle of human progress.

Our mission to serve those who suffer must somehow involve making meaning of suffering. Speyr's claim that meaning can only be found in that which "lead[s] to God, come[s] from him and can be placed at his service" must be central to our project.[6]

The theologian David Tracy has said that the modern period was a turn to the self. He means that philosophers like René Descartes or Immanuel Kant promote the rational mind of man as the arbiter of truth, goodness, and beauty. Rather than Scripture or Tradition, the rational mind properly executing logical thinking establishes the rightness of a thing. The anthropological turn to the self was a dramatic turn in Western philosophy, only superseded by the new turn of postmodernism. The postmodern period, however, should be conceived as a "turn to the other."[7] My question is then, what if that other calls me a stranger, a foreigner, or an exile? In a pluralistic society, we can often choose to be a foreigner. When we move to another country or to another culture, we are recognized and we recognize ourselves as foreigners.

Postmodern thought emphasizes the strangeness of being foreign. Being "other" than the dominant culture sometimes forces

---

4 Ibid., 48.   5 Ibid.   6 Ibid., 47.
7 David Tracy, "The Hidden God: The Divine Other of Liberation," *Cross Currents* 46 (1996): 5–7: "The real face of our period ... is the face of the other."

one to consider oneself foreign and strange to one's self. As our cultures become more pluralistic, we can find ourselves more foreign, more strange than everyone else. Someone somewhere considers you as other, foreign, and strange. Maybe that means we are all exiles. This idea certainly finds acceptance within postmodernism, but is also strikingly similar to the Christian worldview of man.

The Christian would agree with this view to a point. Yes, we are exiles, but we are being called home. It is worth considering this view further. Let's take the postmodern psychoanalyst Julia Kristeva's theory of the other as foreigner or exile.[8] I will then juxtapose that idea with Adrienne von Speyr's, of exiles being called home to the Father.

For Kristeva in particular, "Nowhere is one more a foreigner than in France."[9] She explored this idea in a work called *Strangers to Ourselves* in which she meditates on the psychological, historical, and spiritual meaning of being a foreigner, an other, and an exile. In this work, she argued that, while postmodernism frowns on universals, it is nevertheless universal that ultimately we are all exiles and even strangers to ourselves.

Kristeva first argues that we come to consciousness of ourselves as strangers when difference arises.[10] We have the uneasy feeling that we are in "perpetual transience."[11] As exiles, a search for belonging is always one step ahead: "according to the utmost logic of exile, all aims should waste away and self-destruct in the wanderer's insane stride toward an elsewhere that is always pushed back, unfulfilled, out of reach."[12] We are accustomed to the animosity and annoyance of the other saying to us, "this is not where you belong!"[13] These thoughts are entirely too common, especially if one lives in a foreign country.

According to Kristeva, no harbor of one's homeland can be found. Even in one's family, she thinks, we are viewed as other, even as orphan. There is a natural process of becoming an orphan

---

8 Julia Kristeva (1941–) is a Bulgarian who chose to live in France as a psychoanalyst and is now a professor at the University of Paris Diderot. She often talks about herself being in a common situation with those who have chosen to live in a foreign country. You always know that you will be considered a foreigner no matter how much you choose to assimilate.

9 Julia Kristeva, *Strangers to Ourselves*, trans. Leon S. Roudiez (New York: Columbia University Press, 1991).

10 Ibid., 7.   11 Ibid., 4.   12 Ibid., 6.   13 Ibid.

as we progress from the womb, to the breast, to school, to friends outside the home, to the driver's license, to college, to relocation for work, to marriage, and finally, definitively at the mother's death. Kristeva understands this progress of exile from the womb of the mother to the tomb of the mother as the unavoidable orphaning: "Eventually, though, the time of orphanhood comes about."[14] Even in the family, one eventually feels permanantly unsatisfied, always belonging elsewhere and yet nowhere, forever an exile.[15] Perhaps there are times in our lives that we experience a meaningful encounter with someone as a sort of "crossroad of two othernesses," but the practice of modern life necessitates a constant succession of desired, definitive meetings that never occur.[16] According to Kristeva, we remain permanently orphans, foreigners, and exiles. Even if one is a native, there are these suspicious self-reflections: "Am I really at home? Am I myself? Are they not the masters of the 'future'?"[17] Are we so convinced that we are natural citizens? But who is not these days a hyphenated citizen (Caucasian-American, African-American, Hispanic-American, Hmong-American)?[18] Even though we convince ourselves that we are Native Americans, do we not reserve that title to another group who feel themselves exiled from their homeland onto reservations?

No matter which country, Kristeva says, the native will eventually feel himself "to be more or less a 'foreigner' in his own and proper place."[19] The only universal feeling is that of being a foreigner, an exile: "The foreigner is within me, hence we are all foreigners. If I am a foreigner, there are no foreigners."[20] With this knowledge, we should not deceive ourselves: "Foreigners of the world, unite? Things are not so simple."[21] Kristeva in her postmodern way does not offer the way out of being foreigners and exiles. The question should no longer be "welcoming the foreigner within a system that obliterates him," but instead should be reconceiving society such that it promotes "the togetherness of those foreigners that we all recognize ourselves to be."[22] There are no exits out of perpetual exile. The status of being always in exile, she believes, was discovered by Freud, in that he believed that exilic existence (*unheimlich*) is set so clearly "within us in its

---

14 Ibid., 21.   15 Ibid., 21.   16 Ibid., 10–11.   17 Ibid., 20.
18 Ibid., 19.   19 Ibid.   20 Ibid., 192.   21 Ibid., 24.
22 Ibid., 2.

most bewildering shape" that it becomes "the ultimate condition of our being with others."[23] We only know each other as other. We will only come to know ourselves in as much as we acknowledge our own otherness and the otherness of others.

Here, I think, is a connection point between postmodernism and Christianity. The Christian reading of the Bible forms a narrative of an exiled people chosen in covenant through the Son in the Holy Spirit to return home to the Father.[24]

The exilic existence comes out of a biblical and Trinitarian metaphor for Christians. It is an attempt to give an account of faith in Christ to those who know themselves as foreigners. It comes out of Israel's history of being chosen by God out of a time of slavery in Egypt and Babylon. These two foundational events of being chosen while in exile forms much of the Old Testament understanding of God, covenant, and redemption. The New Testament too is dominated by Jesus Christ, the ultimate exile, who is redeemed by the Father out of the world, out of hell, and returned to the right hand of the Father where all authority in heaven and on earth has been given to him (Mt 28:18). Let us contemplate this idea in light of the thought of Adrienne von Speyr, particularly as expressed in her books *The Countenance of the Father* and *Confession*.[25]

---

23 Ibid., 192.

24 See David Coffey's "return" model of the Trinity in *Deus Trinitas: The Doctrine of the Triune God* (New York: Oxford University Press, 1999) and *Grace: The Gift of the Holy Spirit* (Sydney, Australia: Catholic Institute of Sydney, 1979).

25 Adrienne von Speyr, *The Countenance of the Father*, trans. David Kipp (San Francisco: Ignatius Press, 1997) and *Confession*, trans. Douglas W. Stott (San Francisco: Ignatius Press, 1985). The two works engaged here were dictated and belong to her thematic works. Published in 1955 with a second edition in 1981, the first is *The Countenance of the Father*. It is considered a minor thematic work on the Father and his relation to the Son and creation beginning from before creation to the Eschaton. It is a small but intense work that reveals a central thread of Speyr's works, namely, the inner Trinitarian relations as relations of eternal love. The second work is *Confession*, which is one of her essential major thematic books, first published in 1960. This book is a deep mediation on the confessional attitude and the Sacrament of Confession. All her works are tied up with the attitude of confession in its personal and ecclesial-sacramental relation of God with the sinner. What is enormously fruitful in this work is that the confessional attitude is seen as revealed in the Son's relationship to the Father in the Holy Spirit, not only on the Cross, but also in—and because of—the inner life of the Trinity.

The narration of salvation history begins with the creation of everything, "the heavens and the earth" (Gen 1:1b). All creation and all concepts only find their ultimate meaning in their origin in God. Even within the Trinity, the relations of the Son and the Holy Spirit find their eternal origin in the inaccessibility of the Father.[26] The first chapter climaxes with the creation of the male and female in God's image and likeness (Gen 1:26): "But scarcely has God articulated the goodness of the world, observed its full correspondence to his will, when man falls away from his proper relationship. He no longer wants to remain within it, no longer wants to obey."[27]

Not long after the creation of paradise and of the right relation of humanity with God and with each other, Adam and Eve are exiled from the paradisal existence because of their disobedience: "He drove out the man" (Gen 3:24a). Adam and Eve now experience the strange feeling that they are not where they are supposed to be. The foundational relationship with God and with each other has been ruptured. The story of humanity's primordial state, according to Genesis, is one of exile. It continues in the story of Cain and Abel in which the Lord justly condemns Cain to being "a fugitive and a wanderer on the earth" (Gen 4:12b).

The Pentateuch is a story of Israel formed in exile. After the foolish construction of the Tower of Babel, the Lord multiplies the one language and scatters humanity "abroad over the face of all the earth" (Gen 11:9). God calls Abram in the land of Ur to be an exile from "your country and your kindred and your father's house to a land that I will show you" (Gen 12:1b). The book of Exodus is the story of the chosen people exiled in a foreign land. The Pentateuch ends with its main character as archetype, Moses, remaining in exile. God lets him see the land, "but you shall not go over there" (Deut 34:4) and he dies in the land of Moab.

It will only be in the historical books that Israel returns home. In the Pentateuch, the foundational canon within a canon of the Old Testament, man and society are fugitives, exiles, and wanderers.

As the story moves to the historical books, God's chosen people are trying to rid the homeland of the many foreigners and their influence. It is rare that there is a time when the foreignness of others or Israel's own foreignness is not the driving conflict

---

26 Speyr, *Father*, 9.　　　　27 Ibid., 25.

of the plot. There is campaign after campaign to annihilate the
foreigners. Nevertheless, there are stories like that of Ruth the
Moabite being brought into the covenant. At one point, she falls
to the ground crying before Boaz, "Why have I found favor in your
eyes, that you should take notice of me, when I am a foreigner?"
(Ruth 2:10). Here we have God's acceptance of the radically other,
the outsider, the foreigner. Even the lineages of Matthew and
Luke reveal King David and the Son of Man having Ruth as their
ancestor. The great king has the blood of a foreigner.

Never does the theme of being a foreigner, an exile, appear more
than in the time of the Babylonian captivity. Another nation conquers and enslaves the chosen people to the hell of subjugation. The
great first temple of Solomon lies in ruin. The former greatness
of David's realm lies in rubble crushed under Babylonian boots.
In the hell of slavery, the exiled Jews must prove in Babylon their
commitment to the covenant. The prophet Daniel has his name
stripped away and is called Belteshazzar. He is taught to speak
like a Chaldean, and finally is given the foreign, forbidden food of
the Babylonians. Will Belteshazzar assimilate or will he experience
the loneliness of being a foreigner? We read that "Daniel resolved
that he would not defile himself" (Dan 1:8a). He chose to remain
the foreigner in exile, faithful to God alone in the hellishness of
a godless land. God will reward this covenant faithfulness, this
hesed, but not until after the lions have walked circles around his
appetizing flesh. Only his covenant faithfulness protects him in
this valley of death. And what remarkable miracles happen because
of his faithfulness: the foreign king, Nebuchadnezzar, comes to
believe in the one true God. The Jews in exile are refined by the
furnace of being a foreigner. The groundwork is laid for the great
scribe Ezra to lead the spiritual renewal of the Jews who return
to Jerusalem.

Even though Ezra and Nehemiah will lead "the people gathered
as one man to Jerusalem" (Ezra 3:1b), their restored kingdom is a
temporary rest because ever since the expulsion from paradise, the
people of Abraham, Isaac, and Jacob have never felt finally at home.[28]

God will not forever abandon his people in exile. Through
faith we believe that the Father sent his Son into the world to
become flesh, to become that which is foreign to God who is

28 Ibid., 49.

Spirit. That which the Son is not as God, he has become as man. Divinity has chosen to cross the border to be an exiled foreigner in the Babylon of humanity. In this way, God takes the otherness of humanity into his own self, becoming a stranger to himself because the Incarnation is the assumption of otherness. Within it, the primordial love of the Father is revealed: "The inconceivable is realized: that God the Father should be the Father not only of the eternal Son but also of sinful man."[29] Just as the structure of the face, the style of the hair, and the accent of speech of the foreigner reveal his origin, so too with the Son. When the Jerusalemites look at Jesus some of them see a Galilean face and hear a foreign accent. Some look at Jesus and see the divine face of the foreign Son of God whose home is his Father's house (see Lk 2:49). His origin in the Father becomes manifest.[30]

The Johannine message is that even his own people reject him as a foreigner: "He came to his own home, and his own people received him not" (Jn 1:11). Not only Adrienne von Speyr, but just as significantly, Julia Kristeva recognizes that Jesus defines himself as a stranger.[31] He does not belong to the world and neither do we: "If the world hates you, know that it has hated me before it hated you. If you were of the world, the world would love its own; but because you are not of the world, but I chose you out of the world, therefore the world hates you" (Jn 15:18–19). Rejected as a foreigner, the Son is crucified. Kristeva would accept all of this strangeness of Jesus. In the eyes of Christian faith, Jesus becomes even more a stranger. The Father raises him on the third day and he thus becomes a human who is unlike any other human. Yes, it is promised that humanity will also experience this new homeland of resurrected existence, but now we are foreigners journeying to this new homeland. We will discuss in later chapters the descent into hell that preceded this new life for Jesus, but for the time being the Christian message is that, while appearing even more foreign to us now, Jesus has prepared a place for us (Jn 14:3) which the Father has constructed for all the exiles as a home in him (Jn 14:2). Having come from the Father, humanity, indeed, all that is good in creation, returns to the eternal life with the Father. The Son breathes forth the Holy Spirit on his people (Jn 20:22) causing a

---

29 Ibid., 51, 53.   30 Ibid., 59. See also Speyr, *Confession*, 21–62.
31 Kristeva, *Strangers*, 83.

deep groaning of prayer to the Father (Rom 8:15–16, 26) because breathing in the graced air of the Holy Spirit reminds his people of their homeland. Since the Son has taken our otherness into himself who is one with the Father in the love of the Spirit, the otherness of being a foreigner "ceases within the universality of the love for the other."[32] Together with the Son and the Spirit, humanity will dwell in the heavenly homeland of the Father.[33] In this eternal life, the Father looks at his creation not as foreign, but rather the eternal countenance of the Father "finds in the world the consummated, eternal love of the Son."[34]

We are now prepared to discuss each Person of the Trinity in the following chapters as we think through the implications of the Son of God's hellish exilic descent. In this chapter I have attempted to give a beginning account of the Christian faith in dialogue with postmodernism. From the point of view of Julia Kristeva, the postmodern person sees herself as a foreigner, an exile. The postmodern acknowledges that every man is always different from every other. Kristeva sees this otherness as the only universal: we are all strangers to each other and more fundamentally to ourselves. For Kristeva, acknowledging this strangeness to ourselves prepares the way for an authentically human morality toward the immigrant because the strangeness of the foreigner "disappears when we all acknowledge ourselves as foreigners, unamenable to bonds and communities."[35] This is not enough, but it is a postmodern opening to the message and relevance of Christianity. Far from being a colonizing superpower, Christianity is a religion *of* foreigners *for* foreigners because the Son's compassionate mission radically changes the distance between humanity and divinity.[36] The other of our humanity is being drawn into the compassionate triune being that we may be one as he is one with the Father (Jn 17:22).

---

32 Speyr, *Father*, 84.   33 Ibid., 126–27.   34 Ibid., 131.
35 Kristeva, *Strangers*, 1.   36 Speyr, *Confession*, 195.

2

God the Father

NO CHRISTIAN THEOLOGY CAN BEGIN WITH anything but the revelation of God the Father in Jesus Christ, the Son, who through the Holy Spirit reveals the Father's love for us. The revelation of the Trinity must be our beginning; anything less will be a misstep. The next step must be the recognition that this God is the God who is love. Being God means being love fundamentally. Or to see God is to see the definition of love. This means love is defined by who God is. The greatest commandment is to love God and love one's neighbor as oneself (Mt 22:37–40): thus to love God we need to see how God loves himself. Within the love of the Trinity, we see the love we are to have for God and for each other. God defines who God is. God who is love defines what love is. Foundational to the encounter with God is that this God is love itself. Humanity is not left alone. We are not abandoned.

As a way to examine this primacy of the Father and its importance for Christian spirituality let us look at a contemporary debate in Trinitarian theology. Consider the fascinating debate that takes place between Professors Bruce McCormack and Paul Molnar as depicted in the important book *Trinity and Election in Contemporary Theology*.[1] The debate can be characterized in a few different ways, but one is that each admits the absolute necessity of ending speculation about the immanent Trinity (God in himself), yet they stop at two very different points and for different reasons. The fallout between them results in dramatically different visions of the immanent Trinity, especially on the topic of the divine freedom of the immanent Trinity. Both cite the theology of the major theologian, Karl Barth (d. 1968) as justification, but the debate has become more about the widely different ways contemporary Trinitarian theology has reacted to process theology (that God is ever becoming more) and current debates about epistemology as

---

1 Michael Dempsey, ed., *Trinity and Election in Contemporary Theology* (Grand Rapids, MI: Eerdmans, 2011).

it applies to the possibility of human knowledge of the immanent Trinity. We could get caught up in a quicksand of considering who is right about Barth's writing and the emerging traditions of interpretations, but the really essential question is: How can we know the Father?

Properly in theological academia, we could compare and contrast their views by consulting another Barthian. Hans Urs von Balthasar, the important twentieth-century Catholic theologian, is a Barthian of sorts and he too points to Barth over speculation about the immanent Trinity. But, Balthasar does this at a very different point from that of McCormack or Molnar. In order to make the case, I will focus on the issue of the divine freedom of the immanent Trinity, which is a central question in the McCormack and Molnar debate. The intent of this study is to go to the cutting edge of the wedge that divides the two. I will argue that in the speculation on divine freedom and the immanent Trinity among the three Barthians (McCormack, Molnar, and Balthasar), Hans Urs von Balthasar best articulates the Catholic perspective on the freedom of the Trinitarian Persons.

The speculative views on the immanent Trinity within modern Trinitarian theology can be located within three broad categories: minimalists, medianists, and maximalists.[2] At one end of the spectrum, minimalist theologians want completely to limit speech about the immanent life of the Trinity, and at the other end of the spectrum are the maximalist theologians who are open to broad, imaginative speculation about the immanent life of the Trinity. In the middle are the medianist theologians who want to limit dialectically our speech about the Trinity but also want to follow what revelation has given to us in the incarnate Son of God.

Broadly speaking, the majority of contemporary Trinitarian theologians are minimalists when it comes to speculating about the immanent Trinity with perhaps the Creed of Nicaea as their minimalist framework.[3] These theologians mark their entrance

---

2 While categorizing broadly, I am aware of the very different Trinitarian theologies composed by the different members of these groups. However, this categorizing, if properly executed, will aid us as we speculate about the Father.
3 See for example, Roger Haight's work, such as *Jesus Symbol of God* (Maryknoll, NY: Orbis Books, 2000) or *The Experience and Language of Grace* (New York: Paulist, 1979).

point usually with Karl Rahner's axiom that the economic and immanent Trinity are identical.[4] This axiom means that the Trinity as it is in itself (immanent) is the same as it reveals itself in the world (economic). Within the framework established by Rahner's rule, these theologians also insist on a Trinitarian theology that takes seriously the epistemological limits demonstrated by continental Enlightenment figures likes Immanuel Kant as well as by postmodern figures like Jacques Derrida who are adamant about the human inability to evaluate speech about God objectively.[5] Some contemporary theologians who hold this view include Gordon Kaufman, Catherine LaCugna, Sallie McFague, Elizabeth Johnson, Roger Haight, Douglas Farrow, Robert Jensen, Eberhard Jüngel, and Jürgen Moltmann.[6] A central critique made by minimalists is that other Trinitarian systems, especially those of the maximalists, create two Trinities—one that is revealed here on earth and about which we can know something (economic) separated from the one that is God in and of himself as he knows himself—with little relation between the two.

An extreme example of a minimalist reading of the Trinity would be Immanuel Kant's. He asserts that, "The doctrine of the Trinity, taken literally, has no practical relevance at all."[7] He means by this that when we critique our faculties' way of knowing, there must be an absolutely strict separation between the accessible phenomenal sphere and the inaccessible noumenal sphere of God. The consequence is that even if God is Trinity we have no way of knowing because it is beyond our ability to understand. In a different vein but just as extreme, Hans Küng argued for

4 Karl Rahner, *The Trinity*, trans. Joseph Donceel (New York: Crossroad, 1997).
5 Such theologians also sometimes briefly reference Dionysian negative theology in support of their view. Dionysius, a significant late fifth or early sixth century theologian, taught that negating statements about God helps communicate even greater truths about God. Establishing dissimilarities between our limited concepts of God and the true reality of God helps us to understand who God is and how he is beyond our concepts, words, and theologies. For Dionysius, negation leads to understanding.
6 An example of Roger Haight's minimalism will be found in the above-mentioned *Jesus Symbol of God* and relevant to this issue, see Paul Molnar, *Incarnation and Resurrection: Toward a Contemporary Understanding* (Grand Rapids, MI: Eerdmans, 2007).
7 Immanuel Kant, *Conflict of the Faculties*, trans. Mary J. Gregor (New York: Abaris Books, 1979), 65.

putting a parenthesis around any speculation about the Trinity in order to facilitate interreligious dialogue. As he says in *On Being Christian*, "We [Christians] can no longer accept the mythical ideas of that [New Testament] age about a being descended from God, existing before time and beyond this world in a heavenly state; a 'story of gods,' in which two (or even three) divine beings were involved, is not for us."[8] Küng continues that the doctrine of the Trinity is unsubstantiated, mythic speculation that prevents fruitful dialogue among the monotheistic faiths because, "There is no God but God."[9]

The Trinitarian theology of David Coffey would be a moderate example of this minimalism. In Coffey's analysis of Rahner's axiom, he makes the important point that there are two rightly ordered relationships present, one epistemological and the other ontological.[10] The epistemological order begins with the biblical, economic Trinity and leads to the immanent Trinity. The ontological order makes the immanent Trinity the ground of the economic Trinity. For Coffey, the study of the Trinity should be "not just the biblical doctrine, for while that is its indispensable starting point, it is only the starting point. If we remained there, we would be opting for a biblical fundamentalism. Nor is it just the doctrine of the immanent Trinity, as it has often been assumed to be, for that on its own is unconnected with the mystery of salvation.... The proper study of the Trinity is the study of the economic Trinity, which of course presupposes both the biblical and the immanent Trinity."[11] Coffey believes that an uninhibited speculation on the immanent life of the Trinity without reference to the biblical or economic Trinity has brought theologies of the immanent Trinity into disrepute. Ontologically the immanent Trinity has priority of order, but epistemologically the real Trinity of theology is the economic.

In this minimalist category but certainly not at its extreme end, we can put Bruce McCormack. Interpreting Karl Barth as a critically realistic dialectical theologian, McCormack argues that speculation about the immanent Trinity can only be known through

---

8 Hans Küng, *On Being Christian*, trans. Edward Quinn (Garden City, NY: Doubleday, 1976), 446. 9 Ibid., 476.
10 David Coffey, *Deus Trinitas: The Doctrine of the Triune God* (New York: Oxford University Press, 1999), 14. 11 Ibid., 16.

the doctrine of election. Anything else is a human construct and a false view of God. The decision to elect all of humanity through the humanity of Jesus Christ is our only entrance into understanding the tri-unity of God. McCormack believes we need to revise our understanding of the Trinity according to these epistemological constraints. If we truly take the doctrine of election as the only possible way to know God's being, then "the being of God is itself established in the act of revelation."[12] In other words, the revelation of the tri-unity of God cannot go behind, beyond, or beneath the revelation of God's being other than through the doctrine of God's electing humanity in Jesus Christ. If the doctrine of election is the summation of the gospel then our understanding of the Trinity must be conditioned only by this doctrine. As a critical acceptance of Kant's critique of pure reason, McCormack attempts to minimize speech about the immanent Trinity through the doctrine of election. In the end, McCormack constructs a view of the Trinity in which the Father eternally chooses (elects) to generate the Son, which is in deep disagreement with the traditional view of the eternal patri-generation of the Son.[13]

Whereas McCormack limits speech about God's existence, which leads him to a revision of the traditional doctrine of the Trinity, other theologians believe that we can say more about the immanent Trinity than the minimalists. These theologians, whom we could categorize as medianists, attempt to balance dialectically the minimizing of our speculative speech about the immanent Trinity because of epistemological concerns with the maximizing of our theological speech about the immanent Trinity because of the gratuity of revelation and grace. In an age after Kant's critique, the modern Trinitarian theologian cannot engage in medieval speculation about the immanent Trinity. However, instead of relying on the Kantian critique, the medianist theologian believes that because of the revelation of the Incarnation and the free gift of God's grace in the Holy Spirit we can relevantly and reverently speak about the immanent life of the Trinity. An example of a medianist would be

---

12 Bruce McCormack, *Karl Barth's Critically Realistic Dialectical Theology: Its Genesis and Development 1909–1936* (New York: Oxford University Press, 1995), 460–61.

13 In Thomistic language, the generation of the Son is First Act and not Second Act.

Thomas Torrance, whose work forges a deep connection between the theology of Karl Barth and that of Athanasius.[14]

In this medianist category we can place the theology of Paul Molnar. Mostly through critique of the dogmatic minimalizing work of contemporary Catholic systematic theology, Molnar argues that the revelation of the Word of God, which alone can be trusted, reveals the full divine freedom of the immanent Trinity. Distrusting the enthusiasm for human experience as a way to God, Molnar attempts a neo-orthodox critique of contemporary Catholic Trinitarian theology. Just as Barth can be read as a deconstruction of Schleiermacherian Liberal Protestantism in order to rebuild a neo-orthodox Protestant theology that is faithful to the tradition, so too we can read Molnar as a deconstructor of contemporary Catholic Trinitarian and Christological theologians who argue for a Catholic version of Schleiermacherian or even Hegelian ideas. Molnar is concerned about theologians who exaggerated the human experience as the central way into knowledge of God, which in his view succumbs to the danger of Feuerbachian anthropological projectionism. Molnar instead takes the graced revelation of the Trinity through the incarnate Son formalized in the Church's creeds and living tradition, which is guided by the Spirit, as the right ground. Molnar, of course, attempts this deconstruction in order to return contemporary Catholic and Protestant academic theology to orthodox (or neo-orthodox) Trinitarian roots. Much like his greatest influence, Torrance, Molnar sees that a modern retrieval of Athanasian theology fused with Barthian dialectic must be the right way forward for Christian theologians to speak properly once again about the immanent life of the Trinity. Yet, for all his speculation on the divine freedom of the Trinity, there are definite limits to what Molnar allows to be said about the immanent life of the Trinity. While revelation gives us much to say about the divine freedom of the immanent Trinity, we must only go so far. God is entirely free to reveal who he is and we should not presume more than what the Father has chosen to reveal in his Son through the Spirit.

An example of another medianist is that of Ralph Del Colle. In his work, *Christ and the Spirit*, Del Colle uses Irenaeus's image of the

---

14 See Paul Molnar, *Thomas F. Torrance: Theologian of the Trinity* (Surrey, England: Ashgate, 2009).

"two hands of God" to develop the field of Spirit-Christology.[15] Spirit-Christology is a constructive attempt to expand Christology proper to include a dynamic pneumatological account of Christ. This area of Christology emerged after the Second Vatican Council as a complementary orthodox model to traditional Logos-Christology. Spirit-Christology focuses on "who Christ is" and "what Christ does" from the perspective of the third article of the Creed. In his work, Del Colle concludes that Spirit-Christology brings three constructive points to Trinitarian theology. First, the Holy Spirit has a proper mission to the world just like the Son. Second, a theology of grace must give priority to uncreated grace as the activity of the Holy Spirit. Third, the relationship of the Holy Spirit to Christ in the Gospels is best articulated with a theology of anointing.

All of these points find their place in the Spirit-Christology of David Coffey. In his Bestowal Model (or Return Model) of the Trinity, David Coffey provides a Trinitarian matrix to Karl Rahner's theology of grace and his Christology. He is attempting an articulation of the Love Model of the immanent Trinity in a way that corresponds to what is revealed in the economy. When the Father eternally begets the Son, he also gives the Holy Spirit to him as the eternal object of his love. The Son in his answering love gives the Holy Spirit to the Father. Such is the immanent Trinity. In the economy, the Father bestows his Holy Spirit outside the Trinity preparing all creation to come to radical fruition in the Incarnation of the Son whom the Father sends. The Holy Spirit as entelechy draws and assimilates the world to Christ returning it to the Son and finally to the Father. Anointed by the Holy Spirit, Christ, the Son, gives his answering love to the Father. This answering love of the Son to the Father contains within it the Holy Spirit and the world. The Holy Spirit becomes "christified" as Christ gives his love to the Father.[16]

The last category of contemporary Trinitarian theology—maximalist—argues that theology should say as much as possible about the Trinity while simultaneously respecting the horizon of mystery. I will be presenting Adrienne von Speyr's spirituality and Hans Urs von Balthasar's theology as in this tradition. We will see in

---

15 Ralph Del Colle, *Christ and the Spirit: Spirit-Christology in Trinitarian Perspective* (New York: Oxford University Press, 1994).   16 See Coffey's *Deus Trinitas.*

this theology a harmonious meditation on the compassionate countenance of the Father revealed in the confessional attitude of the Son through the anointing of the Holy Spirit.[17] This chapter in a sense develops Spirit-Christology by meditating on the face of God who has sent his "two hands" into the world.[18]

In my view, the deep connections of Adrienne von Speyr and Hans Urs von Balthasar cannot be overstated.[19] Drawing from Speyr's two works, *The Countenance of the Father* and *Confession*, we will see that the compassionate countenance of the Father is revealed in the confessional attitude of the Son in and through the Holy Spirit. The Father has sent the Son and Spirit so that we might participate in the Son's confessional attitude toward the Father in the Holy Spirit. What is enormously fruitful in these works is that the confessional attitude, defined as a complete openness of total surrender, will be seen as revealed in the Son's relationship to the Father in the Holy Spirit, not only on the Cross but also (and because of) the confessional attitude's origin in the inner Trinitarian life of God.[20]

Eternally present before creation, the Father is essentially united with the Son and Holy Spirit. The fundamental attribute of the First Person of the Trinity, according to Speyr, "is being a father: this is the primary thing the Son and the Spirit experience of him, just as it will be the first thing that man will know of him."[21] The Son too has the fundamental attribute of being a son as in having come from another, from the Father. The Spirit likewise has the attribute of being from the Father and the Son. Both the

---

17 Hans Urs von Balthasar, *Truth Is Symphonic: Aspects of Christian Pluralism*, trans. Graham Harrison (San Francisco: Ignatius Press, 1987).

18 The origins of this chapter can be traced to my course with Del Colle on the Theology of the Trinity at Marquette University during my doctoral work. What was planted in that class blooms here as an offered flower of remembrance.

19 For more on my interpretation of their relationship, please see my article, "Hans Urs von Balthasar and Adrienne von Speyr's Ecclesial Relationship," *New Blackfriars* 94 (2013): 50–63 and my book *Heaven Opens: The Trinitarian Mysticism of Adrienne von Speyr* (Minneapolis, MN: Fortress Press, 2014).

20 As with any mystical writer, the language is highly metaphoric and the reader should be aware that this mode of theological speech could be highly beneficial if understood cautiously. Speyr developed an extensive theory of mysticism that Balthasar collected into a two-volume work published posthumously, called *Das Wort und Mystik*, vol. 5 and 6 of *Die Nachlasswerke* (Freiburg: Johannes Verlag Einsiedeln, 1970).   21 Speyr, *Father*, 7.

Spirit and the Son know the Father as their origin, who is in "a state of being antecedent."[22] The Father experiences this state as a "supra-responsibility" active from eternity to eternity. In his consubstantial unity with the Son and Spirit, he is always the Father; he cannot change.[23]

As unoriginate originator, the Father gives everything of himself except being Father. He allows the Son to be the visible one while he remains "within the reserved mystery of his fatherhood" manifesting himself only through his acts of generating the Son and spirating the Spirit, which is done jointly with the Son.[24] He is the concealed unoriginate originator of all acts of the Son and the Spirit and "is mirrored forth in the Son and the Spirit."[25] All origins (even those performed by the Son and Spirit) are in him as the beginning and all that comes from him will only be understood within him.[26] All concepts will only be known through their origin and only take on their full meaning from a return to their origin in the Father.

How do we know this origin? Statements about the divine essence are possible and pertinent, even to the point of appearing to satisfy our faith and our human understanding. Still we must be mindful that God's essence is infinitely greater than that which is "real" for us. Speyr asserts that in comparison to our reality, God is supra-reality that surpasses us not only in scope but also in substance; indeed, he surpasses our knowledge, belief, and intuition to an infinite degree in every respect.[27] For Speyr, the Son and the Spirit attest to "the idea and reality of the Father"

---

22 Ibid.   23 Ibid., 12.

24 Ibid., 11. This is seemingly contradictory to Thomas and for which Thomas receives many critiques. He maintains the possibility of any one of the Trinity becoming incarnate because of the divine freedom. Speyr says it is the choice of the Father for the Son to be the visible one. In my view, I would ask: Is not the concept of fittingness of the Son becoming incarnate Thomas's attempt to account for a certain necessity within the divine freedom for the Son to be the visible one?   25 Speyr, *Father*, 8.

26 For Speyr's commentary on the Father as the "beginning" in the first words of the prologue of Gospel of John "In the beginning," see Adrienne von Speyr, *John*, trans. Lucia Wiedenhöver and Alexander Dru, 4 vols. (San Francisco: Ignatius Press, 1994), vol. 1.

27 Speyr, *Father*, 16. For more on her understanding of the knowledge of God, see *The Boundless God*, trans. Helena Tomko (San Francisco: Ignatius Press, 2004) and *Light and Images: The Elements of Contemplation*, trans. David Schindler, Jr. (San Francisco: Ignatius Press, 2004).

through the whole of their eternal relation.[28] When Christians, in faith, attempt "to gain some sense of the Father, we must seek our means in the Son."[29] Though the Father is the concealed one, he is not the anonymous one because he is eternally begetting the Son, who is his Word, and with the Son eternally spirating the Spirit, who is their relation of love.[30] The words of the Son and the love of the Holy Spirit are the keys that unlock the door to the Father's countenance because together they are his loving word and the word of love. Thus, the Christian gains access to the compassionate countenance of the Father through the Son and Spirit.[31] The Son's and the Spirit's relation and mission unlock and throw open the mansions of the Father (see Jn 14:2).[32]

Before the world was created, the Father, the Son, and the Holy Spirit were alone in a blessed unity corresponding to the Father's essence, which "already contained all the relations to the Son and the Spirit that are appropriate to that essence."[33] These are relations of love and each Divine Person has a unique countenance that shines love upon the others and manifests the mutuality of the one divine essence.[34]

The compassionate countenance of the Father, according to Speyr, is seen in the confessional attitude of the Son within the inner Trinitarian relations. Father, Son, and Holy Spirit stand before each other in an attitude that is fitting for God: "Analogously, we can designate this as an attitude of confession."[35] The compassionate countenance of the Father is revealed in the Son's confessional attitude toward the Father and in the Holy Spirit. Understood in an analogous way, the true prototype of the attitude of confession is the begetting of the Son by the Father.[36] Similarly, the Spirit issuing from the Father and the Son reveals both and, in this eternal relation of proceeding-from, the Spirit's own confessional identity is revealed.

The confessional attitude of the Son and the Spirit toward the Father is "complete openness, concealing nothing, perfectly

---

28 Speyr, *Father*, 9.
29 Ibid., 8. "'Attempt' is a favorite word of Adrienne's. A Christian can do no more than 'attempt'" (53).   30 Speyr, *Father*, 11.
31 Ibid., 13.   32 Ibid., 12.   33 Ibid., 9.
34 Ibid., 9, 12. We see here the opposition of relation.
35 Speyr, *Confession*, 21.   36 Ibid., 22.

transparent, and always ready to be sent."[37] The insight is fascinating and fruitful because it necessitates that "everything in God is total surrender, trust and love; every Person stands open to every other."[38] From this openness, the Father participates in the Son and the Spirit to such an extent that they cannot but always manifest the countenance of the Father.

All the acts of the Father reveal his countenance, especially in the begetting of the Son and spiration of the Spirit. His countenance is revealed in creation, which happens within the essential interchange of the love of the Father, Son, and Holy Spirit.[39] In this essential interchange that brings to fruition creation in which they all have their role, the Father has his prominence as the beginning. However, the Father points his creation (and his prominence in it) toward the Son whose prominence will occur on the Cross. In a real sense, the Cross will point all creation back to the Father as "an echo of the creation of the world."[40] Creation is a movement toward the Son. The Son on the Cross, in his plea for forgiveness—"Father, forgive them. They know not what they do" (Lk 23:34)—returns creation now redeemed to the Father. They eternally, immanently stand in mutual reflective relationship and reveal their reciprocal unity in the Trinitarian activity of creation and redemption.[41] Each Person is involved in the common work of every activity outside God, but each has his own role in that work.[42] This means that as it is not possible "to replace the suffering Son, on the Cross, with the Father or the Spirit so, too, it is unacceptable to substitute the Son or the Spirit, in an equivalent sense, for the creating Father."[43] As creation emerged into existence, the relations of the Father, Son, and Holy Spirit are revealed in their personal acts outside themselves even though there is a common work.[44]

---

37 Ibid., 23.   38 Ibid., 67–68.   39 Speyr, *Father*, 13–14.
40 Ibid., 14.   41 Ibid.

42 Ibid., 100–101: "Whenever the triune God exerts some effect on the world from within his heaven, each of the Persons sees his own part as linked to those of the others in a complete unity, which corresponds to the essential unity of their triune love. It is not necessary to make continual distinctions among the wishes, intentions, and achievements of the Father, the Son, and the Spirit, because they are always one, always concordant, arising out of one another and returning into one another."   43 Ibid., 14–15.

44 One might read this and think that Speyr would affirm Karl Rahner's *Grundaxiom* that "the 'economic' Trinity is the 'immanent' Trinity and the

The immanent Trinity is always-more love, to use Speyr's term, and all creation is an expression of this inner-Trinitarian, effusive love. And as such, within creation, the law of always-more love is revealed. The Father brings forth creation as an expression and expansion of his love of the Son and the Spirit. With his creation of the world, the Father expands his fatherly care "as accords with God's essence—not at the expense of the other Persons, but in such a way that the Son and the Spirit, and even man are included in the glorification."[45] The triune God has placed within his creation "the law of the 'always-more' love" because the Father himself has adhered to this law.[46] Human beings are created out of the always-more love of the Father that they may offer back to the Father the always-more love he has given them.

The first human couple attempted to look to the Father with this love, but God had scarcely "articulated the goodness of the world, observed its full correspondence to his will, when man falls away from his proper relationship. He no longer wants to remain within it, no longer wants to obey."[47] Their disobedience to love, indeed their lack of love, caused their fall.[48] This disobedience brought about an opaque relation between this human couple and God. The Son is always completely transparent before the Father. The couple was created to imitate this transparency but, falling away, they reached for the fig leaf and hid in the bushes. They abandoned the confessional attitude of transparency, of being naked before God.

Speyr's attractive understanding of this moment of original sin is that this couple's dialogue with God had now become prayer. This couple found themselves "in a kind of tunnel... deprived of vision."[49] They found themselves caught up in an open question that they put to God without being sure what they were really asking.[50] They no longer approached God naturally; it is no longer

---

'immanent' Trinity is the 'economic' Trinity" (Karl Rahner, *The Trinity*, trans. Joseph Donceel [New York: Crossroad Publishing, 1997], 22). If this only means that the same Trinity is meant in both the economy and immanence, then Speyr and all Christians, I think, would affirm this. However, if something more is meant, if all that is revealed of the Trinity economically is all that is true of the immanent Trinity, then Speyr would absolutely disagree.

45 Speyr, *Father*, 19–20.   46 Ibid., 20.   47 Ibid., 25.
48 For Speyr, the essence of all sin is lack of love, see e.g., *Confession*, 69.
49 Speyr, *Father*, 27.   50 Ibid., 27–28.

"the running of the newly arisen creature toward the arms of his Creator, but rather the considered, difficult, halting words of the sinner to his judge."[51] Through all of this, the Father remains Father, but the accused sinner no longer sees him as such. The sinner's guilt, his lack of confessional attitude, veiled his vision and, thus, began his search for confession. The Father replied by preparing to send his Son and Spirit to bring about an even more intimate imitation of the inner-Trinitarian confessional attitude. Speyr believed that as a sinner, one already "unconditionally feels himself to be a sinner," and so one "will expect confession with a kind of necessity."[52] The only choice is to reveal oneself in complete openness and transparency or to isolate oneself in the attitude of indifference and the hell of non-relationality.

The Old Covenant and the prophets were the Father's initiative to prepare the world for the sending of his Son and Spirit, but his human creatures hesitatingly oscillated between the openness of the confessional attitude and the indifference of isolation: "it is as if the Father's revelatory grace were in a competition with sin."[53] Everything hung in a balance and, within the Father's thoughts, "there must be room not only for the darkest of sinners but also for the supremely bright Son."[54] Yet, the Father loves all. The Father extended his com-passion, his suffering-with the sinner through the sending of his Son. In order to offer this compassion, he refined his people to give themselves back to him through one immaculately answering Yes.[55] Through the sending of the Holy Spirit, the Father prepared throughout the generations of Abraham the finally definitive consent—the one complete Yes of the openness and transparency of Mary.[56]

---

51 Ibid., 28.   52 Speyr, *Confession*, 16.
53 Speyr, *Father*, 31–32. For Speyr's theology of the prophets, see her *The Mission of the Prophets*, trans. David Kipp (San Francisco: Ignatius Press, 1996).
54 Ibid., 34.
55 For Speyr's extensive Mariology, see her works *Handmaid of the Lord*, trans. E. A. Nelson, second edition (San Francisco: Ignatius Press, 1985) and *Mary in the Redemption*, trans. Helena Tomko (San Francisco: Ignatius Press, 2003).
56 The rich Mariology of Ralph Del Colle should be cited here. For Del Colle, Mary is "an instance, the exemplary instance, in her person of the in-humanation of the Spirit, an enhypostasis in the Spirit. Her personhood is exemplary of what it means to be with the other. She is an icon of life in and by the Spirit" (Ralph Dell Colle, "Holy Spirit: Presence, Power, Person,"

The Father sent the Son as an expression of his fatherly love to this one Hebrew woman who has said Yes in the complete confessional attitude made possible by the Son and the Spirit.[57] The Father saw in Mary that the earth is not a cold dead place but warm and capable of bringing love to fruition. The incarnate Son reveals the countenance of the Father through his absolute transparency.[58] In this mission of the Son, the Father "wants to extend something of the eternal sonship to man as well."[59] The Father has oriented creation to the Son and, now, the Son in the Incarnation actively takes it over. He enters creation as an expression of the Father's responsibility and took into his care this responsibility as his own (see Jn 4:34).

From eternity and now on earth, the Son expressed the Father's love, his countenance, through his confessional attitude. Speyr believed that the whole of the Son's life could be viewed from the attitude of confession.[60] The Father's countenance is manifested through the Son who "while on earth, maintains a confessional attitude before the Father and draws his fellow men—his emerging Church—closer and closer to this attitude."[61] He does this through his prayer, his body, and the Eucharist.

When the Son prayed, he prayed to the Father.[62] The Jewish prayers he learned from Mary and Joseph are prayed with a divine depth that accords with his essence and mission as being sent by the Father.[63] It is a prayer from the center of the world gathering up all of the halting prayers of earth and bringing them before the Father. He taught the world to call out to the Father in his own words: "Pray then like this" (Mt 6:9).

Theological Studies 62 [2001]: 338). Additionally, Del Colle thinks that the "Marian manifestation of the Spirit's work is a distinct but inseparable dimension of Christ's saving mystery. If the human mediation and manifestation of God's saving mystery, its iconographic representation and illumination, is to be fully diaphanous to the joint mission of the Son and the Spirit then that human mediation communicates an ontology of personhood that is both for us and with us" (ibid., 339).

57 Speyr, *Father*, 51.   58 Ibid., 51: "It is simply all love."
59 Ibid., 54.   60 Speyr, *Confession*, 21–27.   61 Ibid., 132.
62 Speyr, *Father*, 65.
63 On this Trinitarian foundation of prayer, see Adrienne von Speyr, *The World of Prayer*, trans. Graham Harrison (San Francisco: Ignatius Press, 1985). See also her book of prayers, *With God and With Men: Prayers*, trans. Adrian Walker (San Francisco: Ignatius Press, 1995).

The Son also revealed the Father in his body.[64] His particular body is "for him the expression of an idea and a will of the Father's at the time of creation."[65] The Son made "use of his body in order to fulfill his mission."[66] He knew the way in which bodily life can lead one astray into sin and, therefore, he chastened his body. He kept watch. He fasted. He overcame the temptations of living a bodily life "not just, however, because he is God in fleshly form, but because he is man who obeys the Father fully."[67] In his obedience, he oriented his body to the Father and, by this, the Father is revealed. Even in his body stripped naked on the Cross, the Son became physically and completely transparent, revealing his interior confessional attitude.

Connected with the body is the Son's revelation of the Father through the Sacrament of the Eucharist. The Son "imparted to the sacrament the vision of the Father that he possessed when embodied."[68] For the Father, the Eucharist brings to his memory both the fallen Adam and the New Adam.[69] It is a sign to him of his justice and love. For humanity, it presents the Son's real presence as the countenance of the Father. The Son's bodily life is so completely the revelation of the Father that this gift of the Eucharist, which is the Church's access to the whole of Christ including his body, will be any person's narrow way to heaven.[70]

Since the Father alone knows the hour ("the hour of the Cross is the hour of the Father") the Son did not know when it would come, but he chose to accept it in complete obedience in the attitude of confession.[71] The hour began with the seeming distancing

---

64 Here we will see similarities between Speyr's theology of the body (*Theologie der Geschlechter*, vol. 12 of *Die Nachlasswerke* [Freiburg: Johannes Verlag Einsiedeln, 1969]) and the more widely known theology of the body of Pope John Paul II (John Paul II, *Man and Woman He Created Them: A Theology of the Body*, trans. Michael Waldstein [New York: Pauline Books, 2006]). See also Michele M. Schumacher, "Ecclesial Existence: Person and Community in the Trinitarian Anthropology of Adrienne von Speyr," *Modern Theology* 24 (2008): 359–85.

65 Speyr, *Father*, 67.   66 Ibid., 68.   67 Ibid.   68 Ibid., 69.

69 The Son's words "Do this in remembrance of me" (Lk 22:19) is also a request directed to the Father to remember his sacrificial offering (cf. Ps 106:4).

70 Ibid., 69. For more of Speyr's understanding of the Eucharist, see *The Holy Mass*, trans. Helena M. Saward (San Francisco: Ignatius Press, 1999) and *The Cross: Word and Sacrament*, trans. Graham Harrison (San Francisco: Ignatius Press, 1983).

71 Speyr, *Father*, 71. This is the Johannine understanding of hour.

of the Father from the Son.[72] This distancing is hard for us to understand, but Speyr offered the analogy of an earthly father who entrusts a major task to his son to be done independently. Though the father might desire to intervene, the task has been entrusted entirely to the son and the father must restrain himself: "The divine Father, too, does not want to intervene in the Son's work, whose ultimate independent task is his extreme obedience on the Cross."[73] In Speyr's view, even the Spirit abandoned the Son to his task on the Cross.[74]

The suffering Son in his death on the Cross revealed the Father: "The knowledge of the Cross is just as much a knowledge of the absolute fatherhood of the Father as of the absolute sonship of the Son."[75] Taking away the sins of the world, the Son gave to the world in all its remoteness from the Father the full and supreme proof of the intimate love of the Father.[76] The Son revealed the Father's love for his disobedient creation through the presence of the Son hanging on the Cross. The whole of our finite sin hit the Son with such accuracy that it exposed the whole of the Father's infinite love for him.

Now at this point, we are ready for Speyr's critical exegesis of John 14:9: "He who has seen me has seen the Father." We already know that the Son reveals the Father through his confessional attitude.[77] His mission of confession on the Cross manifested the Father's countenance. Seeing him we see the Father at every moment of the incarnate Son's mission, even in the essential words of the confessional attitude "I thirst" (Jn 19:28). The penitent who kneels at the foot of the Cross "must thirst for absolution and

---

72 Speyr is clear. There is no separation of the divine nature: "The Son's death is the exemplification of the supreme aliveness of triune love; it does not alter the relationship between the Father and the Son; the Father does not need to interrupt the eternal act of generation in order to enable the Son's death" (ibid., 77).   73 Ibid., 74.

74 Speyr sees the Son's commending of his spirit as surrendering up the Holy Spirit to the Father that at his death the Son is abandoned by the Father and the Holy Spirit. For more on my developments on this idea, see my article, "A Compelling Trinitarian Taxonomy: Hans Urs von Balthasar's Theology of the Trinitarian Inversion and Reversion," *International Journal of Systematic Theology* 14, no. 2 (2012): 161–76.   75 Speyr, *Father*, 76.

76 Ibid., 77. For more on Speyr's theology of the Cross, see her work *The Passion From Within*, trans. Lucia Wiedenhöver (San Francisco: Ignatius Press, 1998).

77 Speyr, *Father*, 81.

for the nearness to God that he has lost through sin."[78] At the Cross, he finds the Son also thirsting for this absolution: "How long will you hide your face from me?" (Ps 13:1). The confessional attitude means imitating the Son who has become the Naked One on the Cross completely transparent to us and completely transparent to the Father: "Confession means being naked before God."[79] The Son on the Cross is stripped of all clothing. In our artful crucifixes, we cover this exposure out of a type of modesty, but the Son on the real Cross is nakedly transparent, no longer hiding behind a fig leaf and bushes like the first Adam. For Speyr, our imitation of the Son comes through the power of the Holy Spirit who actuates our confessional exposure: "The soul undoes the buttons, the Spirit undresses it; the soul tries to say Yes, the Spirit brings about that Yes."[80]

In the Sacrament of Confession, a distance exists between the confession of sin and the priest's prayer of absolution. The distance, according to Speyr, functions as a sign for understanding Holy Saturday as the day between the confession of Good Friday and the absolution of Easter Sunday. Following the majority of Christian tradition, Holy Saturday can be understood as a time of exhortation—the preaching to the Old Testament saints in Sheol—but it can also be understood as the time when sin becomes separated from sinners and becomes definitively objectified for what it is—a No to the Father. The Son who takes away the sins of the world is taken by these sins to their place in hell, where they are the objectified No to the Father. The complete Yes of the Son plunges him into the complete No of hell. The Son cries out from the depths (*De profundis clamavi ad te, Domine*: Ps 130:1). This is the day of the Father's greatest mercy who has sent his Son, his obediential Yes, to the place of the wicked, objectified No of sin (*Quia apud Dominum misericordia*: Ps 130:7).[81] Holy Saturday reveals the absolute extent of the Father's compassion.

The Resurrection, as an experience of absolution, comes like lightning.[82] The apostles "had hoped" (Lk 24:21) that Christ would come back to them. All they knew was the waiting that

---

78 Speyr, *Confession*, 173.　　79 Ibid., 184.　　80 Ibid.
81 According to Speyr, it is no mere coincidence that confession in the Catholic Church is usually offered on Saturday (ibid., 134).
82 Ibid., 59.

quickly turned to despair. Then, there is the sudden certainty: "it is really he, he is here."[83] The Father accomplished all of this redemption to reveal that, as the source of life, he is the source of all new life.[84] The Son, who makes all things new (Rev 21:5), has returned the new creation back to the Father in the Holy Spirit.

Only now from the standpoint of absolution can the Son institute the Sacrament of Confession (Jn 20:23) and, for Speyr, this institution is bound up intimately with the risen Lord's sending of the Holy Spirit (Jn 20:22).[85] On Easter evening, the Son gives two commands: to receive the Spirit and to remit sins.[86] It comes as a fruit of the Cross because it is the zenith of the Son's attitude of confession.[87] In this sacrament, which is tied up with the Holy Spirit, the apostles are given the ability to imitate the Son's confessional attitude. They are called, as confessors and penitents, to "unconditional submission to God's word for the purpose of approximating the attitude of the Son toward the Father."[88] In these intimate moments with the resurrected Lord, they received the Holy Spirit and the power to confess and remit sins. They saw both present in the Son's life and death, but now they are the ones entrusted with the Spirit and the sacrament that forgives sins.

The Father's countenance revealed by the Son "must be accessible to men" and Speyr believed that here we see the purpose of the Church.[89] The Father uses the Church and her sacraments to show humanity his countenance through the Son and Spirit. He, in turn, will behold the Church, through the all-purifying medium of the Son's Cross and the Spirit's sanctifying. The Father discerns in every received sacrament the radiant obedience of the Son and the love of the Spirit. For him, the Church will become a perpetual interpretation of what the Son and Spirit have accomplished in their missions.[90]

In the sacraments, he will see the Son's work through the Holy Spirit and for us; we will see in the sacraments the Father, Son, and Holy Spirit. There is both a descending and ascending aspect

---

83 Ibid.   84 Speyr, *Father*, 85–88.

85 For more on this topic, see William Schmidt, "The Sacrament of Confession as *Sequela Christi* in the Writings of Adrienne von Speyr," S. T. D. diss., Lateran Pontifical University, John Paul II Institute for Studies on Marriage and Family, 1999.

86 Speyr, *Confession*, 63.   87 Ibid., 146.   88 Ibid., 71.

89 Speyr, *Father*, 97.   90 Ibid., 100.

to the sacraments that coalesce to reveal the unity of Trinitarian grace.[91] By this Trinitarian grace, the Father enacts through the sacraments the attitude of the Son in the Holy Spirit, especially for the Sacrament of Confession. Speyr interestingly sees the Father valuing so much the institution of confession—the disclosure and purification of sins—that he has, in a sense, drawn it into eternity by the institution of purgatory.[92]

The Father's activity in sending the Son has made heaven ready for us and us ready for heaven.[93] The Father overcomes our orphan spirit. From the moment of our creation, we are being made ready for beholding the countenance of *our* Father. By sending his Son and the Spirit, we have found the way homeward to the Father.[94] The Son instituted the Sacrament of Confession as an access to the eternal countenance of the Father that we may stand before the Father in the confessional attitude as he, the Son, does. All this is accomplished in order that the eternal Father may manifest his countenance to us, finding in us "the consummated, eternal love of the Son."[95]

With our theological eyes toward the Father, we have seen how Adrienne von Speyr has led us through salvation history to make the Father known through the confessional attitude of the Son

---

91 Ibid., 114–15. Speyr is exact in seeing grace as Trinitarian: "No more than the Father can be seen as having created the world without the cooperation of the Son and the Spirit can the sacraments be individually correlated with any one Divine Person. The Father is present in all of them as the one who originally bestows everything, accompanies everything in its unfolding, and receives back everything that is accomplished. It is only we who draw boundaries everywhere, who love ready-made formulas so that we are not forced to go farther: formulas that are not false in themselves but are incomplete and, since we are sluggish, tend to impede our supplementing them. But whenever we touch on the essence of grace, we have to move beyond all boundaries until we reach the Trinity" (ibid., 115).

92 Ibid., 106: "One could, from the standpoint of the Cross, regard the institution of Purgatory as a transference of the confessional situation from the this-worldly context of the earthly Church to that of judgment in the next world; one could see this as a case in which an institution of redemption and of the Church has affected, and been expanded into, the order of the Father; and nothing can bring more bliss to the Son than seeing his work glorified by the Father in this way."

93 Ibid., 106.   94 Ibid., 126–27.

95 Ibid., 131. See also Adrienne von Speyr, *The Gates of Eternal Life*, trans. Corona Sharp (San Francisco: Ignatius Press, 1983), 99–108.

in the Holy Spirit. The Father manifests his loving countenance through the confessional attitude of the Son with the Holy Spirit who makes us transparent to the Father in the Sacrament of Confession. Throughout this theological meditation on Speyr's thought, I see the attempted reconciliation of "kneeling" and "sitting" theology, a commingling encouraged by the theology and witness of Ralph Del Colle.[96]

Our reflections on the Father have made everything ready for the Son who has made the Father known most supremely in his kenotic abandonment on the Cross and in hell. God alone could have gone to this utmost extent to be, alone, our salvation. The Father alone could have sent his Son to this utmost extent to be, alone, our way to the Father.

---

96 Hans Urs von Balthasar, "Theology and Sanctity," in vol. 1 of *Explorations in Theology*, trans. A. V. Littledale and Alexander Dru (San Francisco: Ignatius Press, 1989), 181–209 and see, Peter Henrici, "Hans Urs von Balthasar: A Sketch of His Life," in *Hans Urs von Balthasar: His Life and Work*, ed. David L. Schindler (San Francisco: Ignatius, 1991), 26. If I may, I would like to offer a flower of remembrance of Del Colle as a teacher and father. Everything about his teaching was an attempt to be prayerfully faithful and actively curious, to love the Trinitarian nature of the liturgy and the sophistication of academic thought, to think evangelically and live charismatically, and above all to love the Lord with one's mind. Del Colle's teaching was not managing our theological formation, but truly leading us, which is different from managing us, by disrupting our monadic thought into Trinitarian faith. Lastly, let us also remember him as a father. He treasured his children. I remember distinctly my first semester course with him on Systematic Theology and one day in particular. He must have been working hard the whole day and probably was starving when we met for our evening class. Halfway through the class session from the hallway we heard the loud whispering of his son, "I'm just going to do it." Before his mother could stop him, Del Colle's son burst into the classroom, hugged his dad, and set before him a can of soda. Del Colle's eyes sparkled and his smile radiated warmth. After his son scurried out of the room, we saw the compassionate countenance of Del Colle's deep drinking of his son's spontaneous gift. Here we saw his love for his family and his practice of Trinitarian theology. He modeled the compassionate countenance of God the Father toward his family, for which his students are forever grateful.

3

God the Son

ONE OF THE BEST WAYS FORWARD FOR THE-
ology, and specifically Christology, to make the case for its relevance in a postmodern context would be to engage seriously,
thoroughly, and creatively with drama. Hans Urs von Balthasar's
major work *Theo-Drama* argues for re-engagement with the stage
as a constructive development for theology in the twentieth and
twenty-first century.[1] We will be using theo-drama as a way to
construct a postmodern theology of Holy Saturday. Through this
we will see that the theo-drama of the Bible is a narrative about
compassion. The Old Testament reveals the covenant love of God.
The New Testament reveals the extent of that covenant love as
compassion in which the event of Holy Saturday is the dramatic
climax to the theo-drama of God's covenantal involvement with
the world.

It is my conviction that theo-drama is possible in any era. If
theo-dramatic theory can overcome the No of the early Church
to the theatre and the No of modernism to theology, surely it
can overcome the deconstructive No of the theater and theology
of postmodernism. But how?

As is stated in the first chapters of Balthasar's *Theo-Drama*,
strong objections to this convergence existed in every age of Christian history. The early Church, modernism, and postmodernism
have all rejected theo-dramatic theory. Let's examine these three
Nos and along the way I will elucidate the Christological core of
theo-dramatic theory in which all of these Nos can be overcome.

We must remember that the first No to the possibility of theo-
drama comes from Christianity. In its earliest stages, Christianity
begins assimilating Greco-Roman philosophy but not its theatre.
It could be said simplistically that when evangelizing the ancient
Greco-Roman world, Christians chose Plato not Euripides, the
Stoics not the Thespians.

---

1 Hans Urs von Balthasar, *Theo-Drama: Theological Dramatic Theory*, trans.
Graham Harrison, 5 vols. (San Francisco: Ignatius Press, 1988–98).

With Plato, the ambiguities of the illusionary world must not be imitated because imitation (mimesis) is in fact the only true tragedy. Plato commits the lover of wisdom to the just life seeking the Good, rather than the dubious mythic realm of the God of Drama, Dionysus. Plato's decisive No to the theater reverberated through the centuries within Christianity.

The loftiness of the ancient Greek theater had, by the time of the Christians, devolved into bawdy, popular entertainment. Christianity's suspicion of the theater is evident in these early centuries from many different sources. Novatian has no time for any who would use Scripture to justify the lewd theater and admonishes Christians to participate instead in the theater of creation and salvation.[2] Tertullian is particularly anti-theatrical in his *De spectaculis*, agreeing with the Stoic objections to arousing the passions.[3] Augustine recommends that actors should be refused baptism and Eucharist.[4] In his *Confessions*, he claims that one must overcome the curiosity about the theatre and gladiatorial games because it will only encourage bloodlust.[5] Church synods continue in this vein. The Synod of Elvira (c. 300–303) maintained that if actors want to become Christians, "they must first renounce their professions" otherwise "they shall be expelled from the church."[6] The Apostolic Constitutions were quite explicit: "Actors and actresses, charioteers, gladiators, runners, theatrical directors, Olympic competitors, players of flute, zither and lyre, and dancers—these should either abandon their occupations or be expelled from the Church; the same applies to those who are addicted to the madness of the theatre."[7]

---

2 Novatian, "De Spectaculis," in *The Trinity, The Spectacles, Jewish Foods, In Praise of Purity, Letters*, trans. Russell J. DeSimone, *The Fathers of the Church*, vol. 67 (Washington, D.C.: Catholic University of America, 1974), III, 3, 9–10.

3 Tertullian, "De Spectaculis," in *Apology: De Spectaculis*, trans. T. R. Glover (Cambridge, MA: Harvard University Press, 1931), 16, 30.

4 Augustine, *On Faith and Works*, trans. Gregory J. Loubardo (New York: Newman Press, 1988), 18.

5 Augustine, *Confessions*, trans. Henry Chadwick (New York: Oxford University Press, 1991), III, 2.

6 Samuel Laeuchli, *Power and Sexuality: The Emergence of Canon Law at the Synod of Elvira* (Philadelphia: Temple University Press, 1974), canon 62.

7 Apostolic Constitution, VIII, 32, 9 as quoted in Hans Urs von Balthasar, *Prolegomena*, vol. 1 of *Theo-Drama: Theological Dramatic Theory*, trans. Graham Harrison (San Francisco: Ignatius Press, 1988), 97.

By the Middle Ages, the rhetoric against the theater has lessened. Thomas Aquinas allows the actor to be on the stage as long as it is without sin.[8] The world of the mystery play emerges in this era in which the lines between theology and drama, between the sanctuary and the stage, begin to blur. In the mystery plays, theater evolves out of the Christian drama of salvation history. The West saw the liturgy unfold its dramatic character culminating with Holy Week. Medieval theater has its origins in short plays performed by the clergy in the churches. These episodes from salvation history were used to engage the public in the mysteries of faith. Gradually, the performances were imbued with worldly elaboration, mixing religious themes with the comic and grotesque as well as the farcical and satirical. As these plays increased their "worldly" elements, the conflict between theology and drama re-emerged, revealing no inward reconciliation. Throughout the rest of the complex history, particularly during the modern and postmodern age, theology and drama have oscillated between precarious neutrality and outright rejection.

All of this gives a sketch of Christianity's initial No to the theater, which had arguably detrimental repercussions for the history of theology and drama.

Overcoming Resistance

Despite or because of the evidence of history, theology should embrace theo-dramatic theory. Balthasar said that "It is time, therefore, to attempt a synthesis: theology is pressing for it from within, and from outside—from drama—we have so much material at our disposal."[9] Theology—as a study of revelation—calls for theatre because revelation's shape is dramatic. Drama—as a study of existence—presses in toward theology as it calls for transcendence. It is an anthropological and theatrical phenomenon to imitate (*mimesis*) not as mere disguise but more significantly as seeking perfection in remembrance (*anamnesis*). For Balthasar, Christian theology should want to take up drama as an attempt at perfecting transcendence.

Theo-drama performs a task, Balthasar writes, "which is to draw an *instrumentarium*, a range of resources, from the drama of existence

---

8 Thomas Aquinas, *Summa Theologica*, vol. 4, trans. Fathers of the English Dominican Province (New York: Benziger, 1948), II-II, 168, 3-4.
9 Balthasar, *Theo-Drama* I, 125.

which can then be of service to a Christian theory of theo-drama in which the 'natural' drama of existence (between Absolute and relative) is consummated in the 'supernatural' drama between the God of Jesus Christ and mankind."[10] Balthasar attempted what had not been done before because he saw that these disciplines manifest an inward dynamism toward each other.

And here is where Balthasar is superb: that convergent dynamism is Jesus Christ. The drama of the Christian narrative of Jesus Christ (both its promise and fulfillment) dynamically contains already the millions of theatrical plays, tragic inciting incidences, and divinely-inspired climaxes. The dying and rising of every human life is contained within the one dying and rising of Jesus Christ. The one narrative contains within it all other narratives. While the Church has been ignoring this disruptively important idea, the forces of theatre and indeed of theology have been pushing toward it. And Balthasar has discovered it and presented it persuasively.

Just think what would be possible for Christian theology and humanity if it accepted the final concrete universality of the performance of Jesus Christ.

The No of Modernism: What Is the Case?

But overcoming the resistant No of Christian history is not enough. The No of modernism seemingly destroys any possible relation between theatre and theology. Modernism has devastated the whole project of Christendom, which attempted a synthesizing of Christianity and Western civilization. In the words of Orlando Costas, Christendom was "a vision of a society organized around Christian principles and values with the Church as its manager or mentor."[11] Modernism, of course, becomes a project to dismantle this synthesized artifice of Christendom.

As a product of the Enlightenment, modernism was the process by which the person's task became the Kantian "*sapere aude!* (dare to know!)" and to "dare to know" specifically against creedal Christianity. Modernism's mechanisms of revolution, science, and technology were designed to lead humanity into the era of the

---

10 Ibid., 130.
11 Orlando Costas, *Christ Outside the Gate: Mission Beyond Christendom* (Maryknoll, NY: Orbis Books, 1982), 189.

new Metropolis. Theatre often became a tool for the State's Tower of Neo-Babel.

Georg Wilhelm Friedrich Hegel (d. 1831), as modernist heavy-weight, deals the greatest blow against the possibility of theo-dramatic theory. According to Hegel, "Christianity abolishes art." Balthasar believed that his own project would be possible only if Hegel's critique could be countered. Put simply, the theatre, for Hegel, is the unequivocal high point of all art. The first thesis of art is epic poetry which expresses the spirit of the nation. The second antithesis of art is the emergent subjectivity of lyric poetry. Together these art forms come into transcending synthesis with theatre. However, Hegel argued that the incarnational anthro-pomorphisms of Christianity introduced a fall backward from spiritual transcendence to the concretized myth of Jesus Christ. The result is that creedal Christianity is but the mere "image" of the absolute Spirit. To sum up, Christianity abolishes art because it prevents the transcending synthesis toward theatre as pinnacle of the Absolute Spirit.

Overcoming Modernism: What Should Be the Case?

Balthasar argued that Christian theology does not abolish art, but rather fulfills it inwardly. It must be "the task of Christians to lay hold of drama's relevance and interpret it to the world, just as, elsewhere, we have enjoined them to shoulder responsibility for the philosophical task."[12]

And so, Balthasar argues against Hegel's critique by developing an authentic understanding of Jesus Christ. According to Balthasar, if Jesus is the truly universal, he is also the finally valid concrete.

The transcendence of art toward the absolute, on which Hegel insists, ignores the permanently valid concreteness of individual existence and specifically, the concrete existence of Jesus of Naza-reth. The Catholic Christmas Liturgy proclaims: "In the year of the one hundred and ninety-fourth Olympiad; from the founding of the city of Rome, seven hundred and fifty-two years; in the rule of Caesar Octavian Augustus, the forty-second year; the whole world being at peace: Jesus Christ, the eternal Son . . . became man."[13]

---

12 Balthasar, *Theo-Drama* I, 70.
13 USCCB, "The Nativity of the Our Lord Jesus Christ," in *Roman Missal*, Third Edition (Washington D. C.: USCCB, 2011), accessed July 2, 2022, https://

Concrete enfleshment of the Son of God must be central to authentic Christianity, leaving behind Hegel's modernist, hyper-transcendent spirit for the clouds.

The No of Postmodernism: What Is the Case?

While it is important to understand Hegel's critique and Balthasar's response, my question is about postmodernism. Hegel has probably had his days of dominance in academia. Certainly, for Balthasar, Hegel was a central specter of what's fascinatingly wrong with modernism. There are few philosophers as able as Hegel to produce a Tower of Babel so constructed that any theologians intent on accepting the glory of God's revelation must attempt to destroy it.

However, the present dominance of postmodernism (at least within academia) would seem to make impossible a new meta-narrative structure called theo-drama. For the great postmodernist Jacques Derrida, all logocentrism must be undone—whether it is Plato, Hegel, or Balthasar.

Modernism, of course, proposes a universal human nature in that all humanity shares the same capacity for rationality. Postmodernism can be variously defined, but following this line of thought, postmodernist Michel Foucault (d. 1984) states that rationality is so dependent on power structures of multiple communities that no objective knowledge valid for all can ever be obtained. Or for Stanley Fish rationality is so dependent on a particular community's discourse that it is better to speak of multiple humanities who exist in polyrational communities.

At least modernism maintains the idea of truth, albeit an anthropocentric truth as opposed to Christianity's theo-centrism. As we explored in chapter 1, postmodernism denies the possibility of a meta-narrative of "truth." No normative position of observation exists in postmodernism's critique of reason. Richard Rorty's antirepresentationist stance holds that everything is relative to one's context, especially one's attempt to represent "truth" in some other context than one's own.[14]

---

www.usccb.org/prayer-and-worship/liturgical-year-and-calendar/christmas/christmas-proclamation.

14 The reason my students do not laugh at my jokes is that there are no universally valid funny jokes, like the one time this guy goes to a psychiatrist

The other remains always other.

The role for theatre in this new philosophical realm is philosophic problemitizer (such as Tom Stoppard's plays, like *Arcadia* or the popular Broadway comedy *God of Carnage*), contextual advocate (the film *Milk*), or relativistic peacemaker (the musical *The Book of Mormon*).

The modernist critique of theo-drama asked how a universal could be concrete and yet finally valid. The postmodernist critique would ask the exact opposite: how what is limited and concrete could be elevated to be universal and finally valid.

In postmodernism, no normative interpretation of texts exists because an "interpretation" already assumes a structure of meaning that will be, from the start, foreign to the text. If there can be no logos how can there be a *theo*-drama?

Overcoming Postmodernism: What Should Be the Case?

The answer is Jesus Christ, he who is the finally valid concrete universal. Let me explain. Now we have this important Balthasarian idea—Jesus Christ is the finally valid concrete universal who is asymmetrically over and above the universal because more profoundly concrete and particular.

To be authentically concrete, Jesus Christ would need a particular experience of existence. To be authentically universal, he would need to experience all particular existences. If all concrete existences are non-normative (every center is relative to every other center so there is no universal center), then how could Jesus Christ's particular existence be *finally* valid for all? For Jesus Christ to be the finally universally valid man, he would need to contain all existences in him as *the* meaning of them all.

But how could we say that Jesus Christ knows the existence of a Shoah victim in Auschwitz? How could we say he knows the existence of a civilian Sunni in Aleppo? How could we say he contains the existence of a World Trade Center Tower 2 office worker in New York City on September 11, 2001 at 9:59 AM?

---

and says, "Doc, my brother's crazy, he thinks he's a chicken." And the doctor says, "Well, why don't you turn him in?" And the guy says, "I would. But I need the eggs" (Woody Allen, *Annie Hall*). "More than any other time in history, mankind faces a crossroads. One path leads to despair and utter hopelessness. The other, to total extinction. Let us pray we have the wisdom to choose correctly" (Woody Allen, *My Speech to the Graduates*).

While Jesus Christ may not have the particularities of these existences, he has experienced their existences' ultimate core—suffering to the greatest depths. All humans suffer and suffering is universal not in its physical, mental, or psychic disturbances, but essentially in the experience of catastrophic non-relationality. And Jesus Christ has experienced this intense core of suffering in his descent into the intense non-relationality of hell.

To be in hell is to experience non-relation with God. In Christian faith, we believe that Jesus Christ has descended to the dead and experienced the one human universal—suffering death in seeming non-relationality.

For Balthasar, hell is a state of "supreme solitude" in which one's self is made destitute by being in non-relation to all others, especially to God. It is the ultimate suffering and madness of being eternally alone. Jesus descended to this hell.

For Christians, if they hold a full belief in redemption by substitution, it must mean that the God-man took on the whole experience of suffering, death, Godforsakenness, and self-destitution. If "for our sake [God] made him to be sin who knew no sin, so that in him we might become the righteousness of God" (2 Cor 5:21), then he took on the whole experience of sin without having committed the sin.

As Balthasar said, "Christ willed to deliver us by his solidarity with us who were (physically and spiritually) dead." [15] He would have to undergo the fullness of solidarity which means physical and spiritual death. Death and Hades engulfed us all. "That is why Christ did not only come down to earth, but also under the earth ... He found us all in the netherworld ... and brought us out from there not on to earth but into the Kingdom of heaven." [16]

In his vision of sin and experience of the Godforsakenness of hell, Jesus as the Son of God maintains objectively his beatific vision, that is his union with the Father and the Holy Spirit, yet he also experiences the vision of "sheer sin," what Plato called *borboros* (mud, ordure), the leprosy of humanity's liberty.

The suffering of hell is not then something that just touches Jesus's humanity. Rather, "by virtue of his deepest Trinitarian experience, he takes 'Hell' with him, as the expression of his power

---

15 Hans Urs von Balthasar, *Mysterium Paschale: The Mystery of Easter*, trans. Aidan Nichols (San Francisco: Ignatius Press, 2000), 177.
16 Ibid., 179.

to dispose, as judge, the everlasting salvation or the everlasting loss of man."[17] This suffering touches the Son's divine relation with the Father in the Holy Spirit. Although objectively, he is one with the Father and the Spirit, subjectively he experiences the Godforsaken, self-destitution of suffering in hell.

The post-modern critique of religious views finds that in the end there is no redemption, no exit from destitution of the self. We are all closed in by our own parochial spheres without any universally normative objective worldview. I think that the Trinitarian Christology presented here provides the possibility of overcoming the limits of these spheres. We will find in this theology of Holy Saturday ways for dialogue between Christianity and postmodernism.

Nothing belongs more to us than our suffering destitution of self. This Christian view emphasizes God's mission to send his Son into the deepest, inner sphere of our destitution and he suffers with us (*com-passion*) and thereby contains all particular concrete existences. He dwells there and cries for us, as us: "My God, my God, why have you forsaken me?"

In the hellish pit of the ordure of our liberty, the Son cries Yes to God. For the postmodern, what is most compelling in Balthasar's theology of Holy Saturday is that the postmodern man is not alone in the devastation of his personhood. He thought he was suffering the abandonment of God, others, and himself alone. But, in this suffering, he meets the Son of God who is also seemingly abandoned by the Father.

It is not that there are no finally valid universals, there is but one—the Word made flesh who has ascended to heaven. It is not that there are no finally valid concretes, there is but one—the Word made flesh who has descended to hell. But, how do we come to know this Word descended?

God is His Own Self-Diffusive Exegete

God has sent his only Son who has made the Father known.[18] From the Son, we come to know the Father. From the Word of God, we come to know the word of the Scripture. In the Son of God, we come to know God because he is the exegete of God as

---

17 Ibid., 177.

18 These ideas come from my reading of an article by Hans Urs von Balthasar entitled "God Is His Own Exegete," *Communio: International Catholic Review* 4 (1986): 280–87.

it says in the Gospel of John, "No one has ever seen God; the only-begotten Son, who is in the bosom of the father, he has made him known (*exegesis*)" (Jn 1:18).

The Son abandoned himself in obedience to the Father and the Holy Spirit in order that Mary and the Church (and Mary as the Church) would do the same. Jesus Christ is indeed the central dramatic character. He is not acting in isolation from other dramatic characters. The Father has written the play for universal performance. The Holy Spirit as director makes the play concretely present for every audience who, as audience, is already participating in the action. Mary and the Church are at once both the audience receiving the exegetical action and also dramatic characters themselves participating in the christological exegetical action. Indeed, the theo-drama was never meant to be interpreted passively by an objective observer (contra modernism), but was meant to draw the subjective audience (affirm postmodernism) into the interpretive action of the Son. In being drawn into the action, the audience member has the greatest possible chance of becoming fully human, of laying hold of his own authentic substance, of grasping that most intimate idea of his own self and the fuller revelation of God. Man is not yet fully active as person if he looks only at the stage and does not join in the perfect referential action. Man is known in his suffering because Jesus Christ has experienced the depth of his suffering. This world drama is for me, *pro me*, and for us, *pro nobis*. Within the action in Christ, one becomes a full person. In the obedience of the Son, the Church follows the way of obedience into the Triune God. The Holy Spirit as the Spirit of obedience is given to bring about the obedience of the Church.

The Incarnation as the Son's Yes to the Father and the Holy Spirit (and God's Yes to the world) pierced through the sphere of hesitation of humanity's halfway Yes and No. According to Balthasar, the disobedient vacillation of humanity needed an irrevocable *verbum*, an unreserved Yes. Jesus Christ "is something no other man can be, God's ultimate (*end-gültig*, 'finally valid') Yes to the world; he is the Word in whom God resolved to reveal himself, in an unsurpassable manner, to the world."[19] The unreserved Yes

19 Hans Urs von Balthasar, *The Dramatis Personae: The Person in Christ*, vol. 3 of *Theo-Drama: Theological Dramatic Theory*, trans. Graham Harrison (San Francisco: Ignatius, 1993).

opened the stage in Jesus Christ for the dramatic action of God bringing the world into him and out of the sphere of hesitation by the outpouring of the Spirit of obedience. Jesus Christ's Yes plummets through to the depths of man's No in his descent to hell only to bring the whole of creation back into the Father's redeeming love.

The self-abandonment of obedience to Jesus Christ moves one into a state of expanding universality depending upon one's ecclesial mission. Balthasar argues that "Theological persons are not monads ... the theological person radiates as far as his vocation and mission reaches."[20] Through self-surrender, the destruction of the human center causes a de-privatization of the "I" and creates a locus for ecclesial manifestation of Christ's mission. The Church in her Yes and through her sacramental structure does not present a colorful but ultimately unimportant subplot to the theo-drama. On the contrary, she is united in one mission with the Son and gives her own dependent exegetical participation in the exegesis of God by the Son through the Holy Spirit.

The Son reveals who God is through covenantal relationship. By being in intimate covenantal relationship, one comes truly to *know* the other. Through the progressive revelation of the covenantal relationship God desires with his people, the Son has made the Father's heart known.

Beginning with the covenant with Adam and Eve, God has intended men to be in free relationship with him and each other. Reading the Bible as God's own story, at the creation of Adam and Eve, the Lord makes a covenantal relationship in two parts "Be frutiful and multiply" and "Have dominion ... over every living thing" (Gen 1:28).[21] God is allowing the human persons to express their being-in-the-image-of-God through making new humans—a fundamental expression of their sexual identities as a man and woman. He is also allowing them to participate in his paternal care for creation. Everything created is in right relation:

---

20 Balthasar, *Theo-Drama*, III:271. A "theological person" is man as God encounters him as belonging to his triune love.

21 Here we are reading the Bible as God's own story. See William Kurz, *Reading the Bible as God's Own Story: A Catholic Approach for Bringing Scripture to Life* (Ijamsville, MD: Word Among Us Press, 2007). See also the important book by Luke Timothy Johnson and William Kurz, *The Future of Catholic Biblical Scholarship: A Constructive Conversation* (Grand Rapids, MI: Eerdmans, 2002).

there is right relation (righteousnes) between God and humanity, between man and woman, and between humanity and creation.

In the Fall of Adam and Eve (Gen 2), the covenantal relationship is ruptured on humanity's part. God's generous love depicted in the book of Genesis goes about reconciling human persons with each other and with himself as their Creator. The Book of Genesis presents tale after tale of reconciliation, especially between brothers—Jacob reconciled with Esau (Gen 33) and Joseph reconciled with his brothers (Gen 50:15-21).

Within this foundational, revelatory book, God chooses Abraham and makes a concrete covenant with him that is meant to draw the whole world back into right relationship with him. God speaks to Abraham in a three part covenantal promise giving to Abraham a land and nationhood (Gen 12:1), a name and dynasty (Gen 12:2), and a worldwide blessing (Gen 12:3). God desires to create a concrete place for a concrete people that are trained in the freedom to love, which is developed in the sacrificial vision (Gen 15), and which we will find fulfilled in the covenant with Moses (Ex 19). Through the name of Abraham, God desires to create a legacy of faithful generations concretized in the ritual of circumcision (Gen 17), which will find fulfillment in the covenant with David, whose reign begins a king-priest dynasty (2 Sam 7). Through the faithfulness of Abraham, God desires to create a right relationship of sacrificial love for the blessing of the whole of humanity (Gen 22), which will find fulfillment in the New Covenant of Jesus Christ (Mt 26:26-29).

In fulfillment of the first promise given to Abraham, God works through Moses to give his people the land and nationhood that follows in obediential love. After the Israelites have been set free from slavery in Egypt, God brings them to Mount Sinai, where he had revealed his name to Moses (Ex 3:13-22), and makes with them a three part covenant that requires first of all their obedience (Ex 19:5). If they obey his voice and keep his covenant, following the Ten Commandments (Ex 20; Deut 5:6-21), the whole of the Law (Ex 21-23 and Lev), and above all the crystallizing core of the law, namely loving God with their whole being (Deut 6:5),[22] then they shall be God's "own possession among all the people" (Ex 19:5).

---

22 Gerhard Lohfink, *Does God Need the Church?: Toward a Theology of the People of God*, trans. Linda M. Maloney (Collegeville, MN: Liturgical Press, 1999), 74-88.

God "owns" the whole of his creation, but Israel is being named God's special possession; they will be a concrete representation of his overabundant love. He will give them bread and water in the desert (Ex 16:1–17:7), then milk and honey (Ex 3:17), and then his own Body and Blood (Mt 26:26–29). If they obey, they will be made into "a kingdom of priests and a holy nation" (Ex 19:6). As a kingdom of priests, they will collectively mediate God's presence to humanity and humanity's prayers shall be taken into Israel to be raised up to God. In this way, as a nation they shall be made holy, that is set apart for God's specific purposes.

In fulfillment of the second promise given to Abraham, God works through David to make a dynastic name known the world over for kingly and priestly service. It will be a dynasty that lasts forever, a concrete, permanent relationship of love. In the Second Book of Samuel, the Israelite monarchy originating with Saul receives its golden moment in the covenant with David, to whom God promises a great name (2 Sam 7:9). And this name shall be made so great that dynastically, this kingdom shall not end (2 Sam 7:13). And this kingdom will produce a king who is God's Son (2 Sam 7:14). This anointed king will establish the path for all humanity—*wasoth torath ha'adam* "this is the law for man" (2 Sam 7:19).

In fulfillment of the third promise given to Abraham, God works through Jesus to make the New Covenant of reconciled relationship, of compassionate mercy. If they will eat this bread that is his Body and drink this wine that is his Blood, they will receive the forgiveness of sins (Mt 26:26–29). If they take his Body (Mt 27:35) and receive his Blood (Jn 19:34) offered on the Cross, they will be in reconciled, familial relationship with the Trinity which is light (1 Jn 1:5) and love (1 Jn 4:7).

Each of these covenants has its specific contexts in the theological drama, but there is an inner link between them. The Son of God reveals that in God's own self there is relational space for the other to love in freedom. The human other is invited into this divine origin to see God as he is (1 Jn 3:2)—and he is self-diffusive compassionate goodness.

This last phrase is very Bonaventurian so, in reflecting on the Son of God's compassion, let us think about the metaphysical consequences, with Bonaventure as our guide. Let us analyze for a time Chapter Six of Bonaventure's "The Soul's Journey Into

God" and see his understanding of the good as compassionate self-diffusion.[23] I begin with consideration of the historical and structural context. Then, I proceed from Being to the Good (§ 1), from the Good to the Trinity (§ 2–3), from the Trinity to Jesus Christ (§ 4–6), from Jesus Christ to Mystical Ecstasy (§ 7).

At the time Bonaventure (c. 1217–1274) writes "The Soul's Journey Into God" (late September to early October 1259), two diverging Trinitarian traditions have emerged—one relational and one emanational, often attributed to Dominican and Franciscan, respectively. Both traditions begin with agreement that there is one *ousia* (being or substance) of God who is three *hypostases* (persons). From this agreement came reflection on how the three hypostases differ. One believed in the differentiation of the hypostases by relation and the other by emanation and spiration—the former thought was principally held by Dominicans and the latter principally held by Franciscans. Initially these views were not contradictory, but through the late Middle Ages, they began to diverge: "On the Dominican interpretation of the relation account the persons are constituted in opposed pairs (Father in opposition to Son, Father and Son in opposition to Holy Spirit), whereas on the Franciscan interpretation of the emanation account persons are constituted singly on the basis of their unique emanational property."[24]

Bonaventure developed more clearly the Franciscan interpretation. He began articulating his position in his commentary on Peter Lombard's *Sententiae* in 1250, which is also about the time that Saint Thomas Aquinas was writing his commentary on the *Sententiae*.[25] Bonaventure explained his emanation model succinctly in the *Collationes in Hexaemeron* (*Sermons on the Six Days of Creation*): "This is our whole metaphysics: emanation, exemplarity, consummation; to be illumined by spiritual rays and to be led back to the highest reality."[26] The book, "The Soul's Journey Into God," comes out of his matured metaphysics.

---

23 Bonaventure, "The Soul's Journey Into God," in *Bonaventure*, trans. Ewert Cousins (New York: Paulist Press, 1978).

24 Russell L. Friedman, "Divergent Traditions in Later-Medieval Trinitarian Theology: Relations, Emanations, and the Use of Philosophical Psychology, 1250–1325," *Studia Theologica* 53 (1999): 15.

25 Ibid., 17.

26 Bonaventure, *Collationes in Hexaemeron* 17 (V, 332) as quoted by Ewert Cousins, "Introduction," *The Soul's Journey*, 26.

Bonaventure began writing "The Soul's Journey Into God" ("*Itinerarium mentis in Deum*") in solitude at Mount La Verna in Tuscany thirty-three years after the death of Saint Francis of Assisi, which was on October 4, 1226. The site of Mount La Verna was the place where, in the last two years of his life, Francis received the stigmata from a seraph angel who was holding in his wings the Crucified Christ. At the time of the writing of *The Soul's Journey*, Bonaventure has become the minister general of the Franciscan Order which needed his guidance through difficult internal and external struggles.[27] He seems to have retreated to Mount La Verna to draw some peace and wisdom from this mystical moment in Francis's life.[28] The result of Bonaventure's search produces a Gothic cathedral of his theological thought.

Bonaventure structured his work on the image of the six-winged seraph, who appears in the Book of Isaiah (Is 6:2) and, Bonaventure believes, appeared to Francis, because "this vision represented our father's [Francis's] rapture in contemplation and the road by which this rapture is reached."[29] The six wings of the seraph represent the six levels of illumination discussed in the six chapters of his book that culminate with a seventh chapter on the sabbath day rest of God with his creation. During the time of Bonaventure, traditional angelology designated the lower pair of the Seraph's wings embracing the feet of the Crucified. The middle pair designated spiritual flight in that the angel is not limited by material locationality. These wings are often depicted artistically as extended out like a gliding eagle's wings and as representative of the traditionally Christian *orans* prayer position. Lastly, as discussed in the previous chapter, the upper pair of wings designated the angel's spiritual sight that participates in viewing God's radiant being. These wings thrust out, then turn in toward each other forming an arc above the Crucified Christ's head. The divisions of the book are set up as paired chapters about three themes—a sort of six-pack metaphysics. Bonaventure begins the journey rising "from [Christ's] feet to the wounds in his side to his head, once crowned with thorns and

27 Cousins, "Introduction," 19.
28 See Bonaventure, *The Soul's Journey*, Prologue, 1, 53.
29 Bonaventure, *The Soul's Journey*, Prologue, 2, 54.

now crowned with glory."[30] The first two chapters begin with the material world and the process of sensation that represent the lower pair of wings as they embrace the feet or vestiges of God. The third and fourth chapters journey by reason and the soul. They represent the middle pair of wings as meditative and contemplative prayer. The fifth and sixth chapters arrive at God in himself and contemplate God's Being and Goodness. The seventh chapter meditates on stigmatic union with the Crucified Christ himself. The structure of the book also follows the classic mystical ascending to God through purgation (chapters 1-2), illumination (3-4), and unification (5-7). The movement of the work imitates Dionysius's ascent theology from the world into oneself and then into God himself, from the cataphatic to the apaphatic, from positive theology to negative theology.[31]

From Being to the Good (§1)

Having established a historical and structural context, let us spend some time on the sixth chapter to develop our theology of compassion. The sixth chapter, which is called "On Contemplating the Most Blessed Trinity in Its Name Which Is Good," builds on the previous chapter, which was Bonaventure's first explicit engagement with God's Being in itself. The previous chapter outlined Bonaventure's comprehension of God's unity, but the Christian desires more in his contemplation because an authentic Christian metaphysics must seek "to reduce all of reality to one first principle that is origin, exemplar, and final end of all things" and this First Principle is not a divine monad but a divine Trinity.[32] Contemplating God as Being introduces "the essential attributes of God"; however, the principle for "contemplating the emanations" gives rise to the height of "the most blessed Trinity" as Good itself.[33] Platonic meditation is not enough for the Christian mystic. Contemplation of Being itself will only lead to knowledge of the essential attributes of God, whereas contemplation of Good

---

30 Jaroslav Pelikan, *Jesus Through the Centuries: His Place in the History of Culture* (New Haven, CT: Yale University Press, 1985), 127.

31 See Dionysius, "The Divine Names," in *Pseudo-Dionysius: The Complete Works*, trans. Colm Luibheid (New York: Paulist Press, 1987).

32 Delio, "Bonaventure's Metaphysics," 2.

33 Bonaventure, *The Soul's Journey*, VI, 1.

itself will lead to knowledge of the Trinity divinely revealed in the crucified Son.

The shift is from a philosophical metaphysics of Being to a theological metaphysics of Good. Just as in the Aristotelian universe the ultimate ground is the Unmoved Mover, Bonaventure's grounding is the Good that "is the basic and normative reality of the universe."[34] Jesus reveals God as Goodness itself because, "No one is good but God alone" (Mk 10:18). God alone is good, is Goodness itself. All goodness in the created realm participates in God's Goodness.[35] Moreover, "One can no longer talk about being as the ground of reality without talking about God, and one can no longer talk about God who is Trinity without talking about the good."[36]

From the Good to the Trinity (§2–3)

The second paragraph starts fascinatingly with an Anselmian-style argument. Anselm's *Proslogion* sought to arrive at God's existence *a priori*, grounded in the metaphysical maxim that it is better to be than not to be.[37] Bonaventure states that, "the highest good is without qualification that than which no greater can be thought."[38] After the Anselmian major proposition, the minor proposition comes from Dionysius the Areopagite in the definition of good. In his *Celestial Hierarchy* and *Divine Names*, Bonaventure concludes that the "good is said to be self-diffusive (*bonum diffusive sui*)."[39] The conclusion deduced from the major and minor propositions is that "the highest good must be most self-diffusive."[40] He then goes on

34 Kevin Keane, "Why Creation? Bonaventure and Thomas Aquinas on God as Creative Good," *Downside Review* 93 (1975): 112.

35 For a Thomistic interpretation of the transcendentals, see Alice Ramos, *Dynamic Transcendentals: Truth, Goodness, and Beauty from a Thomistic Perspective* (Washington, D. C.: Catholic University of America Press, 2012).

36 Delio, "Bonaventure's Metaphysics," 2.

37 Bonaventure, *The Soul's Journey*, VI, 2, 102. See Anselm, *Proslogion, with the Replies of Gaunilo and Anselm*, trans. Thomas Williams (Indianapolis: Hackett Publishing, 1995).

38 Bonaventure, *The Soul's Journey*, VI, 2, 102.

39 Bonaventure, *The Soul's Journey*, VI, 2, 103. See Dionysius, "Celestial Hierarchy" and "Divine Names" in *Pseudo-Dionysius: The Complete Works*, trans. Colm Luibheid (New York: Paulist Press, 1987).

40 Ibid. We could use another concept, namely self-kenosis. See my chapter, "Does God Suffer?: Hans Urs von Balthasar's Theology of Holy Saturday," in *On Suffering: An Inter-Disciplinary Dialogue on Narrative and the Meaning of Suffering,*

to define self-diffusion as necessarily having these aspects: existing (actual), of its own self (intrinsic), essence (substantial), personal identity (hypostatic), not caused (natural), autonomous (voluntary), not coerced (free), indispensable (necessary), self-sustained (lacking nothing), and complete (perfect).[41] Therefore, the highest good must have these same qualities to the utmost. In addition to these qualities, the highest good, if it is true self-diffusion (self-kenotic), must produce something other than itself "by way of generation and spiration," which are two ways to diffuse the self.[42] From Richard of St. Victor, the generation and spiration are the beloved and co-beloved, the *dilectum* and *condilectio*. In his *On the Trinity*, Richard states that when there is a beloved there is a third who is the co-beloved loved in harmony by the lover and the beloved.[43] Bonaventure holds that charity necessitates a plurality; one is generator, one the generated, and the other spirated, that is, the Father, Son, and Holy Spirit.

Essential to this Trinitarian contemplation is that the generation and spiration are not created. The highest form of self-diffusion, if it is truly the highest, cannot have a point at which it is not self-diffusive. Therefore, the greatest self-diffusion is the entire substance and nature communicated with no instance when this diffusion was not occurring. Bonaventure further defines this fullest of diffusions as coming about "by way of the Word, in which all things are said and by way of the Gift, in which other gifts are given."[44] Thus, the highest communication of substance and nature is by the Word and by Gift, both of which are different ways of diffusing the entire self. Generation comes by Word and spiration comes by Gift: "you can see that through the highest communicability of the good, there must be a Trinity of the Father and the Son and the Holy Spirit."[45]

In the third paragraph, Bonaventure, having named the qualities of supremacy, places them in a coincidence of opposites moving from goodness to "super-excellent goodness."[46] We see the "supreme communicability with individuality of persons, supreme

---

eds. Matthew Lewis Sutton and Nate Hinerman (Oxford: Inter-disciplinary Press, 2012), 171–83.   41 Ibid.   42 Ibid.
43 Delio, "Bonaventure's Metaphysics," 2n15.
44 Bonaventure, *The Soul's Journey*, VI, 2, 104.
45 Ibid.   46 Ibid., VI, 3, 105.

consubstantiality with plurality of hypostases, supreme configurability with distinct personality, supreme coequality with degree, supreme co-eternity with emanation, supreme mutual intimacy with mission."[47] The Trinity is the highest good such that self-diffusion produces a truly distinct self from the origin, which is of the same substance but plural in selfhood or personhood. One is the emanation and the other the producer of the emanation, which is origin. After stating these bold assertions of distinction he comes back to contemplating the unity that must be "in essence, form, dignity, eternity, existence and unlimitedness."[48] This move is explicitly Dionysian. He states positive aspects about the Trinity as the Good, but then he moves to disruptive negation by stating the opposites of the positives. The Trinity is always more.

The relations of origin distinguish the Persons of the Trinity: "The distinction of the divine persons according to origin means that the Father is distinguished by paternity, the Son by generation and the Spirit by spiration of the love between the Father and Son."[49] Bonaventure grounds his theology in emphatic statements of tri-unity in one divine essence. He is clear that the three Divine Persons diffuse themselves into each other.

Some have simply characterized Bonaventure's Trinitarian theology as dynamic and Aquinas's Trinitarian theology as static.[50] This stereotype is truly inappropriate for either.[51] Bonaventure's theology makes room for understanding the Trinity as voluntary, free, and self-contained, and Aquinas's theology meditates on God as pure act, which is hardly static. They both believe that to say God is love, is to say God is triune.

From Trinity to Jesus Christ (§4–6)

The shift in Bonaventure's theological metaphysics scales the mystic heights from the essential and personal properties of God to personal and collective mystical union in Jesus Christ, the God-man. As Bonaventure tells it, in the desire for mystical union the first

---

47 Ibid. 48 Ibid., VI, 3, 106. 49 Ibid., 3.
50 Keane, "Why Creation," 111–12.
51 See Timothy Smith, *Thomas Aquinas' Trinitarian Theology: A Study in Theological Method* (Washington, D. C.: Catholic University of America Press, 2010) and Gilles Emery, *The Trinitarian Theology of Thomas Aquinas*, trans. Francesca Aran Murphy (Oxford: Oxford University Press, 2010).

Cherub of the Mercy Seat (Ex 25:17-22) contemplates the essential attributes of God. In that contemplation, God is understood as divine Being and "supremely one and yet all-inclusive."[52] However, in seeking for more, Bonaventure asks that this contemplation lead to a new height because God who is Being itself became man. The First Principle is joined with the last; "the eternal is joined with temporal man."[53] The Incarnation of Jesus Christ is itself a coincidence of opposites—knowledge of God will come through a supra-negation of all that's earthly so that all can become heavenly.

Continuing with Bonaventure, the second Cherub of the Mercy Seat (Ex 25:10-22) contemplates the properties of the three Divine Persons. He writes that if "you were amazed" at the self-diffusion being coupled with unity of essence and plurality of personhood and the emanation by the Father to the Son and the spiration of both to the Holy Spirit, then make the assent to the greater ascent of union with Jesus Christ.[54] He is "a trinity of substances and a duality of natures."[55] The hypostatic union contains the highest goodness that has overflowed into a human. The incarnate Son of God is "the metaphysical center of the universe" because in the Incarnation "the highest is joined to the lowest," for God desires "all of creation, from the least to the greatest" to be joined to him "through participation in the good."[56]

The origin of the Incarnation is the Father and due to the greatest self-diffusion emanated to the Son, we can speak of the kenosis of the Father. He empties himself of the divine being by sending his Son: "The self-diffusive goodness that identifies the Father means that the Father is totally self-giving and, in a sense, hidden in the object of his love."[57] And the object of his love is his Son. Goodness is properly fecund such that the Father in his highest goodness, being in perfect fecundity, gives himself eternally to the Son and together with the Son to the Holy Spirit. Because it is completely himself, the love the Father gives is hidden in the generation and spiration; thus, "All things have been delivered to me by my Father; and no one knows the Son except the Father, and no one knows the Father except the Son and anyone to whom the Son chooses to reveal him" (Mt 11:27).

---

52 Bonaventure, *The Soul's Journey*, VI, 5, 107.
53 Ibid.   54 Ibid., VI, 6, 107-8.   55 Ibid.
56 Delio, "Bonaventure's Metaphysics," 8.   57 Ibid., 4.

From Jesus Christ to Mystical Ecstasy (§7)

Bonaventure writes that when one contemplates Jesus Christ the mind is illuminated to perfection because it contemplates the perfect image, the perfect vestige of God. Indeed, he remarks this christological contemplation is like the sabbath (seventh) rest at the end of the six days of creation. God has made a perfect new man (a new *'adam*) in his image and God contemplates his own goodness in this new *'adam*.

The final paragraph of Bonaventure's contemplation leads from Jesus Christ to the mystic's intellect that has been lead by God the Son to an ecstatic joy that reaches "the perfection of its illuminations."[58] The door to this ecstatic joy is Jesus Christ, the Crucified One. In the Prologue, Bonaventure quotes from Revelation, "Blessed are those who wash their robes, that they may have the right to the tree of life and that they may enter the city by the gates" (Rev 22:14). This gate is the Crucified One and the culmination of the mystical vision of the seraph who communicated to Francis "in his body the sacred stigmata of the passion."[59] Because Jesus Christ is the perfected image of the Good, nothing more remains but the mystical ecstasy and the subsequent seventh day of rest in the perfected union of First Principle with the last.

I noted earlier Bonaventure's definition of an authentic Christian metaphysic of emanation, exemplarity, and final end. This tripartite definition is completed on the sixth day. He began this chapter with a discussion of the emanation of the Good as basis for the Trinity. This Trinity has one exemplar for humanity who is the Second Person incarnate in Jesus Christ. This moment is the final end of all metaphysics: mystical union with the incarnate, crucified First Principle. The heart of Bonaventure's theological metaphysics is the wounded, resurrected Jesus Christ. He is located as the universal goodness that is singularly personal. Far from being a metaphysic of remoteness as in Neoplatonic thought, emanation and exemplarity is a personal, communicative reality intimately engaged in the actual nature of man. Because of the metaphysical intimate interpenetration of human nature, the final end is union experienced in mystical ecstasy with Jesus Christ, "not simply Christ but the Crucified Christ."[60]

---

58 Bonaventure, *The Soul's Journey*, VI, 7, 109.   59 Ibid., Prologue, 3, 55.
60 Delio, "Bonaventure's Metaphysics," 7.

The sixth chapter of "The Soul's Journey Into God" is crucial to Bonaventure's theological metaphysics. For many theologians in the early Church and certainly during the Middle Ages, the task of theology begins with faith seeking understanding; their method of theology is always infused with their spirituality. Indeed, "neither St. Thomas nor St. Bonaventure was an extremist; both would have rejected more modern attempts to philosophize without love or desire, to make science cover all modes of cognition, or on the other hand to ban logic in the name of religious and aesthetic experience, and set the will to believe in the place of truth."[61] Particularly in Bonaventure, the soul is actively engaged in a mystical journey, a good adventure, if you will. The implication of such a view, while still using an Aristotelian and Neoplatonic system that can err and conclude with a non-loving, remote Mover, is a theological metaphysics grounded in the Good that contemplates the self-diffusive Trinity.

The compassion of the Son of God, the love we see in the face of Jesus, has its source in the self-diffusive goodness of God who as love is compassion. In this chapter on Christology, we began with drama and we end with thinking about the goodness of the three Divine Persons who reveal their love to each other and have chosen to share this love with their creation through the missions of the Son and Holy Spirit.

---

61 M. C. D'Arcy, *St. Thomas Aquinas* (Westminster, MD: Newman, 1954), 12.

4

God the Holy Spirit

WE ARE BETTER READERS OF SCRIPTURE BECAUSE
we come after Geoffrey Chaucer, T. S. Eliot, and James Joyce.[1] Certainly, much has been accomplished in narrative criticism and its
application to Scripture. Narrative criticism of Scripture arose from
the use of secular literary theory in the 1970s.[2] This method has
provided valid but limited insight into the scriptural text: it has
been valid in that Scripture itself is narrative, but narrative criticism is limited in that the method can neither accommodate the
theological "beyond" to which the text points, nor the complexity
of the dramatic creative elements that are involved in Scripture.
When narrative criticism has been applied specifically to the Gospel
of Luke and the Acts of the Apostles (Luke-Acts), for instance,
the Holy Spirit has been categorized as a "character," but this
classification, I will argue, does not adequately explain the Spirit's
role in Scripture nor in the Trinity. Instead, I propose to expand
narrative criticism to include the theodramatic theory of Hans
Urs von Balthasar as an answer to this theological hermeneutical
problem. My central argument is that the metaphor of drama is
more useful to interpreting Scripture than that of strict narrative.
After all, we are also better readers of Scripture because of great
dramatists like William Shakespeare, Thornton Wilder, Bertolt
Brecht, Anton Chekhov, Tennessee Williams, and Tom Stoppard.

Specifically by employing Hans Urs von Balthasar's theodramatic theory, I will argue that in Luke-Acts the Holy Spirit can

---

1 See Robert Alter, *The World of Biblical Literature* (New York: Basic Books,
1992), 20. See also his fascinating study, *The Art of Biblical Narrative* (New
York: Basic Books, 2011).

2 Scholars like David Rhoads, Donald Michie, Jack Dean Kingsbury, Alan
Culpepper, and Robert Tannehill developed narrative critical theory. See
Mark Allan Powell, *What is Narrative Criticism?* (Minneapolis: Fortress Press,
1990), 5-7. See also Stephen D. Moore, "Afterword: Things Not Written in
This Book," in *Anatomies of Narrative Criticism: The Past, Present, and Futures of the
Fourth Gospel as Literature*, ed. Tom Thatcher and Stephen D. Moore (Atlanta:
Society of Biblical Literature, 2008), 245-56.

be understood as the director of the Son who, as the lead actor, must be made obedient to the prophetic script. The Son as actor is conformed to the part given to him by the Father who is the playwright. First, I analyze attempts to characterize the Holy Spirit. Then, I show how the theological hermeneutical problem can be answered by Balthasar's theodramatic theory in which he understands the Holy Spirit as the director of the theo-drama. Finally, I conclude with an outline of the Holy Spirit as director in Luke-Acts by an exegesis of the annunciation, baptism, and temptation passages. The rest of the chapter will continue to develop a spiritual Pneumatology of compassion.

Theological Hermeneutical Problem: Holy Spirit as Character

Originating in literary theory, biblical narrative criticism uses character theory to describe the Holy Spirit's involvement in the narrative of Luke-Acts. Two questions dominate scholarship on the Holy Spirit and Luke-Acts: Who, according to Luke, is the Holy Spirit, and what does the Holy Spirit do? There is somewhat broad agreement on the second question—the Spirit is a spirit of prophecy. However, the first question divides scholars: Is the Spirit an impersonal force or is the Spirit personal being?[3] I will focus on the scholarship that sees the Holy Spirit as personal being, highlighting two important scholars in this area: William H. Shepherd and Ju Hur.

Shepherd, who produced the first and best scholarly example of narrative criticism on the Holy Spirit, employs the character theories of Baruch Hochman, E. M. Forster, and James Garvey. Shepherd argues that "the Holy Spirit in Luke-Acts is best understood as a character in the narrative."[4] He provides a systematic reading of

---

3 Scholars like Michael Hull, Emil Brunner, François Bovon, and Max Turner (indeed much of the patristic tradition) have read the Holy Spirit as personal being, but G. W. H. Lampe, Hermann Gunkel, Hans Leisegang, and Albert Schweitzer have mainly understood the Holy Spirit as impersonal force. For more on this distinction, see William H. Shepherd Jr., "The Narrative Function of the Holy Spirit as a Character in Luke-Acts," *Society of Biblical Literature Dissertation Series*, 147 (Atlanta: Scholars Press, 1994), 2–23 and see Ju Hur, *A Dynamic Reading of the Holy Spirit in Luke-Acts, Journal for the Study of the New Testament*, Supplement Series, 211 (Sheffield, England: Sheffield Academic Press, 2001), 24.

4 Shepherd, "Narrative Function," 2. See also Baruch Hochman, *Character in Literature* (Ithaca: Cornell University Press, 1985); E. M. Forster, *Aspects of*

Luke-Acts and interprets every passage in which the Holy Spirit appears. He concludes that in Luke-Acts the Holy Spirit functions in a character role of ensuring the reliability of other characters in the narrative, "In short: the Spirit does what the narrator does: assures reliability."[5] The Holy Spirit is stylized with a high degree of coherence. The Spirit is both literal and symbolic while also being simple and transparent. Above all, the Spirit has a great dynamism that makes him a completely free character in the drama.[6]

One must commend Shepherd's work. He has accomplished much through methodical attention to the narrative and provides future scholars with valuable material; however, the actual analysis of the Holy Spirit as character is relatively brief. In short, it is too short. Hur comments that what Shepherd actually does show is "the immediate narrative effect of the Spirit in relation to the reader of Luke-Acts."[7] In my own view, the Holy Spirit does more in the narrative than vouch for a character's legitimacy. He makes them legitimate. He makes them obedient. Put differently, Shepherd's use of character theory does not provide him the ability to discuss the narrative's divine frame of reference. In effect, Shepherd only accomplishes a horizontal portrayal of the Holy Spirit.

The other important scholar mentioned, Ju Hur, responds to Shepherd in a way that is informative, systematic, and should be widely appreciated. Hur also uses Hochman's character theory with the Rimmon-Kenan model and concludes that the Holy Spirit functions as a character.

The major function of the Spirit in terms of the causal aspect of the plot is (as "helper" and sometimes as "sender"): empowering and guiding main characters to bear witness to God's Kingdom and the Risen Jesus by inspiring them to speak and perform mighty deeds in accordance with the plan of God.[8]

The character of the Holy Spirit empowers other characters in the narrative to be witnesses to the resurrected Jesus and the coming of the Kingdom of God. Hur's reading provides a better understanding of the divine frame of reference in the narrative

---

the Novel (New York: Harcourt, Brace & World, 1927); James Garvey, "Characterization in Narrative," *Poetics* 7 (1978): 63–78.

5 Shepherd, "Narrative Function," 247.   6 Ibid., 255.

7 Ju Hur, *Dynamic Reading*, 31.

8 Ibid., 278. See also S. Rimmon-Kenan, *Narrative Fiction: Contemporary Poetics* (London: Routledge, 1983).

than that of Shepherd. Indeed, Hur's work makes several strides in advancing narrative critical study of Luke-Acts. However, his methodology causes problems. He calls his method a "dynamic reading," but this is an unclear designation. How are we to judge the difference between a dynamic reading and a static one? As noted, Hur supplements Shepherd's views by including a divine frame of reference. The difficulty is that with his designation of the Holy Spirit as a divine character, he does not provide the right categories to discuss the Holy Spirit's position in the narrative while also being attentive to the dissimilarity of the Spirit to the other characters. He also does not place the creative element of the Holy Spirit above the narrative as a creative force in the production of the narrative. In this way, Hur's treatment also remains horizontal.

From expositing these two approaches, I draw a few conclusions. First, the Holy Spirit as "character" cannot adequately describe the involvement of the Holy Spirit in Luke-Acts. Since narrative criticism draws exclusively from literary theory, it does not have the categories of multiple creative forces that can properly account for the Holy Spirit. Mark Allan Powell points out that narrative criticism uses the speech-act theory of communication, particularly that of Roman Jacobson.[9] In every act of communication, one can see a sender, a message, and a receiver. Applied to narrative, there is only an author, a text, and a reader. The problem with the adoption of this communication theory is that it cannot account for the multiple creative elements involved in the gospel scriptural narrative.

At the same time that we say Scripture is narrative, we must also say that Scripture is the theological expression of the divine drama played on the world stage. The scriptural narrative participates in a reality beyond itself as a text. Secular literary theory can only go so far to explain the elements within a text like Luke-Acts. Secular literary theory does not have within its method the categories to account for divine activity above the text and in the text.

When Scripture was first composed, it was intended not just for the few literates reading it with their eyes, but rather it was to be proclaimed to those listening with their ears. Scripture was not so much read individually as it was performed within the communal liturgy as a dramatic re-enactment. Though the text was

---

9 Powell, *Narrative Criticism*, 8–9.

read as narrative it was meant to be performed as drama. I think that the limitations of narrative criticism mentioned above make it possible for us to consider raising the curtain on a different kind of narrative criticism.

Theological Hermeneutical Answer: Theodramatic Theory

In many ways, especially through his trilogy, Hans Urs von Balthasar continues to influence the theological world.[10] His attentiveness to the voice of Scripture and patristic authors as well as his close collaboration with Adrienne von Speyr provided rich resources for biblical hermeneutics that have yet to be engaged. At the outset, it is necessary to discuss briefly Balthasar's foundational view regarding the relationship between theology and spirituality as necessary aspects of the Christian life.[11] In his essay, "Theologie und Heiligkeit," Balthasar does not denounce the Protestant Reformation as the greatest tragedy to Christian theology and spirituality. Rather, he claims, the greatest tragedy in Christian history was the separation of "sitting" theology and "kneeling" theology.[12] The one who sits and thinks for insight into the nature of God should be the one who kneels and prays for insight. According to Balthasar, influenced by Adrienne von Speyr, the realm of *sacra doctrina* must be reunited with the realm of *vita sancta*.[13] As an extension of this unity, Scripture should also be

---

10 Peter Henrici, "Hans Urs von Balthasar: A Sketch of His Life," trans. John Saward, in *Hans Urs von Balthasar: His Life and Work*, ed. David L. Schindler (San Francisco: Ignatius Press, 1991), 31.

11 "These fundamental mystical and spiritual patterns are so much a part of von Balthasar that he draws on them with great frequency, sometimes overtly, but often seemingly unconsciously. He employs the schemata and the imagery of the spiritual life as a framework and vocabulary within which he can make prominent in Christ's journey certain features which, apart from the language of spirituality, might remain inexpressible or even unrecognized. Von Balthasar uses mystical patterns as a lens to see more deeply into the mystery of Christ" (Mark A. McIntosh, *Christology from Within: Spirituality and the Incarnation in Hans Urs von Balthasar* [South Bend, IN: University of Notre Dame Press, 1996], 4).

12 Hans Urs von Balthasar, "Theology and Sanctity," in *Explorations in Theology*, trans. A. V. Littledale and Alexander Dru (San Francisco: Ignatius Press, 1989), 181–209. On this point, see also his earlier essay, "Patristics, Scholastics, and Us," trans. Edward Oakes, *Communio* 24 (1997): 347–96.

13 John Saward, *Mysteries of March: Hans Urs von Balthasar on the Incarnation and Easter* (New York: HarperCollins, 1990), xviii.

reunited with theology not in exclusion of the historical-critical method or literary-critical method, but in a legitimate relationship with Scripture as "the very soul of sacred theology" in which the text is read and prayed.[14] In Balthasar's view, theodramatic theory consciously attempts to be a marriage of "sitting" and "kneeling" theology. It is a marriage in which Scripture is not just narrative, but truly the script of the theo-drama.[15]

With this in mind, one must gather the resources of the method in order to understand the involvement of the Holy Spirit in Luke-Acts. Theodramatic theory, quite simply, uses dramatic theory to expound theology:

> Thus arises our task, which is to draw an *instrumentarium*, a range of resources, from the drama of existence which can then be of service to a Christian theory of theo-drama in which the "natural" drama of existence (between the Absolute and the relative) is consummated in the "supernatural" drama between the God of Jesus Christ and mankind.[16]

The natural drama of existence, Balthasar is saying, can serve to articulate the supernatural drama. According to this theory, Scripture is not an object to be antiseptically analyzed with an Enlightenment subject-object hermeneutic.[17] Scripture is not only an object narrating God's creative and dramatic action in

---

14 *Dei Verbum*, in vol. 1 of Vatican Council II, New Revised Edition, ed. Austin Flannery (Northport, NY: Costello Publishing Company, 1996), no. 24. See also Johnson and Kurz, *The Future of Catholic Biblical Scholarship*.

15 *Theo-Drama* is the second part in Balthasar's trilogy. The first is *Theo-Phany* [The Glory of the Lord] and the third is the *Theo-Logic*. The setup of the trilogy comes from his phenomenological understanding of revelation, "A being appears, it has an epiphany: in that it is beautiful and makes us marvel [hence, Theo-phany]. In appearing it gives itself, it delivers itself to us; it is good [hence, Theo-Drama]. And in giving itself up, it speaks itself, it unveils itself: it is true (in itself, but in the other to which it reveals itself) [hence, Theo-Logic]," Hans Urs von Balthasar, *My Work: In Retrospect*, trans. Brian McNeil, Kenneth Batinovich, John Saward, and Kelly Hamilton (San Francisco: Ignatius Press, 1993), 116.

16 Hans Urs von Balthasar, *Prolegomena*, vol. 1 of *Theo-Drama: Theological Dramatic Theory*, trans. Graham Harrison (San Francisco: Ignatius Press, 1988), 130.

17 "God's revelation is not an object to be looked at: it is his action in and upon the world, and the world can only respond, and hence 'understand', through action on its part" (Balthasar, *Theo-Drama* I, 15).

the theo-drama; it also participates in this theo-drama. In strict narrative criticism, as Powell says, "the text is the thing."[18] In theodramatic theory, the "theo-drama is the thing." Scripture as script participates in this thing.

Drama often points to a reality beyond itself because theatre itself intends to interpret the relative in terms of absolutes—the struggle of this family, Stella and Stanley Kowalski with Blanche DuBois points to the dysfunctional reality of all families. The audience escapes the world from which they live to the seeming unreality of the drama. In truth, the audience does not escape from the world; they experience the world in greater relief. What had been dismissively relative is now in the drama more intensely absolute. The audience leaves themselves to find out more about themselves because "the task of the stage is to make the drama of existence explicit so that we may view it."[19] In the theatre, one experiences a kind of transcendence that is a looking from above at one's world below.[20] Applying these concepts about drama to Scripture, we could say that in Scripture readers can experience transcendence. The readers are invited to assess their world from God's point of view.[21]

---

18 Powell, *Narrative Criticism*, 19.

19 Balthasar, *Theo-Drama* I, 17-18 and further along he says "Nowhere is the character of existence demonstrated more clearly than in stage drama: we are drawn to watch it, and initially it is immaterial whether, in doing so, we are searching for or fleeing from ourselves, immaterial whether the performance is showing us the serious- or the play- dimension, the destructive or the transfiguring aspect, the absurdity or the hidden profundity of our life. Probably nowhere else but in this interplay of relationships (which is the essence of the theatre) can we see so clearly the questionable nature and ambiguity not only of the theatre but also of existence itself, which the theatre illuminates."

20 "Dramatic theory (*Dramatik*) is concerned with what-is-going-forward (*Agogik*), and, as in the relationship between life and the stage, the boundaries between the two are blurred, so it is in God's dealings with mankind: the boundary between the actor or agent and the 'auditorium' is removed, and man is a spectator only insofar as he is a player: he does not merely see himself on the stage, he really acts on it" (Balthasar, *Theo-Drama* I, 18).

21 "For the moment, however, it is not this ambiguity which is to the fore but rather the abundant wealth of material, relationships and connections; these provide a complete, ready-made set of categories—hardly noticed by theology up to now—which can be used to portray God's action" (Balthasar, *Theo-Drama* I, 18).

Theological Hermeneutical Answer: The Holy Spirit as Director

In narrative criticism, there is one element of creative originality, namely that of the author. In theodramatic theory, however, there are three elements of dramatic creativity—the playwright, actor, and director. Let us not miss the Trinitarian connection. The Father can be considered the playwright. The Father composes the redemption play for performance to the world audience. The playwright has two creative positions.[22] As originator of the play, he is above the drama. But in another way, the playwright also sustains the play as his words become the actor's words. The Father as playwright enters into their depths (*prosopopeia*). The playwright "has power to make himself present in the actor, and only in him."[23] He provides the area of creativity (i.e., the setting, characters, and plot) and gives the area his imaginative vision.[24]

The Son comes on stage as the actor. The playwright's work only becomes concrete in the actor. He causes the idea of the play to be embodied, "The Actor puts himself and all the powers of his soul, including his emotions, at the service of the work of art, at the service of the part he is to play."[25] In this, he is obedient in a kenotic way to the will of the playwright and the director. The Son as the actor real-izes the vision of the drama. As the incarnate one, he embodies the idea by acting in obedience to the author's vision.[26]

The Holy Spirit creatively engages the play as director. The director translates the idea and script of the author into concrete existence. The director's task "is to transpose the play's ideal content as a whole into the reality of the performance as a whole."[27] He ties the two ends, "a stage script . . . on the one hand and the available actors on the other."[28] He coordinates his actors and the action, as if he is saying "move toward this part of the stage" or "say your line in this manner." As a director, he must be present to the actor, but he also "must disappear, as it were, in order to be a

---

22 Balthasar, *Theo-Drama* I, 270.   23 Ibid., 278.   24 Ibid., 268–69.
25 Ibid., 281, 287: "The playwright's work is potentially drama: it only becomes actual through the actor."
26 Ibid., 281, 284: "There is nothing mechanical about this making-present; it is a creative act for which the poet explicitly and necessarily leaves room in his work, both in terms of the depth of inspiration (the details of gesture, intonation, and the 'higher task') and so forth."
27 Ibid., 262.   28 Ibid., 298.

medium and an atmosphere present to all."[29] The Holy Spirit as director spans the chasm between the author and actor to make the play responsibly present for the audience.[30] As Paraclete, he guides the actors, principally the main character, in obedience to the vision of the author in order to present the play's theme to the audience. In a sense, the Holy Spirit is also in the dramatis personae as impermanent forms (dove, fire, breath); however, his principal role is as a director.

Having gathered an overview of Balthasar's treatment of the Holy Spirit as director, I would now like to engage with the text of Luke-Acts. I focus on four aspects of the Holy Spirit as director in Luke-Acts: first, the Holy Spirit is in and above the theo-drama depicted in Luke-Acts; second, the Holy Spirit makes the Son obedient as the lead actor; third, the Holy Spirit actualizes the theo-drama in the present here and now; and finally, the Holy Spirit is the proper exegete of the theo-drama.

Let us take up the first point. The Holy Spirit as director can be seen to be both in and above the Son as actor. The Spirit is in the Son as his possession or as a directorial, creative element within the Son. Yet, the Spirit is also above him as a director driving the Son forward.[31] In drama, the actor experiences this as a meeting of minds as he and the director incarnate the play, but at other times, the actor experiences the cruel and unconditional decision of the director to push the actor into a conflagration to transform him into his role. The Spirit is in Christ as his interior *intimo meo* (more inward than myself) and at the same time above him rigid and pitiless, pushing him to the Cross.[32]

The Holy Spirit as director makes the actor obedient to the text of the play. In the words of the French playwright and director, Gaston Baty, "Without doubt, the first commandment for the director is obedience to the text."[33] The director fulfills the first commandment of obedience to the text by making the actor obedient to it—memorizing the lines to the point of identification.

---

29 Ibid., 301.   30 Ibid., 298–99.

31 Saward, *Mysteries of March*, 24. Balthasar thinks that "When it comes to the actors, the director's task is much harder, for they, since they are responsible for bringing their roles to life, can also claim a primacy over him" (Balthasar, *Theo-Drama* I, 299).

32 Balthasar, *Theo-Drama* I, 262, 298.

33 As quoted in Balthasar, *Theo-Drama* I, 299n5.

In this theodramatic interpretation, the text is the Father's will of creation and redemption. The Holy Spirit must be obedient to this text, but his mission in the world, at least in relation to the Son, is to make the Son perform this text obediently. The idea is captured in Jesus's proclamation that his presence fulfills the Scriptures in the audience's hearing (Lk 4:21). The Son as the actor must be obedient to the text (will) of the Father and he lives this obedience through the Holy Spirit as director within him. In this way, we can understand Balthasar's statement that the Son's obedience to the text is "directed to the Father, but it is lived out in the Holy Spirit."[34] The obedience of the actor is to have no other desire than to enact creatively the desire of the author and director.

In dramas, the main actor thrusts open the stage of redemption for the other actors. So too does this happen in the theo-drama. By the masterful, obedient performance, the lead actor exemplifies and provides the space for the other actors to be obedient to the director. Applying this idea to the theo-drama, the Son, as the lead actor in his obedience to the Holy Spirit as director, opens the space for the obedience of the other actors. Where the other actors have failed to obey the director, the masterful, lead actor obeys.

The director is given the creative role of making the play present here and now. The performance of the drama necessitates the director meaningfully actualizing it in the present for the here and now. The director puts on the play by illustrating it, translating it into three-dimensionality. But, putting on the play "also implies penetrating the dramatist's mind and heart in order to prolong his thoughts and feelings over and above the words."[35] The director presents the play not as a static reproduction, but as an unrepeatable, interpretively meaningful performance.[36] He is responsible for the whole performance, which means he will intervene implicitly behind the scenes, but also explicitly in the concrete performances. We see this with the Holy Spirit who at

---

34 Saward, *Mysteries of March*, 23.

35 Balthasar, *Theo-Drama* I, 299.

36 Ibid., 301–3: "Here the director meets his hardest task: he must be committed enough to make the play relevant and at the same time civilized enough not to equate this here-and-now relevance with a narrow doctrine of society. The theatre is a political reality, in a lofty and noble sense, but it should not be misused for political party propaganda."

times is absent from the action but at other times appears. The Holy Spirit intervenes within the drama itself, only when necessary, but in a self-effacing way as if he were disguised (e.g., as a dove, fire, water).[37]

At first glance, Scripture presents a difficulty with the Holy Spirit as director because he does appear on stage. However, a closer analysis of dramatic theory need not go far to find instances of directors on stage. An ancient instance is in Greek drama. One sees gods entering into the play. For example, in Aeschylus's trilogy of the Oresteia, particularly *The Eumenides*, the gods (Athena, Apollo, etc.) enter the drama (*deus ex machina*: the actors were lowered on to the stage via crane) in order to stop the cycle of bloodguilt by introducing justice to humankind. Though directors are offstage, some have so significantly imbued the play with themselves that they are present to the whole. The Holy Spirit has so infused himself into the world theatre that he even acts on the world stage directing all the actors in their roles.

A final aspect of theodramatic theory regarding the Holy Spirit as director is that authentic exegesis is possible only in the Holy Spirit. This aspect is related to Balthasar's theology that God is his own exegete.[38] In relation to making the play here and now, the director is also responsible for writing the script of the play. If the Holy Spirit as a creative element was involved in the writing of the script (indeed, he is responsible for the action from which the script derives), then one must also read in the Holy Spirit. If one is to be in the audience and have a full understanding of the performance, one must know (intuitively if not explicitly) the director's interpretation of the play. The Twelve "understood none of these things ... and they did not grasp what was said" (Lk 18:34), but when the Spirit descends, "they were all filled with the Holy Spirit and spoke the word of God with boldness" (Acts 4:31). We can then say that the script "of God's saving drama which we call Holy Scripture is worthless in itself unless, in the Holy Spirit, it is constantly mediating between the drama beyond and the drama

---

37 Ibid., 301: "As a figure he must disappear, as it were, in order to be a medium and an atmosphere present to all."

38 "How then can man, who is created with an orientation towards God and constantly seeks him, begin to interpret him? Only God, who has the vision of his own wisdom is able to reveal his wisdom" (Hans Urs von Balthasar, "God is His Own Exegete," *Communio* 4 [1986]: 280–87).

here."[39] Reading Scripture is a re-presentation of the theo-drama made here and now by the working of the Holy Spirit as director.

An Outline of the Holy Spirit as Director in Luke-Acts

Having searched through theodramatic theory for resources, we turn to the task of evaluating the fruitfulness of the theodramatic theory of the Holy Spirit as director by looking at Luke-Acts. Does theodramatic understanding of the Holy Spirit as director account for the figure of the Holy Spirit presented in Luke-Acts? While space restricts a full commentary on the Holy Spirit in Luke-Acts, I think that I can make the case by an interpretation of the annunciation, baptism, and temptation scenes (Lk 1:26–38; 3:21–22; 4:1–13).

Let us first look at the Holy Spirit as in and above the Son as actor. From theodramatic theory, one can see the involvement of the Holy Spirit as director in the Son as the actor. Christ, the anointed one, is the one who will baptize "with the Holy Spirit" (Lk 3:16) because the Holy Spirit has come in to him at his Incarnation and baptism. He is in possession of the Spirit within him and will send that power to others (Acts 1:8). Christ has received the Holy Spirit in baptism. The Holy Spirit immediately directs him into the desert. Luke emphasizes the interior guiding of the Holy Spirit in Luke 4:1, saying that the Son was "full of the Holy Spirit . . . and was led by the Spirit." The interior location of the Holy Spirit continues with Jesus's preaching, which is "in the power of the Spirit" (4:14). Acts also contains a reference to the location of the Holy Spirit within Jesus's interior (Acts 10:38). Central to Luke's understanding of the Spirit is that the Spirit is in Jesus Christ.

Another important aspect of theodramatic theory is that the Holy Spirit be above the incarnate Son. In the annunciation scene, one of the characteristics of the child being formed within Mary is that "the Holy Spirit will come upon" her (Lk 1:35a). Similarly, in the baptism scene, the Holy Spirit descends upon Jesus (Lk 3:22) and therefore he is considered the Father's "beloved Son" (3:22b). In Jesus's first preaching, he uses Isaiah to show the Spirit's origin above him and the Spirit's dwelling place in him: "The Spirit of the Lord is upon me, because he has anointed me to preach good news to the poor" (Lk 4:18). Luke presents the Spirit's location above Jesus as central to Jesus's role as the Son.

---

39 Balthasar, *Theo-Drama* I, 22.

Theodramatic theory also sees the role of the Holy Spirit as the director who makes the Son as actor obedient to the script. The Son is the one who is led, who receives, who follows, and who responds to the Holy Spirit. The Holy Spirit guides the Son. The Spirit acts directly upon Mary bringing about Christ within her virginal womb. The directing activity of the Holy Spirit continues in the temptation scene. In this scene, Christ is "led by the Spirit ... into the wilderness" where he is starved and tempted (Lk 4:1-2). By his direction, the Spirit brings about the occasion for the Son to be tempted like Israel in the wilderness. Whereas Israel had been disobedient when tempted in the wilderness, Christ does not resist the Holy Spirit. Wherever Israel disobeyed as in the stories of the manna from heaven (Ex 16), the temptation of the Canaanite kingdoms and cults (Deut 12:30-31), and at Meribah and Massah (Ex 17:1-7; Ps 95:8), Christ obeys in the temptations of the manna from stones (Lk 4:3-4), the temptation of the kingdoms of the world (Lk 4:5-8) and the testing of the Lord (Lk 4:9-12). A theodramatic reading of these episodes in Luke-Acts discerns the Holy Spirit as director who makes the Son as actor obedient to the script of redemption.

An equally important theme of theodramatic theory is that the Holy Spirit as director has the responsibility of making the play present. Mary asks, "How can this be, since I have no husband?" (Lk 1:34). The answer is that "the Holy Spirit will come upon you" (Lk 1:35). The Holy Spirit sets the stage for the drama. He makes the main protagonist (the Son as the Christ) take stage at this moment and in this particular way. He sets the play in Nazareth in Second Temple Judaism during the Roman occupation. The Spirit descends upon the Son at the Jordan River (Lk 3:22). The Spirit turns the Son's face to Jerusalem and toward the Cross (Lk 9:51). We can conclude that the action area becomes concrete for the interaction between God and man in this moment of Incarnation.[40] As director, the Holy Spirit has brought about the concrete existence of the theo-drama.

The sending of the Holy Spirit makes the drama of redemption a truly divine play.[41] The sending of the Holy Spirit is revealed

---

40 Balthasar, *Theo-Drama* III:41.
41 "The idea of a divine person being sent to be and do something in the world is an essentially dramatic idea, elevating and fulfilling 'role' in the theatrical and psychological sense" (Saward, *Mysteries of March*, 18-19).

in his being sent to "come upon" and lead the Son interiorly. Being obedient to the designs of the Father's will, the Holy Spirit makes the play present and the Son obedient. The Holy Spirit acts as a creative element for the fulfillment of the Father's will. As the director, the Spirit is the one who will teach you "what you ought to say" (Lk 12:12).

Examining even these brief passages at the beginning of Luke-Acts, we can interpret the Holy Spirit theodramatically as the director of the theo-drama. He has shown himself both in and above Christ. He has made the Son as actor obedient to the play the Father has written. He has opened up the whole of the drama to us by carrying the performance through the ages, continually making anew what has been performed throughout the millennia. Scripture reminds us of our parts in this play and the Holy Spirit directs our roles. As readers of Scripture, we are also invited by the director to be audience-performers. The Holy Spirit has made the play for us and with us.

Secular literary theory, particularly in its postmodern forms of characterizing the Holy Spirit, limits analysis of the role of the Holy Spirit in Luke-Acts. By thinking of Scripture as theo-dramatic script rather than narrative text, I have argued that Balthasar's theodramatic theory can better articulate the person of the Holy Spirit. If we designate the Holy Spirit as director rather than as character, we can better explain his involvement in the theo-drama as depicted in the script of Luke-Acts. The Holy Spirit as director makes the play present by being both in and above the Son as actor making him obedient to the Father as author of the theo-drama.

5

Come, Holy Spirit

THE HOLY SPIRIT GIVES LIFE AND SO IN SCRIP-
ture we hear the Spirit directing the Church so that the Church
can "become partakers of the divine nature" (2 Pet 1:4). To articulate this life in the Holy Spirit, I would like to offer reflections
on four Pneumatologies that capture the compassionate life in the
Holy Spirit. Learning from Basil, Gregory of Nazianzus, Seraphim
of Sarov, and Pope John Paul II we can develop a compassionate
theology of the Holy Spirit.

Basil's Pneumatology

St. Basil the Great (329–379) was born in Pontus, Asia Minor,
and was raised in a family of saints. His father, Basil the Elder,
and his mother, Emilia, are venerated as saints along with three
of his siblings, Macrina, Gregory of Nyssa, and Peter of Sebaste.
He excelled in the study of rhetoric in Constantinople and Athens
and became a close friend to Gregory of Nazianzus, who I will
consider next. After his studies, Basil sought a life of holiness
and was baptized in 358 describing it as waking from a deep
sleep. Influenced by Eustathius of Sebaste, he began the ascetic
life in imitation of his sister Macrina and visited monasteries
throughout Egypt, Palestine, Syria, and Mesopotamia.[1] On his
return home, he founded his own monastery in Pontus adding a
community form to his rule, which has been imitated by many
other religious founders. He can rightly be called the father of
Eastern monasticism. His return to Asia Minor thrust him into
several theological controversies with Apollinarianists, Eunomians,
and Pneumatomachians. After his ordination, he worked alongside
Eusebius, bishop of Caesarea. Basil succeeded Eusebius as bishop of
Caesarea in 370. He is known for his defense of Nicene orthodoxy,
his charity to the poor, his administration in the Church, and his
establishment of Eastern monasticism.

---

1 See Gregory of Nyssa, *The Life of Saint Macrina*, trans. Kevin Corrigan
(Toronto: Peregrina, 1998).

We have many writings from him, but I would like to consider his work *On the Holy Spirit*.[2] This small treatise defends the divinity of the Holy Spirit as being of equal rank and dignity with the Father and the Son. He began the work by offering the two common doxologies in use at the time that have slight but significant variations.

1) Glory to the Father through [*dia*] the Son in [*en*] the Holy Spirit.

2) Glory to the Father with [*meta*] the Son together with [*syn*] the Holy Spirit.

The first doxology was the more traditional one and was used by Catholics, Eunomians, and Pneumatomachians. The second doxology was novel for that age and seems to take a significant step in the Trinitarian theology of the time particularly with regard to the divinity of the Holy Spirit.

Basil defended both of these doxologies as essential to authentic Christian belief in the Trinity. These prepositions make all the difference. The first doxology gives glory to the Father (seemingly alone) and then shows how that glory arrives to him, namely "through" the Son and "in" or "by" the Holy Spirit. The second doxology, however, gives glory to Father, Son, and Holy Spirit by using the preposition "with" as if to imply that the glory is shared among all three Divine Persons. If the glory is given to all of them, then they must be of equal dignity and divinity. Basil perceived the importance of defending both these doxologies against the Pneumatomachians, Eunomians, and Arians (he names these groups in the work) in order to defend the full divinity of the Holy Spirit.

Basil addressed the document to Amphilochius, answering information he requested about these doxologies' legitimacy. He writes that Scripture equivocally uses "in" and "with" when referring to the Holy Spirit and uses "through" and "with" in regard to the Son.

Since the Son's divinity is not the problem, Basil examines Scripture's definition of the Spirit and concludes that throughout Scripture, "the Spirit is spoken of together with the Lord in precisely the same manner in which the Son is spoken of with the Father."[3] The Spirit must be thought of in the same terms as the Son.

---

2 Basil, *On the Holy Spirit*, trans. Blomfield Jackson (Crestwood, NY: St. Vladimir's Seminary Press, 1980).

3 Basil, *On the Holy Spirit*, IX.22, XVII.43.

In Basil's view, the baptismal language of the Church also provides evidence of the legitimacy of the equal glory of the Father, Son, and Holy Spirit. The conjoining of the three names in baptism points to the equal dignity and divinity of all and thereby, "The Lord has delivered to us as a necessary and saving doctrine that the Holy Spirit is to be ranked with the Father."[4] In baptism all three must be named and, thus, through all three come salvation. This shows that all three must receive glory for their work.[5] The Spirit, according to Scripture, is essential in baptism because the water brings death, but the Spirit brings life: "the water receiving the body as in a tomb figures death, while the Spirit pours in the quickening power, renewing our souls from the deadness of sin unto their original life."[6]

The Holy Spirit operates with the Father and the Son in a common work though executed differently. According to Basil, the original cause of all things is the Father, the creative cause is the Son, and the perfecting cause is the Spirit.[7] The Spirit also confirms the creating and ordering of the Father and the Son as well as sanctifying the creation. All creation needs the Holy Spirit, even the angels and the humanity of Christ.[8]

Basil continues his argument in defense of the divinity of the Holy Spirit by using language of three hypostases and one monarchy, which will become influential for the tradition: "we both confess the distinction of the hypostases, and at the same time abide by the Monarchy."[9] The Spirit proceeds "out of God, not by generation, like the Son, but as Breath of His mouth."[10] He concludes that "the way of knowledge of God lies from One Spirit through the One Son to the One Father, and conversely the natural Goodness and the inherent Holiness and the royal Dignity extend from the Father through the Only-begotten to the Holy Spirit."[11] Therefore, one must acknowledge the three hypostases and the one monarchy.

If the Spirit is of the one community of nature then he ought to be glorified "with" the Father and the Son.[12] The Spirit deserves equal glorification because he is good by nature "in the same way as the Father is good, and the Son is good" because "there is not

---

4 Basil, *On the Holy Spirit*, X.25.   5 Ibid., XII.28.   6 Ibid., XV.35.
7 Ibid., XVI.38.   8 Ibid., XVI.39.   9 Ibid., XVIII.45.
10 Ibid., XVIII.46.   11 Ibid., XVIII.47.   12 Ibid., XVIII.45, XIX.48.

even one single gift which reaches creation without the Holy Spirit" and "not even a single word can be spoken in defense of Christ except by them that are aided by the Spirit."[13]

Basil returns to the doxology and resumes his rhetorical study of the prepositions, concluding that "whenever we have in mind the Spirit's proper rank, we contemplate Him as being with the Father and the Son, but when we think of the grace that flows from Him operating on those who participate in it, we say that the Spirit is in us."[14] Thus, both doxologies should be used in the Church ascribing "glory to God both 'in' the Spirit, and 'with' the Spirit."[15]

Gregory Nazianzus's Pneumatology

We now turn to Gregory of Nazianzus, who used the image of light to communicate the full divinity and glory of the Holy Spirit. This image characterized the Trinity as "a single intermingling of light,... in three mutually connected Suns."[16] The three Suns are so close that they partake and emit the same light, yet each is a distinct Sun. He called the Trinity "light and light and light."[17]

In the fourth century, there was hedging—notably by Basil of Caesarea—from boldly saying the Holy Spirit is God.[18] The Council of Nicaea (325) left the phrase "and [we believe] in the Holy Spirit" uninterpreted.[19] Heresies abounded arguing against the Holy Spirit's divinity by such as the Neo-Arians, the Eunomians, and the Pneumatomachians, but unfortunately orthodox theologians had no council to argue definitively against these interpretations of the limited divinity of the Holy Spirit. The battleground was Constantinople because it was a principal city for influential heretics. Orthodoxy needed its best theologians in Constantinople to defend the divinity of the Holy Spirit with powerful reason and eloquent rhetoric. In 379, Basil of Caesarea,

---

13 Ibid., XXIV.55–56.   14 Ibid., XXVI.63.   15 Ibid., XXVII.68.
16 Frederick Norris, *Faith Gives Fullness to Reasoning: The Five Theological Orations of Gregory Nazianzen*, trans. Lionel Wickham and Frederick Williams, vol. 13 of *Supplements to Vigiliae Christianae* (Leiden, Netherlands: E. J. Brill, 1991), 31.14. For the critical edition Greek text, see Hermann Josef Sieben, trans. and ed., *Gregor von Nazianz, Orationes Theologicae—Theologische Reden*, vol. 22 in *Fontes Christiani* (Freiburg im Breisgau: Herder, 1996).
17 Ibid., 31.3.   18 Ibid., 189.
19 Patrick Carey, ed., "The Creed of Nicaea," vol. 1 of *Marquette History of Theology: From the Primitive Church to 1350* (n.p., n.d.), 70.

on his deathbed, recommended his friend Gregory of Nazianzus to be bishop in Constantinople. As bishop of Constantinople, Gregory wrote prodigiously for the orthodox view and was given a villa, which he made into the church of St. Anastasia, a base for the resurrection of the faith. Among the many works that were written during this period was his famous and influential *Theological Orations* (in his corpus they are *Orations* 28–31) defending and spreading Trinitarian orthodoxy with his skilled rhetoric.

Building upon Basil's theology of the Holy Spirit discussed above, I will now examine Gregory's theological argument in Oration 31 wherein he defended and developed the Holy Spirit's consubstantiality with the Father and Son as ontologically and soteriologically necessary.

Gregory Nazianzus (c. 325–390) yearned for a life of monastic contemplation.[20] Instead, he was forced into action in defense of the Father's consubstantiality with the Son and Holy Spirit. He sought the role of Mary but was always thrust into the role of Martha.[21] His Christian parents had sent their gifted child for education to Caesarea where he grew in friendship with Basil and Gregory of Nyssa (d. 604). His education continued in Alexandria and Athens, where he again met with Basil. At the culmination of his career, he may have been asked to accept the post of rhetorical master at his Athenian school.[22] His father fought for him to be the bishop of Nazianzus, but during his tenure as bishop, he would often retreat into monastic life. Basil, the expert administrator of the Cappadocians, called Gregory to the backwater Sasima to be its bishop and to defend against any Neo-Arian encampment in the city. He accepted the task but detested it. This active life caused

---

20 I imagine that with any Church Father the text is directly tied up with the personality writing the text. With Gregory we have a wealth of autobiographical evidence that demonstrates the theological work necessarily bound up with his personality: "Fundamental to Gregory's relationship with his readers, meanwhile, is the sheer obtrusiveness of his self and his sufferings in his works, both poetical (the Maurists catalogue ninety-nine poems under the category de se ipso) and oratorical: in his very first sermon he describes his experience of being crucified beside Christ, and rising with him" (Neil McLynn, "A Self-Made Holy Man: The Case of Gregory Nazianzen," *Journal of Early Christian Studies* 6.3 [1998]: 466).
21 It shows that Gregory had a sense common to Byzantine saints: "contemplation first, service second" (Norris, *Faith Gives Fullness*, 8).
22 Ibid., 6–7.

friction with his friend Basil. Also Gregory's political skills were weak and he was ousted by the Neo-Arians.[23] This Holy Saturday experience caused Gregory to retreat into monastic contemplation for four years. But this Mary was called to be a Martha again, this time in Constantinople where he led the orthodox in defending against the strong presence of the Neo-Arians, especially the Eunomians.[24] The opportunity at Constantinople was irresistible and it is here that Gregory wrote the majority of his orations including the *Theological Orations*.[25]

The *Theological Orations* were written at an immensely important time in the summer or autumn of 380. Emperor Theodosius, in February 380, made Nicaea the official teaching of the Roman Empire. In November of that year, Theodosius forced the Arian bishop, Demophilus, to assent to the Nicene Creed or be exiled. Demophilus chose exile and in 380–81 Gregory of Nazianzus became the bishop of Constantinople, a seat of great ecclesial and political power. In the midst of these maneuvers against Neo-Arianism, Gregory's *Orations* became the theologically decisive blow and helped lay the groundwork for the monumental First Council of Constantinople (381).[26]

Let us consider the fifth of the *Theological Orations* (numbered 31 in his corpus). The four preceding orations speak on what a theologian ought to be, the limits of reason in understanding the unknowable God, and the defense of orthodox Christology.[27] These four orations end with the statement that the Holy Spirit is not a "strange, unscriptural God."[28] Gregory's opponents seem to be the Neo-Arians as well as Pneumatomachians—especially given his assessment of this group being "fairly sound so far as the Son is concerned."[29] And yet, the Holy Spirit is not a strange or unscriptural God.

---

23 Ibid., 11–12.   24 Ibid., 8–9.   25 Ibid., 9.

26 The orthodox power over Constantinople did not hold because soon Gregory was politically outmaneuvered by Neo-Arians. His brief bishopric and the eloquence of the *Orations* warrant the claim that Gregory of Nazianzus "was both a bumbling administrator who possessed few political interests or skills and a talented literary figure who understood the relationship between philosophy, rhetoric and theology" (Norris, *Faith Gives Fullness*, 12).

27 Frederick W. Norris, "Gregory the Theologian," *Pro Ecclesia* 2 (1993): 473.

28 Norris, *Faith Gives Fullness*, 31.1.

29 Ibid., 31.1. A segment of the Pneumatomachians maintained the divinity of the Son, but denied the divinity of the Spirit (ibid., 184).

Gregory thinks that what is truly strange is the foreign position that says that the Holy Spirit who is properly called Holy is not God.[30] The Father must have always been holy from the very beginning. If there was a time when the Son or the Holy Spirit was not God, then there was a time when the Father was not holy. If the Holy Spirit is not God from the very beginning, how could Christians have been made holy by a created being?[31]

Gregory goes further in his ontological argument. The Holy Spirit must be either an existing being with the Trinity or an inherent property of the Trinity. Using Aristotelian metaphysics, Gregory concludes that the Holy Spirit is either an accident or substance, either an activity of the Trinity or a subject of the Trinity. If he is an accident or activity of the Trinity, then he is directed rather than being the director because "he has no active power and ceases with the cessation of his production."[32] Yet, in the Scriptures the Holy Spirit is revealed to decree, grieve, and speak.[33] He directs the actors rather than being the activity of the actors. The Holy Spirit begins motion and is not the one put in motion. He is "a substance, not the attribute of a substance."[34] Gregory turns next to the baptismal prayers of the Church that speak of being baptized *in* the Father, Son, and Holy Spirit as opposed to being baptized *about* the Holy Spirit as an attribute of the Father. Some Arians held the Holy Spirit to be an activity, the Eunomians a creature, and the Pneumatomachians an unknowable aspect of God. But, Gregory argues, Scripture speaks of the Holy Spirit as a *subject* of divinity as opposed to being just an activity, creature, or unknowable.

The main task for Gregory is describing how the Son and the Spirit differ from each other. The Father is the Ingenerate One, but both the Son and the Spirit come from the Ingenerate. In the previous orations, we learned Gregory's argument for the Son's generacy contained in the nonsubordinationist term of *homoousios* (one substance). There is the Father who is the Ingenerate One and the Son who is the Generate One. For Gregory, the Holy

---

30 Ibid., 31.4.   31 Ibid., 31.4.

32 Ibid., 31.6. Hence the importance of the previous chapter on the Holy Spirit as the Director.

33 The Holy Spirit "says things (Acts 13:2), he decrees (Acts 13:2), he is grieved (Eph 4:30), he is vexed (Is 63:10)—all of which belong to a being with motion, not to the process of motion" (Norris, *Faith Gives Fullness*, 31.6).

34 Ibid., 31.6.

Spirit is the mean between these two; he is the Processed One, as the Scripture says, "The Spirit of truth, who proceeds from the Father."[35]

Gregory warns that we must continue to safeguard the unity and distinctiveness by saying that the Trinity is "three persons within the single nature."[36] He strikes a balance between Sabellianism and Arianism. He recognizes in both of these Trinitarian theologies the destruction of the quality of the Godhead.[37]

Gregory's analogy to demonstrate three persons with a single nature in differing relations is that of Adam, Eve, and Seth. Adam as the "molded creation" is analogous to the Father, Eve as "a portion of the molded creation" to the Holy Spirit, and Seth as the "offspring" to the Son. While the analogy is imperfect, we can begin to see biblically two types of manifestations from an original source while all are of the same substance.

The second section of this oration defends the Holy Spirit's divinity revealed in Scripture. Gregory writes that there are statements said about God that are clearly accepted by Christians but are not explicitly in Scripture. He points out, for example, that Christians use the words "ingenerate" or "unoriginate" to speak about God the Father. Both words are not in Scripture, yet they can be inferred as true from such passages like, "I am the first and I am the last" (Is 44:6), "Before me no god was formed, nor shall there be any after me" (Is 43:10), "I AM who I AM" (Ex 3:15).[38]

Gregory offers his now famous position that the divinity of the Holy Spirit can be learned in Scripture from seeing the progressive revelation of the Trinity in the gradual enactment of the covenants.[39] The Old Testament covenants revealed the divinity of the Father. With the New Covenant, the Father revealed his Son to a people who are now capable of understanding more about the nature of God. In the present age of covenant faithfulness,

---

35 Ibid., 31.8 quoting John 15:26. Siben, *Gregor von Nazianz*, 31.8.

36 Sieben, *Gregor von Nazianz*, 31.9. Norris maintains that "Yet even here it is easier to specify what he intended to avoid than to state exactly what he wished to confess" (*Faith Gives Fullness*, 194).

37 "Thus there will be no Sabellian 'One,' no three to be mischievously divided by our contemporaries" (Norris, *Faith Gives Fullness*, 31.9).

38 See Norris, *Faith Gives Fullness*, 31.23.

39 An idea that Joachim of Fiore (c. 1132–1202) will take to more radical conclusions.

the Father and Son have revealed the divinity of the Holy Spirit from Pentecost and through every sacrament and ecclesial action. The progressive revelations of the triune nature of God were proportionate to the capacity of developing humanity to receive them, like light that "shines on us bit by bit."[40] For Gregory, Scripture, Tradition, liturgy, and salvation necessarily urge the Church to continue to affirm the full divinity of the Holy Spirit.[41]

Building to a rhetorical climax, Gregory concludes, "Thus do I stand, thus may I stand, and those I love as well, on these issues, able to worship the Father as God, the Son as God, the Holy Spirit as God."[42] With these bold statements, he presents "a swarm of proof-texts" for the divinity of the Holy Spirit clearly inferred from Scripture.[43] When Christ is born, the Holy Spirit overshadows Mary; when Christ is baptized, the Holy Spirit descends upon him; when Christ is tempted, the Holy Spirit leads him into the desert; when Christ performs miracles, the Holy Spirit attends to him; when Christ ascends to the Father, the Holy Spirit descends on the Church: "Is there any significant function belonging to God, which the Spirit does not perform?"[44] He lists about seventeen titles and over fifty operations of the Holy Spirit that demonstrate the ubiquitous presence and activity likened only to that of God himself.[45]

Emperor Theodosius appointed Gregory presider over the Council of Constantinople to articulate the full divinity of the Holy Spirit as dogmatically normative for the Church. Gregory did not believe the council went far enough in its statements about the Holy Spirit and resigned in anger during the council. From his letters after the council, we can see the bumbling administrator, and tragic figure, as well as the heroic theologian defending the full divinity of the Holy Spirit with rhetorical gift and theological passion.[46]

What comes through the continued importance of Gregory's *Theological Orations* and the Creed of the Councils of Nicaea and

---

40 Norris, *Faith Gives Fullness*, 31.26–27.
41 Norris, "Gregory the Theologian," 483.
42 Norris, *Faith Gives Fullness*, 31.28.
43 Ibid., 31.29.
44 Ibid., 31.29. See respectively, Luke 1:31, 35; Matt 3:13–17, Luke 3:21–22; Matt 4:1, Luke 4:2; Matt 12:22, 28; Acts 1:9, 2:3–4.
45 Ibid., 31.29–30.
46 Norris, "Gregory the Theologian," 483.

Constantinople is the faithful confessing of the glory given to the Father, to the Son, and to the Holy Spirit. Through the centuries, the continual confession of the full divinity of the Holy Spirit was not due just to the Emperor making normative the council's creed, the intense warring of political and ecclesial powers at the council, or the rhetorical verve and persuasive argumentation of Gregory Nazianzus.[47] For me, continual confession of the Nicene-Constantinopolitan Creed can only be found in the faithful through the centuries who see in it the truth of their Christian faith and their present experience of the risen Christ through the gift of the Holy Spirit by the Father and Son. In the adequate image of "a single intermingling of light... in three mutually connected Suns," the faithful have a vision of God and see the goal of their life in the three-fold vision of light.[48] Living in this divine Holy Spirit is the true gift of God. Living in the Spirit means being made holy by the Holy One.

The Three Gifts of Seraphim of Sarov

On July 19, 1903, Tsar Nicholas II and Tsarina Alexandra descended from imperial glory to become pilgrims of devotion to the poor monk of Sarov. The canonization of Seraphim on this day was to be a catalyst of spiritual and national unity for Russia. The rabble and the royal couple mingled in united devotion to bow before the holy relics and plead for the intercession of this new saint for Russia.[49] For Nicholas II, "the glory of the reign and the glorification of the holy and humble man of God were somehow mysteriously connected."[50] In addition, it is no small matter that Alexandra, after having four daughters, claimed a miracle of giving birth to a long sought for male heir after bathing in the Sarov waters.

---

47 Ibid., 484.

48 John Anthony McGuckin, "The Vision of God in St. Gregory Nazianzen," *Studia Patristica* 32 (1992): 151.

49 The canonization "confirmed [Nicholas's] own self-image of a noble and benign monarch, and he believed that in their mutual devotion to St. Seraphim, tsar and people were as one" (Robert D. Warth, "Before Rasputin: Piety and the Occult at the Court of Nicholas II," *The Historian* 47 [1985]: 334).

50 Robert L. Nichols, "The Friends of God: Nicholas II and Alexandra at the Canonization of Serafim of Sarov, July 1903," in *Religious and Secular Forces in Late Tsarist Russia: Essays in Honor of Donald W. Treadgold*, ed. Charles E. Timberlake (Seattle and London: University of Washington Press, 1992), 212.

Seraphim was actually quite different from what he was made out to be as a national patron of the Eastern missions.[51] As we study an account of his life we will see in the figure of Seraphim a new way to see what it means to live in the Holy Spirit.

In this work by a disciple of Seraphim, we have a presentation of "poor Seraphim" as a *starets* in Russian (*geron* in Greek), as a wise elder, as a warrior saint, and even as a holy fool, that figure so important in Eastern Orthodox spirituality. In what is often taken to be the best source for Seraphim's teaching, *A Conversation of St. Seraphim of Sarov with Nicholas Motovilov Concerning the Aim of the Christian Life*, we see Seraphim as more of a latter-day Elijah than a patriotic rallying point for the Romanovs.

The starets origin can be traced to the Egyptian Desert Fathers, like Saint Anthony, as well as the hesychast tradition.[52] He is a spiritual father or charismatic figure whose actions and words receive special guidance from the Holy Spirit. The starets is the trusted healer and prophet given at a specific time for a specific mission. He usually lives much of his life in hesychast fashion. The word *hesychia* means peace, silence, or quietness of heart.[53] To achieve this peace, the starets lives in solitude as vast as the Black Sea, continually searching for God. He goes out to the desert to achieve this quietness because "A hesychast is someone who longs, whose heart is full of desire for God, and because of that goes out to learn how to free his heart from its passions in order to meet God."[54] His spiritual dwelling is with the prophet Elijah who taught that God does not speak in the strong wind, the earthquake, or fire, but in the "still small voice" like the subtlest of breezes (see 1 Kings 19:11–13). In the desert he repeats in unceasing, self-activating prayer, "Jesus Christ, Son of God, have mercy on me, a sinner."[55] After years spent in

---

51 "It is instructive to realize that the first foreign language accounts of Serafim's life and glorification were written in Japanese by Akil Kadzim for distribution in Japan's Orthodox churches" (Nichols, "Friends of God," 225).
52 Kallistos Ware, "The Spiritual Father in Orthodox Christianity," *Cross Currents* 24 (1974): 296. We also have the wonderful work in the hesychast tradition called *The Way of the Pilgrim and the Pilgrim Continues His Way*, trans. Helen Bacovcin (New York: Doubleday, 1978).
53 Igumen Symeon Cossec, "The Search for God in the Hesychast Tradition," *Sourozh: A Journal of Orthodox Life and Thought* 73 (1998): 30.
54 Ibid., 31.
55 The Jesus Prayer of the hesychast tradition had gradual developments. For a short history of the prayer, see Olivier Clément, *The Roots of Christian*

the spiritual desert, God ordains the starets to come back in order to bestow wisdom and healing on those who visit him. From this solitude with God alone, the starets saves because "If you have peace in your heart," as Seraphim said, "then thousands of souls around you will be saved."[56]

Prochur Moshin (July 17, 1759–January 2, 1833), later to take the name Seraphim, was surrounded by war, Westernization, enlightenment, military expansionism, the French Revolution, and Napoleon's invasion of Russia. The modern life of progress did not draw him into business or the intelligentsia. Like Gregory Nazianzus, he desired the desert of the monastic life: "'Poor Seraphim' was neither hostile nor critical; he simply lived in another world, in direct contact with the patristic age of the Church and with the primitive monks of Egypt and Syria who first instituted Christian ascesis."[57]

He entered into the Sarov monastery, becoming a tonsured monk, deacon, and ordained priest. From 1794–1804, he lived as a hermit in the woods according to the rule of Saint Pachomius. Like the stylite Desert Fathers before him, Seraphim spent 1,000 days and nights on a large stone. He returned to the monastery where he lived fifteen years, never leaving his cell and staying in complete silence. Prompted by a vision of the Blessed Virgin Mary, the secluded hesychast opened his door to the world and lived the rest of his eight years as a starets to the many visitors that came to Sarov.

During his time as a starets, Seraphim cured Nicholas Motovilov. After Motovilov's healing he came again to Seraphim and this conversation is the best source of Seraphim's teaching. We will examine the text to learn what it means to live in the Holy Spirit.

The first gift of living in the Spirit is that of insight and discernment. The starets has been given "the ability to perceive intuitively the secrets of another's heart, to understand the hidden depths of which the other is unaware."[58] He perceives by the light of the Holy Spirit the inner spiritual life of another. The soul is disclosed before the starets so that both the problem and its solution are apparent.

Mysticism, trans. Theodore Berkeley, 2nd ed. (Hyde Park, NY: New City Press, 1995), 202–7.

56 Ibid., 34.

57 A. F. Dobbie-Bateman, "St. Seraphim of Sarov," in *A Treasury of Russian Spirituality*, ed. G. P. Fedotov (New York: Sheed and Ward, 1948), 247.

58 Ware, "Spiritual Father," 301.

Evidence of this first gift appears at the beginning of Motovilov's meeting with Seraphim. They sit down facing each other. "The Lord has revealed to me," says Seraphim, "that in your childhood you longed to know the aim of our Christian life and continually asked questions about it of many and great ecclesiastical dignitaries."[59] Motovilov had been searching earnestly for God all his life, but he has never told anyone this: "Let me here interpose that from the age of twelve this thought had ceaselessly vexed me, and I had, in fact, approached many clergy about it; but their answers had not satisfied me. This was not known to the elder."[60] Seraphim could not have known of this search for the aim of the Christian life, yet the Lord has revealed it to the wise starets. Now that the Lord has revealed the problem, Seraphim seizes the opportunity to ameliorate the soul of Motovilov.

The second gift of the starets is that he can love others by making their suffering his own.[61] The starets gives up the seclusion of his former life precisely to meet with others and show them God's love by suffering with them. He brings the love of God he has experienced to those who do not know this love, consoling them with the same love that they have received from the Lord. Very often in starets narratives, the manifestation of this gift is through bodily and spiritual healing.[62]

In this first meeting, Seraphim accomplishes a miraculous healing of Motovilov.[63] But what's more, Motovilov reveals to Seraphim a deeper spiritual wound and Seraphim answers:

> no one ... has given you a precise answer. They have said: Go to church, pray to God, fulfill the commandments of God, do good; such is the aim of the Christian life.... And

---

59 Seraphim of Sarov, "A Conversation of St. Seraphim of Sarov with Nicholas Motovilov Concerning the Aim of the Christian Life," in *A Treasury of Russian Spirituality*, ed. G. P. Fedotov (New York: Sheed and Ward, 1948), 266–67.

60 Ibid., 267.

61 Ware, "Spiritual Father," 303.

62 We see this manifestation in the development of the starets narrated in *The Way of the Pilgrim and the Pilgrim Continues His Way*.

63 "In 1831 Seraphim cured the pious landowner, Nicholas Motovilov, of rheumatism and sores. 'Do you believe,' he asked, 'that the Lord Jesus Christ is God and Man, and that His spotless Mother is ever Virgin?...Then, if you believe, you are well already.' Seizing Motovilov by the shoulders, he slowly and firmly made him walk" (Dobbie-Bateman, "St. Seraphim of Sarov," 251).

now poor Seraphim will explain to you in what really this aim consists. Prayer, fasting, watching, and all other Christian acts, however good they may be, do not alone constitute the aim of our Christian life, although they serve as the indispensable means of reaching this aim. The true aim of our Christian life, is to acquire the Holy Spirit of God.[64]

Seraphim makes clear to Motovilov the difference between the necessary way of the Christian and the end of the Christian. Prayer, fasting, and giving alms are the way of the Christian, but they are not the end; the Christian end is living in the Holy Spirit. Receiving this wisdom, Motovilov is restored to spiritual health.[65] As the starets has lived in the Holy Spirit so now the disciple sees the true reason for all the various Christian practices. To live in the Spirit, to live in his presence, is the goal of the Christian's life. In him we live, move, and have our being.

The third spiritual gift of the starets is the ability to transform human perception to see the environment the way God sees it. The starets gives his disciples the vision to see "everything in the light of Mount Tabor" as if everything can, with the Lord, be transfigured to reveal its relation with divinity (Mt 17:1–9, Mk 9:2–8, Lk 9:28–36).[66] What were ordinary clothes become in the Holy Spirit brilliantly white as snow. The material environment is transfigured to radiate the immateriality and truer reality of the glory of God.

Toward the end of the conversation with Seraphim, Motovilov questions whether he is really living in the Spirit of God. Seraphim does not debate; instead he prays, "Lord, vouchsafe to him to see clearly with bodily eyes that descent of Thy Spirit which Thou vouchsafest to Thy servants, when Thou art pleased to appear in the light of Thy marvelous glory."[67] At this prayer, Motovilov sees

---

64 Seraphim, "A Conversation," 267.

65 He promises his spiritual children constant care even after his death. On his gravestone, he wanted these words: "When I am dead, come to me at my grave, and the more often, the better. Whatever is on your soul, whatever may have happened to you, come to me as when I was alive and, kneeling on the ground, cast all your bitterness upon my grave. Tell me everything and I shall listen to you, and all the bitterness will fly away from you. And as you spoke to me when I was alive, do so now. For I am living, and I shall be forever" (Ware, "Spiritual Father," 303).   66 Ibid., 305.

67 Seraphim, "A Conversation," 274.

himself wrapped around by "dazzling brilliance" and a blinding light "spreading several yards around and throwing a sparkling radiance across the snow blanket on the glade and into the snowflakes which besprinkle" them with radiating light.[68] Furthermore, Motovilov begins to speak about the new feelings of stillness as well as majestic sweetness, joy, and especially warmth. With this prayer of Seraphim, the tangible human environment gives way to the intangible and greater sphere of divine presence. The sensory becomes periphery as the spiritual becomes foundational. In the woods far from the Holy Land, Seraphim's prayer brought Mount Tabor close. Wherever the Spirit is there is a true, glorious holy land.

If you read the text, you'll also come to learn of the uniquely Catholic and Orthodox movements. This recently narrated "living in the Spirit" has already earlier in the text been tied to the sacraments and it's Seraphim who makes this connection as he reminds Motovilov of his baptism. Seraphim's prayer unlocks the already divine reality of Motovilov's living in the Spirit that has been present since his baptism. The senses just needed to be awoken. The starets opened Motovilov's eyes to the presence of the Spirit already surrounding him from the moment of his baptism.

As we can see, the three gifts of the starets are manifested in the life of Saint Seraphim of Sarov. He can read the soul of Motovilov, show him love by healing him bodily and spiritually, and transform the disciple's perception in order to see the divine life in the human environment.

Seraphim does not conquer the great political enemies of Russia, even if Tsar Nicholas II believed that the saint's glorification "projected a new solidarity that was as patriotic as it was spiritual."[69] At the canonization, Psalm 135 was read in the Tsar's presence: "Praise the LORD .... For the LORD has chosen Jacob for himself, Israel as his own possession" (Ps 135:3-4). For Nicholas II, the glorification of Jacob and consequently Seraphim was connected necessarily to the glorification of Russia as a new Israel. The canonization marked the unity of the sanctity of Seraphim and the holy empire of Russia. Seraphim fought the spiritual battle that won his glorification and now Tsar Nicholas II would have him fight for the empire to win Russia's glorification. And yet, the real Seraphim was he who witnessed to the transfigured living in the Spirit.

---

68 Ibid. 69 Nichols, "Friends of God," 229.

Come, Holy Spirit, Today

Living in the Spirit can be dismissed as premodern, maybe even outmoded. Perhaps this new life in the Spirit is impossible for a postindustrial, postmodern, and even post-Christian world. The explosive and, we could say, destructive forces of atheistic humanism in the twentieth century that have woven narratives of materialism under the banner of scientific methodologies would have us believe that living in the Spirit has no longer any relevance to authentic, intelligent living today.

When Karol Wojtyła (May 18, 1920–April 2, 2005) became pope in 1978, he intended to focus his pontificate on developing a new and authentic Christ-centered humanism with his first encyclical *Redemptoris hominis* (1979). However, this work on Christ as the true revealer and redeemer of humanity grew into two more encyclicals: one on the Father, *Dives in misericordia* (1980), and the other on the Holy Spirit, *Dominum et vivificantem* (1986). In his reflection on the humanity revealed and redeemed by Christ, John Paul II came to anchor this new humanism in God's Trinitarian being and activity in the redemption and salvation of man.[70] *Dominum et vivificantem* is the longest and theologically richest papal encyclical on the Holy Spirit.[71] One must read this encyclical, in fact all the works of John Paul II, in light of the Second Vatican Council, especially the documents *Lumen gentium* and *Gaudium et spes*. Pope Paul VI saw that the Council itself was calling for a new study and devotion to the Holy Spirit as a necessary complement to its teaching.[72] In this way, Pneumatology must be the bedrock for theological reflection on the Church and the Church's engagement with the world. It should also be mentioned that *Dominum et vivificantem* was written for the year of the Holy Spirit (1998) in preparation for the celebration of the Jubilee in 2000. Pope John Paul II consciously provides this document as the complement to the Council, in the stream of the Catholic Church's heritage, and meant for third-millennium Christianity.[73] This encyclical is an

---

70 George Weigel, *Witness to Hope: The Biography of Pope John Paul II* (New York: HarperCollins, 1999), 386.

71 It is important to mention what documents led up to this. Pope Leo XIII wrote *Divinum illud munus* (1897) on the Holy Spirit and Pius XII wrote *Mystici corporis* (1943) on the Church, which has the Holy Spirit as its vital principle.

72 John Paul II, *Dominum et vivificantem* (Vatican: Libreria Editrice Vaticana, 1986), 2.   73 Ibid.

exegesis of Scripture on the Holy Spirit—particularly Genesis 1:3, John 14–16, and Romans 8—together with the Tradition of the Church in service of his theological meditation. He states that this is not an exhaustive Pneumatology. The main purpose is "to develop in the Church the awareness that 'she is compelled by the Holy Spirit to do her part towards the full realization of the will of God, who has established Christ as the source of salvation for the whole world.'"[74] It is a work that reflects on (I) the Holy Spirit as the Spirit of the Father and Son given to the Church, (II) who convinces the world of sin in the human heart thereby participating in the redeeming work of Christ, (III) in order to bring forth in man the life of grace which means life within God's triune love.

The first part of the encyclical places the Holy Spirit in relation to the Father and the Son by an exegesis of John 14–16. In this Farewell Discourse, "we can say that the highest point of the revelation of the Trinity is reached."[75] We see in this passage a revelation of the Trinity of Persons, their intimate bond, and their joint salvific work. Christ promises to the Apostles that he will send another Counselor who will continue to work in the world through the Church bringing the Good News of salvation (3, 14). The Holy Spirit "will ensure continuity and identity of understanding" and "that in the church there will always continue the same truth which the Apostles heard from the Master" because he will "teach you all things," "bring to your remembrance," and "bear witness" to Christ.[76] The Spirit and Christ have an intimate relationship that draws in the Church to participate in the redeeming and saving work of the Trinity. The sending of the Holy Spirit will come after Christ has departed, "because of the Redemption accomplished by Christ, through the will of the Father."[77] Christ is the one anointed and exalted in the Holy Spirit who comes in the Holy Spirit, possesses the Holy Spirit in himself, and sends the Holy Spirit to others.[78] In this the Holy Spirit is understood as personal love or Person-Love. He is the uncreated Love-Gift or Person-Gift, who "being consubstantial with the Father and the Son in divinity is love and uncreated gift from which derives as from its source (*fons vivus*) all giving

---

74 Ibid. He is also quoting here a section of *Lumen gentium* 17.
75 Ibid., 9.   76 Ibid., 4–5.   77 Ibid., 8.   78 Ibid., 15–17.

of gifts vis-à-vis creatures (created gift)."[79] The Spirit of God is given at the departure of Christ through the Cross in order to accomplish the entire salvific plan in us, bringing about a new beginning as he did in the original beginning (Gen 1:3). The one who was Crucified and Risen is the one who sends the Holy Spirit to carry out the redemption in human hearts that was won by Christ in his self-emptying. The gift of the Holy Spirit was given to the Apostles, to the Church, and for the whole world such that he "guides the Church into the fullness of truth ... [and] makes the Church grow, perpetually renews her and leads her to perfect union with her Spouse."[80]

John Paul II continues his exegesis of the Farewell Discourse in part two, focusing on the Holy Spirit as the one who will "convince the world of sin" (Jn 16:8). The convincing of sin is seen in light of Peter's speech on the day of Pentecost—"this Jesus ... you crucified and killed" (Acts 2:23)—in which he links the descending of the Holy Spirit, the convincing of sin, and the rejection of Christ. The Holy Spirit convinces the world of what it has just done and what it always does in sin. It rejects Christ.[81] This "convincing of sin" is at the same time a call to the remission of sin, a call to repentance. There is a double gift in the "convincing": the gift of the truth given to the conscience and the gift of the certainty of redemption given to the person.[82] He convinces that the world committed the greatest sin, "the killing of Jesus, the Son of God, consubstantial with the Father!" but at the same time he convinces that "the sin of having crucified the Son of God 'conquers' human sin!"[83] The Spirit of truth that "searches" the "depths of God" searches the depths of the human heart, in one's conscience, while also giving the person a conviction that sin and death have been overcome by Christ.

The rejection of Christ is linked to the original rejection of God in the beginning so that John Paul II turns to a discussion of the original reality of sin. The original rejection is disobedience, a turning away and closing in from God and also an opening up to the "father of lies." The eating of the tree of the knowledge of good and evil is an enticement to go beyond the limit set by the Creator as impassible for the creature. It was a rejection of

---

79 Ibid., 10.   80 Ibid., 25.   81 Ibid., 30–31.
82 Ibid., 31.   83 Ibid.

the source of all giving of truth and love, a rejection of the gift. The one who can "convince of sin" is the one who is the gift and the source of all giving of gifts.[84] The convincing shows the evil contained in the sin and reveals the pain, the very "fatherly" pain of God. At the same time he reveals the love of the Father and Son for man in Christ who offered himself without blemish to God and did this with an eternal Spirit (Heb 9:14). In this sacrifice of the Son, the Holy Spirit is present and active.[85] The Holy Spirit acts as the "fire from heaven" together with the oblation sacrifice of supreme love in order to bring about the redemption and obedience of the world by a purification of the conscience.[86]

The third part uses the exegesis of Romans 8 and Galatians 5:17 to show how the Holy Spirit is the source of divine life, adopting man into a divine filiation. The Spirit of the Father and Son makes sons and daughters of the Father. The Spirit is the uncreated gift to the human heart that brings about the created gift whereby Christians "become partakers of the divine nature" (2 Pet 1:4). The Holy Spirit gives life, divine life, and gives to the created human spirit the life of sanctifying grace.[87] He is "the source of all God's salvific activity in the world."[88] He strengthens the "heart of man" and the heart of the Church, bringing about a union of the Bride with the Bridegroom: "The Spirit and the Bride say to the Lord Jesus Christ: 'Come'" (see Rev 22:17).[89]

---

84 Ibid., 37.   85 Ibid., 40.   86 Ibid., 41.
87 Ibid., 52.   88 Ibid., 54.
89 Ibid., 58, 65. Here also he invokes *Lumen gentium* 4.

6

Man

WE DRAW ON CHURCH TEACHING FROM IRE-
naeus through to the Second Vatican Council: the glory of God
is man fully alive and the one human who is fully alive is Jesus
Christ who, though he suffered and died and was buried, rose
again on the third day. In this way, biological living has entered
into resurrected, eternal life. *Gaudium et spes* 22, so often quoted
in the writings of John Paul II, states that in Christ divinity was
revealed but also the fullness of our humanity was revealed. The
revelation of our humanity in Christ includes our human experience of being broken and dead in order to be brought to a new
resurrected, eternal life.

We can begin to see that the definition of man should include
becoming destitute and destroyed in the self in order to be fulfilled in new life. In Jesus's teaching about humanity, we have
this important verse, "Truly, truly, I say to you, unless a grain of
wheat falls into the earth and dies, it remains alone; but if it dies,
it bears much fruit" (Jn 12:24).

Yes, obviously we should do whatever we can to alleviate suffering, but also we need to acknowledge that personhood realized
and fulfilled necessitates this breaking open. It is essential to living
the fullness of our human biological and soul-filled life.

In Finitude Infinitude

Let us understand that within the finiteness of man we experience the infinity (ever more) of God. Being human, we need
to know what is authentically human. By experiencing multiple
cultures, we come to transcend the parochial to find truly *human*
cultures. Daily we drink the water of our human neighborhood, but
can we for a moment, for a Sunday, drink the wine of humanity?
I mean that there is a desire within us to discern the authentically
human. Is this not something of the striving of evolutionary biol-
ogy, cross-cultural sociology, and even the various medical sciences?
Do we not, even in postmodernism, seek to lift up our eyes to

some eternal objectivity above us? And yet are we not trying to find some transcending of our finitude? Are we not longing to transcend into infinitude?

Our existential experience of suffering finitude is compassion—sharing the suffering of others, and letting the divine share in the suffering through one's humanity. All compassion becomes incarnational and the suffering is taken over into God's compassionate presence. In my view, one person's suffering and another's response becomes a kind of incarnation of the infinite compassionate presence of God alone.

In Adrienne von Speyr's work, we find this idea expressed in her theological anthropology. Let us focus on this aspect of her thought—the finiteness of our life, the boundary, the limit of our existential power, the impeded horizon. Imagine your finite existence as a box, like one you might use for moving your books to a new apartment. First of all, it is important to grasp the finiteness of your life. This finitude of your life can be filled with only a finite number of days, projects, people, ideas, and activities. You can read only a finite list of books in your life. It is a tragic thought! Without reflection, one's finitude could be filled with meaninglessness, yet much of our striving in this life is an attempted transcendence of this finitude. Knowing one's finitude is a pathway to wisdom as the psalmist prays, "So teach us to number our days" (Ps 90:12; cf. 34:4). Here's the conundrum of our human experience. Objectively, our existence is finite, but subjectively, we desire and we even live as if we are infinite.

According to Speyr, we must open ourselves to the compassion of God. Speyr believes that "The only thing you can say about the love of God is: it leaves behind scorched earth."[1] Or as it says in the Torah, "God is a devouring fire" (Deut 4:24; cf. Heb 12:29). Sometimes we think that "God" is just another finite compartment in our finite box—finding a hour on Sunday to go to church. But in reality, he is "always more."[2] If God were to enter into our life, we would discover that he is a devouring fire. He takes up all aspects of our life. He brings the scorching of his compassionate love to overtake all of our finitude by his infinitude. When we are

---

1 Adrienne von Speyr, *Lumina and New Lumina*, trans. Adrian Walker (San Francisco: Ignatius Press, 2008), 15.

2 This is one of Speyr's favorite phrases: God is "always more [immer grösser]."

encountered by God as God, God's infiniteness overcomes any of our preconceived finite boundaries of him.

The ultimate human finitude is death. An end to all our striving. Some choose to fear this finality. Woody Allen has said it perfectly, "It's not that I'm afraid to die, it's just that I don't want to be there when it happens."[3] But we find another perspective in Speyr: "Death is God's invention that finally prevents the sinner from resisting His grace."[4] Why do we die? It is a gift in God that finally presents us with God's irresistable grace. He is a devouring fire. He leaves behind scorched earth. Speyr reminds us that death, as an allowed intervention by God to his irresistible, efficient grace, confronts us with his potent, unavoidable presence. It is like the unavoidable presence of a parent extending his arm to his child saying, "Hold my hand." What child will not accept that invitation? Why do we not see death as the Father extending his arm and saying, "Hold my hand." Certainly, in death there will be no other hand to hold. One should not fear death because, as Speyr says,

> To fear death means to shift it completely into the temporal and to forget the power of the sacraments that ferry us over to the other side, that prepare and purify us. To know death, by contrast, means to know that God remains the eternal giver and that out of a kind of yearning He already uses the moment we pass over to manifest His presence more clearly.[5]

Shifting from alive to dead is not shifting from something to nothing, but from beginning to eternity, from finiteness to infiniteness.

Let's approach this topic from another angle by thinking about loneliness. Modern and postmodern man, if he is anything, is perpetually lonely as was discussed in the first chapter. A wonderful image that depicts this loneliness is the painting by Edward Hopper (d. 1967) called "New York Movie" (1939). The woman is isolated to the side of a movie theater self-absorbed in thought. She's in a room full of other people engaged in the movie, but for herself she seems tragically alone. However, because of the

---

3 The character Kleinman in a short play by Woody Allen, *Without Feathers* (New York: Ballantine Books, 1986), 99.

4 Speyr, *Lumina*, 59.   5 Speyr, *Lumina*, 60.

fullness of her coloring, she's also a kind of hero of the only one who is acknowledging her perpetual loneliness. At least she knows she's lonely.

* * *

Let us consider Saint Augustine (340–430). For many of his years, he lived a life of hedonism that only later became a life of holiness—from a life of the lonely pursuit of things to a life in relationship with God alone. In his autobiography, *Confessions*, we read Augustine's honest assessment of his life and ours, "Our hearts are restless until they rest in you."[6] When one's relationship with God is alive, healthy relationships begin to fall into God's plan for eternal life in his loving compassionate presence. God says it quite clearly, "It is not good that the man should be alone" (Gen 2:18). His desire is that we would not be alone. It is not good that we are alone. The biblical understanding of man and woman expresses God's sincere desire that we not be alone.

Let us consider more of Augustine's spirituality. He finally encountered God through a mystical turn inward to go upward—to know oneself in order to know God. In his major work on the Trinity, specifically in Book X, he seeks to know himself as he is known in his mind.[7] His "exact purpose" he sets before himself: How do I obey the Delphic Oracle, "Know thyself?" The inward turn is a turn to the mind—whole and always already present. It is Augustine's position that a whole and self-present mind already knows itself when it understands the command "Know thyself."

Augustine first addresses the question of how one can love the unknown and his answer is one cannot. Earlier in the extensive masterwork, Augustine came to the conclusion that one can only love what one already knows. Here he states again that no one can love a thing of which he is "absolutely ignorant."[8] One must in some way know a little bit about a thing in order to desire to love it more. In other words, one must have some knowledge of a thing in order to seek to know more of the thing. The more

---

6 Augustine, *Confessions*, trans. Henry Chadwick (New York: Oxford Press, 1991), 3.

7 Augustine, *The Trinity*, trans. Stephen McKenna (Washington, D.C.: Catholic University of America Press, 2002), X.1.1.

8 Ibid., X.1.1. For Augustine's conclusion about knowledge preceding love, see Book VIII.

one knows of a thing, the more one desires to know everything about it. One could say that he loves to know the unknown, but, in Augustine's mind, one cannot say that he loves the unknown.[9]

Augustine now moves toward the relationship of the love and knowledge of one's self. If the mind loves to know itself, how is this possible if it does not yet know itself? This paradox seems like a formidable objection to the conclusion that one must know in order to love. But doesn't the mind love itself before it knows itself? Don't we love to seek the knowledge of ourselves because we do not know ourselves?

In order to answer this, Augustine says that the mind certainly loves something in its seeking to know itself.[10] But, what is this something? Does it know the genus that makes the mind desire the knowledge of the species? Is it the known thing that we love leading us to know something about the unknown? Or is it just that we are curious about the unknown?

All of these have more or less something to do with Augustine's position. He answers the problem this way. In our experience, the mind is seeking to know itself: "it is inflamed with this desire."[11] It loves, but what in the mind does it love? The mind does know what knowing is. It knows itself as seeking to know itself. What the mind knows is that it is seeking itself. For Augustine, the mind loves to know more of itself because it knows itself as seeking. The mind seeking to know itself clearly shows that the mind "is more known than unknown."[12] We will come to see that this answer is only tentative because he wants to say more than that the mind only knows itself in seeking to know itself.

The third step that Augustine takes in his desire to obey the command, "Know thyself," moves him to ask whether the mind is a whole without parts or a whole with parts. The mind, Augustine says, "knows itself as a whole."[13] To him, there can be no parts to the mind because the mind is incorporeal or spiritual. If it is spiritual then it is simple. In the ancient world, the assumption of Platonic and Aristotelian metaphysics was that the spiritual realm is whole in that it does not have parts, but the corporeal realm is filled with a multiplicity of parts. Augustine and his readers would see that the mind, being spiritual, would be a whole without parts.

9 Ibid., X.1.3. 10 Ibid., X.2.4. 11 Ibid., X.3.5.
12 Ibid. 13 Ibid., X.4.6.

This idea does not mean that one cannot make distinctions, but the spiritual is the more simple, wholly, and holy.

The next step for him is that the mind as a whole seeks to know itself but it is not really seeking because it is already always available. The mind is always present to oneself. Augustine earlier said that "nothing can be more present to itself than itself."[14] The external world of things comes and goes, but the interior of one's own self is always present. Setting out on the adventure of self-discovery is no journey. The mind is already present. One is already present to oneself. It seems to him absurd to suggest that there is one part of the mind here that is seeking to know the other part of the mind over there. What needs to be present is the decision to know oneself and that decision may take us down the longest road, which we will see below. But first we need to grasp the concept that since there are no parts in the mind because it is whole, then the mind is present to itself as a whole.

If the mind as a whole is not seeking for itself because it is already always present to itself as a whole, then "the mind does not seek itself at all."[15] The significance of this discovery cannot be overstated. Augustine has said that the mind is always available to itself and that it is a whole mind. The mind is already and always wholly present to be wholly known. One does not "seek" for what one has wholly. So in this sense, the mind does not seek itself because it is always already available to itself.

Now we come to the fourth move that Augustine makes in order to know himself. It could be called the ascetical move. The mind must know itself as it is in itself, in its own nature.[16] To see truly the mind as it is in itself, one must cast aside images from the exterior world. Sometimes the mind desiring to know itself draws into itself "those things upon which it has long reflected with love."[17] If the mind focuses all its attention on the exterior world, then it will bring those images into itself as it is trying to know itself. The mind has been impressed with these images so strongly that they cannot be cast away: "the mind errs when it binds itself to these images with a love so strong as to regard itself as something of this kind."[18] Since the mind is incorporeal substance, it cannot be understood with corporeal images.[19] One

14 Ibid., X.3.5.   15 Ibid., X.4.6.   16 Ibid., X.5.7.
17 Ibid.   18 Ibid., X.6.8.   19 Ibid., X.7.10.

must let go of all bodily images in order to know the spiritual mind and, in this way, one will go "more deeply within."[20]

If the mind has abandoned all images of the corporeal world, then it will see itself as not being absent and will come to the conclusion that "there never was a time when it did not love itself and never a time when it did not know itself."[21] Thus we come to the fifth and final phase in Augustine's obedience to the command to "Know thyself."

The mind knows itself because it is completely available to itself as a whole: "it knows itself for no other reason than that it is present to itself."[22] The self-presence of the mind, or self-awareness makes self-knowledge instantly available. As soon as one hears and understands the words "know" and "thyself," the mind immediately knows itself. All of this implies that one has gone through the process of purifying the mind from the corporeal, letting the mind be as it is without external images. For Augustine, this is a considering of the mind's "nature." Knowing oneself implies knowing one's nature and being ruled by that nature "under Him by whom it must be governed."[23]

In Augustine's view, this self-knowing is linked to discernment of self-presence, the ability "to distinguish itself from that which it knows to be another thing."[24] If the mind carries out this discernment and obeys the command "Know thyself," it truly does know itself at the very instant it understands the command. Since the mind is instantly accessible as a whole, the mind can know itself.[25]

In order to know the Trinity, one must know one's own mind because the spiritual mind is closer to the Lord's nature than any other aspect of the world or ourselves. Since we are made in the image of God, knowing one's own mind is to begin to know God. The final part of Book X introduces how knowing one's own mind

---

20 Ibid., X.8.11.   21 Ibid.   22 Ibid., X.9.12.
23 Ibid., X.5.7.   24 Ibid., X.9.12.
25 Certainly, we must realize that Augustine has been influenced by Neoplatonism, though there is debate among early church scholars about the extent of this influence and its relationship to the even more important biblical and theological influences. The assumption that Augustine takes from this influence is that the more inward is the more true because the more inward is more simple. Whereas the exterior world contains multiplicity, the inner world of one's own mind consists of simplicity because of its spiritual nature.

leads one to knowing not only God as unity but also as triune. Knowing the mind as it is in itself directs one to know God as he is in himself as triune. We can see this in the *Confessions*, where knowing one's own self is also a knowing of God. As one goes more inward, one finds that God is more inward than one's own self (*interior intimo meo*).[26] Augustine helps us understand the *modo interior* of the Christian life as the way to seek more and more knowledge of the triune God who loves us more than we could possibly know.

Mission of Service as Compassionate Confession

What do we come to know of ourselves when we know ourselves in God? We are directed toward others in a mission of service, but specifically service as compassionate confession. Here's where we're heading as I close this chapter on the human person: "There is no mission that is not determined decisively by one's confessional attitude."[27]

This quotation is from Adrienne von Speyr. You can read more about her in my previous book, *Heaven Opens*.[28] Now I'd like to help us arrive at that connection between one's confessional attitude and one's mission of service. To do that I'm going to concentrate on a central theme of her writings and the principal subject of this book, the theology of Holy Saturday. For Speyr, God unveils his deep, intense love to the utmost extent on Holy Saturday. We'll be examining her mystical theology through one of her central books, *Confession*. It is a very encouraging book, a very warm and opening book that teaches the grace of the Sacrament of Confession. This sacrament is often forgotten, but as one gives one's self over to this sacrament one realizes what a gift it is from God and how everything, especially one's missionary life, changes.

In whatever area one is called to be a missionary as one discovers oneself in the Lord, the confessional attitude makes all the difference. As one grows in being a missionary, one begins to discern clearly what is authentically human. We all grow up in our little parochial spheres in which we think everything we

---

26 Augustine, *Confessions*, 201.
27 Speyr, *Confession*, 208.
28 See especially Chapter One, which provides a biography of her life as a doctor and mystic.

do is right and what everything everybody else does is strange or weird. I'm normal, everybody else is a foreigner, an other.

One of the things you learn as a missionary, especially as an international volunteer, is just what is authentically human of your experience and of other cultures. One of the things you learn to see is that everyone suffers. No matter where you are, be it in the richest land, in the poorest land, or in all the lands in between, wherever you are, there is suffering. Everyone suffers, everyone experiences a destitution of self, everyone experiences loneliness no matter how rich, or how poor. Everyone experiences a suffering loneliness.

The Christian must respond in his missionary life to that loneliness with compassion. Compassion means "suffering with." Compassion does not mean to go galloping in like a white knight scattering money, buildings, or social programs, as important as these offers can be. The Christian missionary life is that of suffering with the lonely by offering your presence. Hearing their cry. Recording their cry in your heart so it becomes your own. The missionary says, "You are suffering, you are lonely and now so am I, and I'm going to be with you and suffer with you."

This mission of presence heals. The services of social programs, buildings, and feeding the hungry can accomplish much good in the world, but the one thing that every human needs is a balm for loneliness. The central mission is compassion.

To be compassionate your attitude must be confessional. You don't descend from your lofty tower to serve your inferiors (the queen having pity for the less fortunate). The truly Christian understanding of kenosis is that you are, in a confessional sense, so low that you become the servant. You realize all the ways that you have excluded God from your life and prevented others from loving you. You see that, in a sense, you're serving upwards to the lowly from your position of even greater lowliness. You see that even these, the least of his brothers, understand God better than you do. Saint Vincent de Paul has this insight. The reason we serve the poor is because we're poorer than they are. That is the attitude that must be brought to one's mission.[29]

For Speyr, the concept of serving up is the confessional attitude. First, before one enters into the Sacrament of Confession,

[29] Vincent de Paul and Louise de Marillac, *Rules, Conferences, and Writings*, ed. Frances Ryan and John Rybolt (New York: Paulist, 1995).

the attitude matters. How should we enter into this sacrament? Speyr thinks that:

> In all events which are not inevitable and in whose course freedom and inclination can intervene, a person usually searches for a solution or a way out and often for a reason or cause as well....Only when this success fails to materialize according to his wish does he look for the causes behind the failure, and it is in this search that he first encounters the question concerning the state of his own life....Yet it is precisely when he justifies himself and concludes that he is innocent that his deeper discomfort—the feeling of a hidden guilt—begins.[30]

She begins with the truism that when we have a problem, we look for the solution. If our solution works, the search is over. Problem, solution, problem, solution. We don't look further.

The same is true in a sense for the most serious things in life. You can run a list in your head of the different solutions that you have tried for your own loneliness and the loneliness you have seen in others. When that solution doesn't work, you start to reflect more deeply about the problem. When you feel the loneliness, you insert your routine strategy. But then, it does not work and you are still lonely. Now, you start to wonder what it is that went wrong with that solution. That moment there—the beginning of reflection—is an invitation to the confessional attitude. So often, we refuse it and prefer to justify ourselves. Still, there is in that moment the possibility of saying, "I'm not the answer to my problem. I must look outside." That's the moment of invitation.

Knowing myself means knowing I'm not the savior of me. According to Speyr,

> Ultimately, only the Creator of the human soul will be able to treat it so that it becomes the soul he needs. Only he can heal it, and he does this in ways that only he knows and discloses and prescribes for healing....The decisive way of God—confession—is based on obedience: more specifically, on the obedience to God.[31]

Think about that. If God made us he knows what we need. When we are sick he knows what heals us.

---

30 Speyr, *Confession*, 11.   31 Ibid., 15.

The early Church theologian, Ignatius of Antioch, has a deep understanding of God as the Divine Physician and of the Eucharist as the medicine of healing immortality. The Creator knows what is ailing his creation. The Eucharist is the healing presence of Jesus Christ, and the Sacrament of Confession as the outflow of the Eucharist ("Do this in remembrance of me, for the forgiveness of sins"). These sacraments heal us from our sin. That is the medicine. Whatever way we look for solutions to heal loneliness, it is Confession and the Eucharist that heal us. It is forgiveness and presence that heal us. That is the medicine. Only God knows what truly heals and he's offered us this.

Continuing with Speyr's thinking, we come to this next insight about the desire to confess: "If a person ... comprehends himself as standing before God, and if he knows that he, like Adam, was created by God and redeemed by Christ and that Christ opens for him the way to the Father and the doors of heaven, then ... he will expect confession with a kind of necessity."[32] As this person starts to acknowledge God over and above, he will come to realize that he is not right in his relationships. He will see that things are not as they are supposed to be. He will find a way to confess this disconnection. He expects a way of confession as a necessity for healing and beginning again.

Even though one expects some way to confess, not everyone takes the next step. Speyr says, "As long as a person is not confessing, he feels free to speak or keep silent about whatever he wishes."[33] When we don't confess we regulate what we say to others. We prevent certain things from being revealed. We feel in control when we decide what to reveal and what not to reveal. Speyr continues, "What he then hates in confession is not the humbling experience of revealing himself, and not the fact that he is a sinner—he already knows that somehow—but the necessity of capitulating before and within total confession, the fact that the freedom of selection has been withdrawn and that the only choice remaining is to reveal everything or nothing."[34]

The Sacrament of Confession requires you to reveal everything of yourself. The sacrament demands a revealing of everything or nothing. That is the choice that God gives in confession. One

---

32 Ibid., 16.   33 Ibid., 18.   34 Ibid.

reveals everything or nothing—not some, not half, not most. Everything or nothing.

The disease of the moment in much of modern society is compartmentalization. Modern man has placed his life into different compartments that are not associated with each other. On Monday, he has a certain group of people that he relates to, perhaps it is in a classroom or in an office. He has certain ways of behaving in this compartment, revealing some small aspect of himself, but not everything. He's a good student or he's a good worker. He takes his notes. He answers his emails. He's complimented for his correct compartmentalized behavior. That covers the first few days of the week.

As he makes his way through the week, his Thursday, Friday, or Saturday night is party night. Work is no more, he now plays the party guy, revealing only that aspect of his being. He has his Thursday night friends, who are different from his Saturday night friends. He's no longer the diligent student taking notes or productive worker complimented by his boss. He's the chaos maker unleashing his bravado ego.

On Saturday morning, he is yet another person. He calls his parents. He drives his child to the next soccer game. He's Dad who has everything under control. He's the athletic man who takes time to coach his child.

And then there is Sunday morning and he goes to "church" in his more formal clothing, on his best behavior, and with appropriate tedium. He does not pray for his salvation—he is already right and just and says the words "It is right and just" thinking it refers to him and not the sacrificial atonement completed by his Lord. He says he lifts his heart up to the Lord as a phrase he memorized long ago. He's saying all the right words so he must be doing all the right things. He'll make sure to put some money in the collection basket because he is right and just.

This man we've created has all these different behaviors for all these different compartments. He doesn't mention what happened on Sunday morning to his friends on Thursday night. He doesn't bring his Friday night into his Sunday morning prayer. He's not one man. He's at least five different men and he protects these boundaries. He's not sure who he really is, but he does know in some fundamental way this is not how it's supposed to be.

Speyr says this compartmentalizing of the life of the modern man is overcome by developing a confessional attitude. The walls that divide his identity are torn down by the grace of the Sacrament of Confession. If he will enter into the fullness of the sacrament, his risen Lord will appear within all of these locked rooms.

That's the grace that's given in the Sacrament of Confession. There is no possibility of "oversharing" in the grace of the Sacrament of Confession. The Lord already knows, he is only asking for cooperation.

> [The penitent] is sick as a whole person and must be healed as such, and not eclectically. That is the first humbling experience. The second is that he is only one of many and has to accept the same conditions as do the others ... [he experiences] the elimination of all external differentiation ... merely one penitent in the line of other sinners. The peculiarities of my particular "case", which made it seem so interesting to me and which I would so gladly have explained to the listener, do not matter at all any more.[35]

Jesus Christ's forgiveness of sins in the Sacrament of Confession separates the sin from the one who has sinned. In this sense, Speyr sees in Confession that the sin is objectified and separated from the subjectivity of the person. Sin is separated from the man, who is restored to who he is meant to be in God.

We still have more to consider. Speyr says that, "Whoever would learn how to confess must first look at the life of the Son of God."[36] You want to confess, you want to reveal everything. The model is the Son of God. He knows how to confess. He is not another sinner trying to become a saint. He confesses toward the Father in a completely different way. He is always Son speaking everything toward the Father. Here is how Speyr puts it:

> God stands before God in the attitude that is fitting for God. Analogously, we can designate this as the attitude of confession, since it is the attitude in which God shows himself as he is .... When the Son institutes confession at Easter, he does so to bring this divine attitude closer to human beings, to mediate to them part of the trinitarian life.[37]

---

35 Ibid., 18. 36 Speyr, *Confession*, 20. 37 Ibid., 21.

The Father and the Son and the Holy Spirit relate to each other in a confessional attitude. They reveal everything to each other. They hold back nothing. The Son reveals everything to the Father. We can call that by analogy the confessional attitude. The Son relates to the Father in this attitude of revealing everything, hiding nothing, being completely transparent. This is a big step in thinking with Trinitarian faith.

Here we have the next step that is critical in thinking about the confessional attitude:

> One can say that the Lord lives on earth before the Father in the same condition in which the perfect penitent should live before his own confessor, before the Church and before God: in complete openness, concealing nothing, always ready in every moment to expect the intervention of the Holy Spirit, drawing security from the Father and his Spirit instead of from within himself. The Son lives in perpetual contact with the Father, and the expression of this contact is his word, "Not my will, but thy will be done."[38]

That is the confessional attitude, and the Son lives in that state in heaven eternally and while he was on earth. He invites all into the confessional relationship that he has with the Father. He prays, "that they may all be one; even as you, Father, are in me, and I in you, that they also may be in us" (Jn 17:21).

The Church teaches that the Sacrament of Confession it is not just one sinner speaking to another (that would be therapy), but a sinner speaking of his sins to God through a priest invested by Christ with the authority to act in his name.[39] As Speyr points out, the Sacrament of Confession is Trinitarian and therefore is a kneeling with the Son and confessing with him toward the Father in the Holy Spirit.

The Sacrament of Confession is, as are all the sacraments in the Catholic Church, an entrance into the union and communion of the Divine Trinity.[40] The Son takes all of the sins of the world and reveals them to the Father—"Father, forgive them," he says on the Cross, "for they know not what they do" (Lk 23:34). In

---

38 Ibid., 23.   39 See CCC 1441.
40 I explore the Trinitarian nature of all the sacraments in Chapter 9 of my book, *Heaven Opens*: see pp. 209–23.

this moment on the Cross and in all instances of the Sacrament of Confession as a kind of re-presentation of the Cross, the Son takes all the sins of the world and presents them to the Father. In this sacrament, one learns to say with the Son, "Not as I will, but as you will" (Mt 26:39).

Speyr insists on the connection between confession and mission:

> Anyone who has recognized, in confession and in the prayer belonging to it, the possibility not only of ridding himself of his own sins through the grace of the Lord but also of helping others at the same time will suddenly realize that there is a place where confession and mission encounter and permeate one another to the point of coincidence.[41]

It is important to understand that confession is a letting go of sins, but that is not all. It is also taking on the sins of the world or more accurately, taking with one the sins of the world (of one's mission) into confession. There is a sense that, yes, you are saying, "Father, forgive me; I know not what I do," but more profoundly, you are coming to say, along with the Son, "Father, forgive them; they know not what they do."

In the Sacrament of Confession it is not just you and God, it's the whole big mass of sinners (including you) and God. You take everyone with you in union and communion as you come into union and communion with the Trinity.

I should clarify. This confession of the sins of the world in one's own confession comes from the Lord's teaching about not judging other people, but instead seeing the sin in oneself. Seeing the sin in others, we are invited by the Spirit to see that sin in ourselves, how we are connected in greater ways that we think. Yes, it is a grace to see clearly and hate sin in all its forms, but we need to go the whole way with this grace of the discernment of spirits to see clearly the sin in us. As an example, consider Thomas Merton, the great American spiritual writer. As he read reports of the Second World War expanding in its most gruesome stages, he experienced a spiritual conviction that his sins contributed to this war.[42] He saw that the sins of the world—the treachery, the

---

41 Speyr, *Confessions*, 206.
42 Thomas Merton, *The Seven Storey Mountain: An Autobiography of Faith* (New

dehumanizing—was already in him in his anger. He may not have murdered with his hands, but he had murdered with his heart.

Speyr has a unique way of talking about the objectivity of sin, as opposed to the subjectivity of sin (which would be thinking about sin as only related to a specific sinner). She says Jesus on the Cross is carrying sin in its objectivity. His work on the Cross is separating the sin from the sinner, leaving the sinner saved. In confession, the Lord objectifies the sin from the subjectivity of the sinner. You confess the sin itself and in a very real sense you represent the whole of humanity committing that sin yet again. But, then as you confess it, you're giving it over into the Son's substitutionary sacrifice.

The Son's mission is a completely divine one and as you and I join in that mission it takes on the divine purpose of reconciliation and recapitulation of all things in Christ (Eph 1:10). In order to carry out his divine mission, the Son remains eternally in the attitude of complete openness before the Father and the Spirit and that means the attitude of confession. This attitude always allows him to do the will of the Father and the Holy Spirit and to carry out his mission as personally and at the same time as obediently as possible.

Now we are able to come back to the central quotation for this section, "There is no mission that is not determined decisively by one's confessional attitude."[43] The Son's mission, the Church's mission, and our mission are all determined by our confessional attitude, our being completely open to God alone—to being alone with God alone.

The Son's attitude of openness and his actions of reconciliation comprise a single unity such that his whole mission of reconciliation is tied up with his attitude of openness. As he is on the Cross reconciling the world toward the Father, he must be open to this long drawn-out Godforsakenness. He cries, "My God, my God, why have you forsaken me?" (Ps 22:1). Open to the abyss, he

---

York: Harvest, 1948), 272: "There was something else in my own mind—the recognition: 'I myself am responsible for this. My sins have done this. Hitler is not the only one who has started this war: I have my share in it too...' It was a very sobering thought, and yet its deep and probing light by its very truth eased my soul a little. I made up my mind to go to confession and Communion on the First Friday of September."

43 Speyr, *Confessions*, 208.

reconciles everything, and speaks by his action, "in God alone is my salvation" (see Ps 62). Even as he feels he is "a worm, and no man" (Ps 22:6), even as "dogs are round about me" and "they have pierced my hands and feet" (Ps 22:16), Jesus "will tell of your name to my brethren" and in their midst he "will praise you" (Ps 22:22). While for a time he seems forsaken, God "has not despised or abhorred the affliction of the afflicted; and he has not hidden his face from him, but has heard, when he cried to him" (Ps 22:24).

All the various differentiated missions in the world take their point of departure from the Cross. The Lord promises that from the Cross, "the afflicted shall eat and be satisfied" (Ps 22:26) and they will be fed from here where God alone died for all: "All the ends of the earth shall remember and turn to the Lord; and all the families of the nations shall worship before him" (Ps 22:27). To join oneself to the Cross of Christ is to join oneself to the mission of the Son, confessing toward the Father the sins of the world that he may "make all things new" (Rev 21:5).

The Sacrament of Confession has a richness to it that we need to reflect on. I think it is really the sacrament for the twenty-first century, for this postmodern age. Yes, true, all the sacraments are for every century, but in particular there's something here that is missing and is critically needed for humanity's future.

One's mission is decisively determined by one's confessional attitude. How completely you let go of yourself determines how well you will serve in whatever mission God has called you to.

Hans Urs von Balthasar collected a book of prayers from Adrienne von Speyr's writings, journals, and dictations. This is from her prayer for thanksgiving after confession:

> Lord, we thank you for the gift of confession, for having taken away all our sins by your death. When you did this, you showed us how total nakedness before the Father, how standing ready before him, doing his will, remaining where he has placed us all belong to the essence of true confession.
>
> And now, as we come to the end of this year, we are conscious of having often done wrong. We have neglected so many things that, in keeping with your will, we ought to have attacked with gusto. We have not paid enough attention to your voice, we have not truly lived for you alone. For we should have sought you in all things, we

should have relished this year's joys as coming from you, we ought to have taken on ourselves its sufferings as willed or permitted by you, we ought to have followed every path you opened to us....

And if we have not discovered you in all things and have failed so often to meet your expectations, today your grace permits us to have the refuse cleared away from us. You cleanse, you mend, you make all things new in us and together with us. And you do all this by the power of your Cross.

You suffered this Cross on Good Friday, and, in spite of our denial, you made so many feasts of redemption come after it on the strength of your Resurrection. And the absolution you give us is a perfect one: you give us the gift of a new purity, in union with the Father in your common Holy Spirit, in the eternal purity of the Trinity.[44]

---

44 Speyr, *With God and with Men*, 31–33.

7

Mary

AS WE EXPLORED THE CONFESSIONAL ATTITUDE
in the previous chapter, we now need to explore the Yes of Mary.
The Yes and No dialectic of the Old Testament is able to receive
the irrevocable Yes only when it, too, answers a definitive Yes,
breaking out of its finitude into the infinite. God accomplishes
this breakthrough in his centuries-long purification of Israel culminating in one Israelite who says Yes completely. With this one
Yes, the bridge to the New Testament has been constructed, a
bridge that crosses over to the new beginning.[1] We also see the
beginnings of ecclesiology. In this section, I will consider these
two aspects, first, the Marian Yes and second, the Ecclesial Yes.

The Yes of Mary, the "let it be to me (*fiat mihi*) according to
your word" (Lk 1:38b), makes possible the Yes of the Son: "for
without her he would not have a human nature and thus a human
will with which to obey the Father."[2] God could not violate
the freedom of his own creatures.[3] Thus, for Balthasar, "it was
essential, therefore, if God's Word willed to become incarnate
in the womb of a woman, to elicit the latter's agreement and
obedient consent."[4] And where does true consent come from if
not from the Cross? "And the Cross itself is rendered possible
only through Mary's consent."[5] The paradox is evident: How is
it possible that the Cross, the pinnacle of all fiats, be "rendered
possible" through an antecedent fiat? According to Balthasar,
Mary's Yes is an anticipatory participation: "It is true that the
priority of Mary's 'immaculate' consent owes its existence to grace,
to the fullness of grace that is 'merited' on the Cross; but it is
equally clear that, by grace, the possibility of this fullness on

---

1 "As a fleshly Mother she stands in direct continuity with the generations
who descend from Adam via Abraham, whereas, as a virgin Mother, who
became pregnant on the basis of her consent to the overshadowing Spirit,
she signifies a hiatus and a new beginning" (Balthasar, *Theo-Drama*, III:328).
2 Saward, *Mysteries of March*, 69.
3 *Non enim invite tantum beneficium praestari debebat* (Thomas). See Balthasar,
Theo-Drama, III:297.   4 Ibid., III:297.   5 Ibid.

the Cross is dependent, in part, on the Mother's consent."[6] The effect is the cause of the cause.[7] An effect is only possible because of the breach of the temporal realm by the transcendent Word becoming flesh. This is a work of God's grace, his covenantal Yes to the world.[8]

The Yes of Mary coincides with the action of the Holy Spirit. She had the indeterminate readiness that was made determinate mission by the Holy Spirit. Mary's readiness to obedience is all that the Spirit needs, such that, "The Spirit overshadows her in the moment in which she opens herself to him; it is like a stroke of lightning which fuses together God's question and man's answer, man's readiness and God's answer, into one infinite, fruitful unity."[9] The Spirit's overshadowing "made her perfectly obedient to that self-communication of God."[10] In this, the Spirit is the Spirit of obedience for Mary as it is for the Son.[11]

Marian consent is the fundamental attitude: "Only in this yes can the Son of God become man: at that time in Mary, and now, anew in each one who attempts to join in her consent."[12] This point cannot be stressed enough for both the theology and spirituality of Hans Urs von Balthasar and Adrienne von Speyr.[13] The

---

6 Ibid., III:352. See also Saward, *Mysteries of March*, 69: "The Mother's obedience is an anticipated participation in the obedience of the Son. Her freely given assent to the Incarnation is prepared for in advance by the 'retroactive' application of the merits of Christ."

7 Balthasar, *Theo-Drama*, III:297.

8 "God initiates a new chapter in the history of salvation by a new inbreaking of his grace, so that Jesus enters into the world *by means of a human assent, a finite Yes* that is itself entirely an act and a creation of his grace and unmarred by the failures that affect all other responses to God's covenantal love" (Edward T. Oakes, *Pattern of Redemption: The Theology of Hans Urs von Balthasar* [New York: Continuum, 1994], 252).

9 Adrienne von Speyr, *Handmaid of the Lord*, trans. E. A. Nelson (San Francisco: Ignatius Press, 1984), 34.

10 John Paul II, *Dominum et vivificantem*, 51.

11 "In Mary, he [the Holy Spirit] was the Spirit of obedience, love, and attachment to the Son, as was called for through the Son's Incarnation" (Adrienne von Speyr, *Mary in the Redemption*, trans. Helena M. Tomko [San Francisco: Ignatius Press, 2003], 88).

12 Hans Urs von Balthasar, *First Glance at Adrienne von Speyr*, trans. Antje Lawry and Sergia Englund, O. C. D. (San Francisco: Ignatius Press, 1981), 53.

13 "The Church of redeemed sinners participates in the pre-redeemed consent of Mary, which eschatologically is to become the consent of the entire

Yes of Mary "is the most humble thing that the maiden can say or accomplish, and for that very reason, her greatest, her perfection."[14]

The Word of God appears on the stage (is the stage itself) as the Second and Last Adam. The first Adam called out for an answer. The answer given by God was a woman. Eve fashioned from the side of Adam is the "at last," the "bone of my bones and flesh of my flesh" (Gen 2:23). Woman is the essential answer (*Ant-wort*) to the word spoken out by man. Adam speaks out his word (*das Wort*) that is received by an answer (*die Antwort*; note the feminine gender of the German term). The *ant* means "over against" and even "toward" that which is the word; thus, "if man is the word that calls out, woman is the answer that comes to him at last."[15] The word of the man calls out. Though primary, the word remains unfulfilled and only attains fulfillment with the answer of the woman. Though secondary, the answer of the woman is of equal rank and dignity. The two are mutually dependent such that "there can be no word without an answering word" or an answering word without an original word spoken.[16] Their mission is in the command "be fruitful" (Gen 1:28), a fruitfulness received in the woman, uniting the man and woman within herself, and is thus "the fruit-bearing principle in the creaturely realm" that makes a new something.[17]

The masculine calling word and the feminine answering word indicate an analogy for the relationship, the *diastasis*, between God and creature. God as masculine word calling out is received by his creatures (both Adam and Eve) and responded to with the feminine answering word. The Son as the Second and Last Adam and as Word of God calls out for a necessary "helpmate." The Son as man calls out for an individual female answer; the Son as Word of God calls out for a creature as feminine answer.[18] The

---

people of God.... The charism of Adrienne von Speyr can be understood only from this perspective" (ibid., 52–53).

14 Ibid., 51.   15 Balthasar, *Theo-Drama*, III:284.   16 Ibid.

17 Ibid., III:286.

18 "Now what he [Balthasar] means can easily be misunderstood, and to speak of masculine and feminine as symbols of the divine-human relationship has become a matter of intense debate and controversy in the past few years. But no one denies the symbolic power of these images as applied to the God/creature relationship, and so it is important to understand what Balthasar means by his insistence that the finite response to God (in both sexes) is essentially a feminine one" (Oakes, *Pattern of Redemption*, 254).

Marian consent is the necessary feminine answer to the primary calling out of the Son as man; we also see the necessity of the Ecclesial (and still Marian) consent as the feminine and creaturely *Antwort* to the Son as the Word of God. The translation of the analogy also happens on the mission to "be fruitful." Within the female (womb of Mary) the answered word and answering word in a dyadic union make incarnate the divine Word. [19] That which the heavens could not answer was answered by the womb of Mary.

In her feminine creaturely answer, Mary becomes the *Realsymbol*, type, exemplar, pattern, and goal of Ecclesia as the feminine answer to the incarnate Son; we move into a fruitful intersection of Mariology and Ecclesiology. [20] The path continues from the Son's obedience, to Marian consent, and thence to the Ecclesial Yes in Christ that has always been a response of obedience made possible and fruitful by the Holy Spirit.

The Church shares in the obedient Yes given by the Son by giving her own obedient Yes already archetypically given by Mary. [21] The Ecclesial Yes is *in Christ* because he has opened up the acting stage for consent in his obedient descent into humanity's disobedience. [22] The fellow actors obey the same director, but continue to take their cues from the lead actor. The *in Christ* attitude is that of obedience shown by Christ's obedience, who is "both the '*exegesis*' of the Trinity's life of love and the '*epitome*' of the creatures' proper attitude to God, and especially that of the Church, his Body and Bride." [23] The way of obedience of the Son is the

---

19 Balthasar, *Theo-Drama*, III:290.

20 The movement between Mariology and Ecclesiology is justified because in her obedience Mary "is the prototype of every future instance of Christian obedience" (Speyr, *Handmaiden*, 27).

21 "A really adequate history of liberation is to be found where there is a humanly adequate response to the word of Jesus, in an unconditionally trusting discipleship of him; that is, in Mary, who is the innermost core of the Church, and in the genuine saints assembled around her" (Balthasar, *Theo-Drama*, III:29).

22 For *in Christ*, see Romans 3:24, 4:5,24, 6:11,23, 8:1-2, 39, 9:1,33, 10:11,14, 12:5, 15:12,17, 16:3,7,9-10. Not only is this a Pauline insight, it is also Johannine. For Speyr, Christian prayer is the human's interior life and word of Yes originating *in Christ*, in the Divine Word living with the Father. See Speyr, *John*, vol. 1, 31-37.

23 Saward, *Mysteries of March*, 26: "As Christ in the Spirit obeys the Father, so the Church in the Spirit is to obey Christ."

way of obedience back to the Father in the Holy Spirit.[24] The disposition of Church is always Marian and thus always in Christ.

The Ecclesial Yes imitates the Son's obedient attitude toward the Father and Holy Spirit that is the way of self-abandonment. For Balthasar, sin, the No of man, is self-enclosure to God's call, whereas obedience, the Yes of the Church, is self-openness and self-abandonment to this call. The turn into oneself in spite of the divine beckoning spurns the self-emptying way of the Son, indeed the inner way of the Trinity. Abandonment (*Hingabe*) is a coming-out-of-oneself, a response of self-surrender to an antecedent self-surrender of divine love.[25] The Ignatian indifference, a passionate indifference (Teilhard de Chardin), is the first principle and foundation by which "our one desire and choice should be what is more conducive to the end for which we are created."[26] The attitude of self-abandonment is not Puritanical or a spiritual Quietism; authentic self-abandonment is the opposite of these: "Therefore, we must make ourselves indifferent to all created things, as far as we are allowed free choice and are not under any prohibition. Consequently, as far as we are concerned, we should not prefer health to sickness, riches to poverty, honor to dishonor, a long life to a short life."[27] Whether one possesses or does not possess, the obedience to God through the direction of the Holy Spirit is the all-consuming vision. The end is all and indifference to all else.[28]

---

24 "The Incarnation took place precisely to make it possible that men should thus accompany and be carried along by him" (Balthasar, *The Glory of the Lord: A Theological Aesthetics*, ed. Joseph Fessio and John Riches [San Francisco: Ignatius Press, 1981], vol. 1, 459).

25 See McIntosh, *Christology from Within*, 66–67.

26 Ignatius of Loyola, *The Spiritual Exercises of St. Ignatius: Based on Studies in the Language of the Autograph*, trans. Louis J. Puhl (Chicago: Loyola, 1951), 23.

27 Ignatius, *Spiritual Exercises*, 23. In addition, when making the choice of one's way of life, "It is necessary to keep as my aim the end for which I am created, that is, the praise of God our Lord and the salvation of my soul. Besides this, I must be indifferent, without any inordinate attachment, so that I am not more inclined or disposed to accept the object in question than to relinquish it, nor to give it up than to accept it" (ibid., 179).

28 For Speyr, self-abandonment and indifference necessitates the destruction of the human center: "Our whole performance before God is a pharisaical program, the center of which is our own perfection, with the result that it is blind to the word spoken to us, the ever-new and ever-unexpected word. The whole of man's progress consists in the perpetual destruction of the human center, thus making way for the ever-new beginning in which is

Self-abandonment moves one into a state of expanding universality depending upon one's mission. Balthasar argues that "Theological persons are not monads . . . the theological person radiates as
far as his vocation and mission reaches."[29] Through self-surrender,
the destruction of the human center causes a de-privatization of
the "I" and creates a locus for ecclesial manifestation of Christ's
mission.[30] The Church joins the Yes of the Son and his mission.
She is given a participation in the sending of the Son through
the Holy Spirit to the world. The Son's mission continues in the
Church. The theo-drama continues even after the main protagonist
has left the stage.[31]

The participation in the Son's mission must always be anchored
in obedience as following the Crucified Lord.[32] The Spirit directed
Christ in this way; it will be the same way that the Spirit directs
the Church. The theo-drama happens in the vivid tension point-
ing to the Cross. The antagonistic No of the world's disobedience
appears to triumph over the Father's Yes to the world through
the obedience of his Son. The script points to the heightening of
this action, driving the protagonist into the midst of it. The Holy

---

heard the word . . . . The only way to love is to overcome one's own point of
view" (Speyr, *Word Becomes Flesh*, 24).

29 Balthasar, *Theo-Drama*, III:271.

30 "If the mission is accepted and carried out, it de-privatizes the 'I', causing the latter's fruitful influence (through grace) to expand into the whole
'Mystical Body' of Christ. In this way, there is a mutual interpenetration of
the diverse missions and the persons who identify themselves with them:
this is what is meant by the *communio sanctorum*" (ibid., III:349).

31 We see this in Shakespeare's *Julius Caesar* in which the title character
dies halfway through the play, yet the play continues.

32 See Maximilian Greiner, "The Community of St. John: A Conversation
with Cornelia Capol and Martha Gisi," in *Hans Urs von Balthasar: His Life and
Work*, article trans. Michael Waldstein, ed. David L. Schindler (San Francisco:
Ignatius Press, 1991), 94 (here Martha Gisi is speaking): "I believe what the
Herr Doktor's and Adrienne's reflections had in common with the view of
St. Ignatius lies in the idea of obedience as following the obedient Christ.
This is really the central idea. And when one speaks in this context about
our community one can understand obedience only in the light of this
theology: obedience as following the crucified Lord. This is what was alive
in him and in Adrienne as something coming from Ignatius, and it is here
that one can see the true core of their Ignatian thinking and faith." See also
Hans-Peter Göbbeler, *Existenz als Sendung: Zum Verständnis der Nachfolge Christi
in der Theologie Hans Urs von Balthasars (unter besonderer Berücksightigung der Gestalt
des Priestertums und von Ehe und Familie)* (St. Ottilien: EOS-Verlag, 1997), 49–52.

Spirit pushes the Son forward into the obedient abandonment of the Cross. It is within this action that the Church participates. The Church follows every contour of the Lord's mission. She does not just participate in the Resurrection without having joined Christ on the Cross. Balthasar states that the fundamental insight of any theology of the Resurrection must be that the Risen One is the Crucified One.[33] The form of the Christian life ought to be the *Ernstfall*, the crucial moment of Christian witness as one's own martyrdom, which is participation with the Crucified One.[34] The Church must never lose its focus on the obedience of the Son on the Cross: "For the Church is a product of Christ's absolute obedience, an obedience that brought him to the Cross." The sacrifice of Christ on the Cross, a sacrifice "through the eternal Spirit" (Heb 9:14), also draws the Church in obedience to the Spirit's overshadowing at the annunciation, the Pentecost, and the epiclesis of the Eucharist.

The way of obedience *pro nobis (for us)* began with the original No of disobedience that cascaded into the post-Christian culture's rejection of God. This led to the finally valid, perfectly obedient Yes of Christ, which could only be discussed in terms of Balthasar's theodramatic theory of the Holy Spirit as director, who is in and above the Son making him obedient and making the play present for us. The Holy Spirit overshadowing in the annunciation and the Pentecost reveals the Marian Yes that has opened up the Ecclesial Yes and now, through the centuries, in the epiclesis of the Eucharist. The Yes of the Son has pierced through the sphere of hesitation that was answered and made fruitful by the Marian and Ecclesial consent. Thus, the Holy Spirit is the one sent by the Father who made Christ obedient and now is making us obedient to the Father's will. It is a play still needing completion. The libretto of Scripture speaks of the fifth act that "must soon take place" (Rev 1:1). Until then, the Holy Spirit and the Church call out to the Lord: "The Spirit and the Bride say, 'Come!'" (Rev 22:17).

Our Lady of Compassion

Mary's Yes opens her to the mission of the Son to bring the compassion of the Father in and through the Holy Spirit. This

---

33 Saward, *Mysteries of March*, 134.
34 See Hans Urs von Balthasar, *The Moment of Christian Witness*, trans. Richard Beckley (Glen Rock, NJ: Newman, 1969), 5-31.

Yes reverberates in compassion for centuries. Since this Yes was of God it becomes timeless. Mary's compassion extends throughout the centuries always in service of her Son. I wish to explore how three modern twentieth-century conflicts were preceded by Marian apparitions imploring for conversion and peace.[35] What does the claim of Mary's appearance before major conflicts of the twentieth century tell us about who God is and how God may use Mary in the twenty-first century?

Toward the end of the twentieth century, Pope John Paul II said that Mary's appearance at Fátima in 1917 contained messages of conversion and repentance particularly geared toward the horrors of the first decades of the twentieth century, but these messages reverberated throughout the rest of the century.[36] If in any century humanity needed the message of forgiveness, peace, and hope it was this past century.

In 1917, the world was suffering from the devastation of the First World War, which claimed the lives of 20 million. 1917 also saw Tsar Nicholas II of Russia abdicate in face of the Russian Revolution.

In the midst of this chaos, Pope Benedict XV began a novena of prayer for peace.[37] On the eighth day of that novena, the Feast of Our Lady of the Blessed Sacrament, May 13, many believe that Mary appeared to three shepherding children (Lucia dos Santos 10, Jacinta Marcos 7, Francisco Marcos 9) in a rural area outside Fátima, Portugal.

Lucia said of this visit that she saw a lady "all dressed in white, more brilliant than the sun, radiating a light clearer and more intense than a crystal glass filled with clear water pierced by the most burning rays of the sun."[38] Mary then revealed to the chil-

---

35 While the Church does not require belief in any claimed appearances and messages of Mary, many of all classes and educational backgrounds in the Catholic Church, as well as other churches, have come to see them as a sign of God's continued compassion for the world, especially given the horrors humanity experienced in the twentieth century.

36 John Paul II, "Message of Mary's Maternal Love," Homily at Mass in Fatima, May 13, 1982: http://w2.vatican.va/content/john-paul-ii/it/homilies/1982/documents/hf_jp-ii_hom_19820513_fatima.html.

37 For a scholarly history of the events surrounding what is claimed in the apparition contextualized with events in the twentieth century, see Hilda Graef and Thomas Thompson, S. M., Mary: A History of Doctrine and Devotion (Notre Dame, IN: Ave Maria Press, 2009), 431-34.

38 Andrew Apostoloi, Fatima for Today: The Urgent Marian Message of Hope (San Francisco: Ignatius Press, 2012), Kindle, loc. 704 of 4024.

dren that they were "going to have much to suffer, but the grace of God will be your comfort." She asked that they not be afraid and that they "Recite the rosary every day in order to obtain peace for the world and the end of the war."[39]

Every 13th of the month until October 13th, Mary appeared to the children who were accompanied by larger and larger crowds. At this last apparition, there is evidence that a crowd of roughly 70,000 gathered. On that day, Mary said, "I want to tell you that a chapel is to be built here in my honor. I am the Lady of the Rosary. Continue always to pray the Rosary every day. The war is going to end, and the soldiers will soon return to their homes."[40] After these words, several thousands believed they witnessed the sight of the sun seeming to dance in the sky.

Now, at the beginning of the twenty-first century, Fátima continues to be a place of pilgrimage for Christians to connect with God's plan of salvation. If we believe that these events were authentic, I want us to think about: Why at this time? The world had been through the horrors of the Great War and many were saying, "Never again." It seems that that Lord knew something even worse was about to happen, not only with the Second World War, but also the Cold War. The twentieth century was an era most in need of reconciliation to the Lord.

In 2010, on May 13th, Pope Benedict XVI, like his predecessor, John Paul II, called attention to Fátima and its message. He said there,

> At this time when the human family was ready to sacrifice all that was most sacred on the altar of the petty and the selfish interests of nations, races, ideologies, groups, and individuals, our Blessed Mother came from heaven, offering to implant in the hearts of all those who trust in her the love of God burning in her own heart.[41]

At Fátima we see how God used Mary as a compassionate presence for a world at war.

Moving from western Europe, we now consider the Vatican-approved Marian apparition in central Africa that occurred before

---

39 Ibid., loc. 754 of 4024.   40 Ibid.
41 Pope Benedict XVI, "Homily at Esplanade of the Shrine of Our Lady of Fátima," May 13, 2010: https://w2.vatican.va/content/benedict-xvi/en/homilies/2010/documents/hf_ben-xvi_hom_20100513_fatima.html.

the Rwandan conflict in 1994 in which genocide took the lives of at least 800,000 people. The Hutu-led government, alarmed by an inflow of armed Tutsi refugees, unleashed mass killings of the Tutsi minority. In 1995 the Tutsi Rwandan Patriotic Army, in reprisal, closed in on Kibeho, the site of a refugee camp for displaced Hutus. They opened fire killing at least 4,000 people. The massacre in Kibeho was one of the worst during a conflict which saw many indiscriminate mass killings.

It is believed that in 1981, fourteen years before that massacre in Kibeho, Mary appeared on the outskirts of the town to three school children, Alphonsine, Anathalie, and Marie-Claire.[42] Later a few more would see her. Mary told them that they needed to pray to prevent a terrible war, to prevent the river of blood that was shown to one of the visionaries. Some of these visionaries died in the genocide and their blood joined that prophesied river.

Mary asked the children to pray with her as the Lady of Sorrows, as the lady who suffers with her people.[43] One of the visionaries said of the message of Kibeho,

> Our Lady says that she will console you; she hears the prayers of all who call on her, and she watches over you. . . . She says "Love my son, love each other, and care for the poor and the sick. Do not let jealousy and anger into your hearts; fill them with kindness and be willing to forgive. If you are weak in spirit or lacking in faith, pray to me, and I will bring you comfort and strength."[44]

She was described by one of the visionaries:

> the most lovely woman she had ever beheld emerged from a cloud, floating between the floor and the ceiling in a pool of shimmering light. She wore a flowing, seamless white dress with a white veil that covered her hair. Her hands were clasped in front of her in a gesture of prayer, her slender fingers pointing toward heaven. . . . Waves of love emanated from the majestic lady.[45]

---

42 Immaculee Ilibagiza, *Our Lady of Kibeho: Mary Speaks to the World from the Heart of Africa* (Carlsbad, CA: Hay House, 2008).

43 The devotion to Our Lady of Sorrows is an ancient and traditional title practiced in Eastern and Western Christianity. For more, see Graef and Thompson, *Mary*.

44 Ilibagiza, *Our Lady of Kibeho*, 113–14.   45 Ibid., 35.

One of the visionaries, Anathalie, said that Mary's message was clear, "If you will work with me, I shall give you a mission to lead those lost souls back from the darkness." Mary tells Anathalie: "Because the world is bad, my child, you will suffer—so if you accept this mission, you must also accept all the sufferings I send you with love, joy, and patience."[46] Mary was inviting Anathalie to suffer with her, having compassion, so that they can both participate in leading the people from darkness into light. Today, Kibeho is a major site of pilgrimage and center for continued reconciliation in Rwanda and throughout central Africa.

Mary's mission in the twentieth century and into the twenty-first is a continuation of her mission with her Son at the foot of the Cross. She suffers with her son and with us. Simeon prophesied "a sword will pierce through your own soul also, that thoughts out of many hearts may be revealed" (Lk 2:35). At the Crucifixion of her Son, "standing by the cross of Jesus [was] his mother" (Jn 19:25). She is not powerless but faith-filled, not inanimate but active, not passive but compassionate. Her presence at the Cross of her Son brings to fruition a motherhood to others: "Behold, your mother" (Jn 19:27).

In the first century, she stands by her Son, suffering with him. In the twentieth-century world of wars, massacres, and genocides, she stands by her sons and daughters as she holds humanity close to her heart, without judgment, but only forgiveness, without aggression but only compassion. She offers compassion and she wishes for that compassion to be shared. As our world slips deeper into passions of destruction, her compassion at the Passion of Jesus Christ reveals our heart's true need—to receive a love as unconditional and intense as only a mother's love can be.

Mary as Free to Love

A friend of mine was featured in a *New York Times* article about a group called Con-solatio, a community of religious and volunteers who meet with the poorest of the poor in more than twenty countries.[47] They have a presence in the government housing

---

46 Ibid., 49.
47 See Corey Kilgannon, "Nestled in the Projects and Nourishing Souls," *New York Times*, https://lens.blogs.nytimes.com/2012/09/28/nestled-in-the-projects-nourishing-souls/?_r=0, accessed 09/28/2012.

projects near downtown Brooklyn. A volunteer and friend, Marian West, said in this article that she moved to Manhattan when she was in her mid-twenties as a massage therapist and dancer with a dream to be a performer in the capital of the artistic world. For her, the mission quickly became "all about making the money to pay the rent and stress, stress, stress." She said, "One day I met a woman in the subway feeding the poor and she told me, 'I sold everything I had and now I'm free to love.'" I would like to examine this freedom to love as it pertains to Mary.

In this postmodern culture, "freedom" means different things to different people. For instance, because of the origin of the United States, freedom in American culture can mean personal autonomy. We could spend time tracing the origin of freedom as autonomy from its philosophical development in continental Europe from the Enlightnment to the French Revolution.

Throughout the history of the West, freedom has usually been understood as a gift from God or the gods. In Western cultures, for example, the origin of the concept of freedom as a positive condition began with early Judaism. Let us look at the Book of Exodus. This book is about the escape (exodus) of the Israelites not into autonomy, but freedom in the God of Abraham, Isaac, and Jacob. It is an exit to a commitment. The book is really a book about godly freedom. It begins with Israel enslaved in Egypt and ends with Israel freed to worship their God at Mount Sinai.

Israel was saved from slavery to receive the law, to receive the Torah. They are free now to respond to the Lord in faithfulness. Their life is now a freely given response. They are free to commit to a new kingdom, not the kingdom of the pharaoh but the kingdom of God. That kingdom's law is a way of life in relationship to the Lord. The Torah is way of life and not just a matter of legalistic duty fulfillment. It's a regulating of the whole of one's life: one's personal life, one's spiritual life, one's moral life, one's community life. The whole of the Torah is the whole of life and the whole of life is the Torah.

In the Old Testament, freedom is understood not as individuated autonomy; it is understood as being free within the right law, being alive within the right way of living. This relationship between freedom and the law differs markedly from the way contemporary Western culture understands freedom.

The perfect interpretation of the meaning of freedom is Jesus Christ, who is our definitive interpreter of Scripture, and also the fulfillment of freedom and freedom's relationship to the law. He was clear that his mission was fulfilling the law: "Do not think that I have come to abolish the law and the prophets; I have come not to abolish them but to fulfill them. For truly, I say to you, till heaven and earth pass away, not an iota, not a dot, will pass from the law until all is accomplished" (Mt 5:17–18).[48] And then we must join Jesus's teaching to his relationship with the Holy Spirit because, "Where the Spirit of the Lord is, there is freedom" (2 Cor 3:17). The Holy Spirit brings freedom and with this freedom we have not been given "a spirit of timidity but a spirit of power and love and self-control" (2 Tim 1:7). The Spirit empowers and fear disappears. The perfect love of being in the Holy Spirit brings power, love, freedom, and "casts out fear" (1 Jn 4:18).

Jesus Christ explains to us that the law is about freedom, freedom in the Holy Spirit. Because freedom and law are united in the person of Jesus Christ, he promises, as it were, that "if you follow me you'll be free. I will set you free. I am the way, the truth, and the life. I am freedom." In Christ, the law is not a matter of merely following precepts but of following a person, *the* person. Here we arrive at a proper understanding of Christian freedom. The Christian can say, God has given me the freedom to have a beautiful intellect and a beautiful free will, and all that free will and intellect can be used in the service of Jesus Christ. Freedom is a complete following of Jesus Christ. This yoke of Christ is an easy yoke for me because my identity is no longer tied to my performance—which was always marred by sin—but rather to Christ's offer of freedom and redemption. He calls you sinner no more. He calls you his.

The woman caught in adultery, whom the Pharisees want to stone to death (Jn 8:1–11), is brought before Jesus for judgment. The letter of the law calls for her to be stoned to death; the law interpreted through Jesus Christ brings her freedom. Jesus speaks to her, "Neither do I condemn you; go, and do not sin

---

48 See "Jesus and the Torah" in Gerhard Lohfink, *Jesus of Nazareth: What He Wanted, Who He Was*, trans. Linda M. Maloney (Collegeville, MN: Liturgical Press, 2012), 190–215.

again" (Jn 8:11). By God's redeeming grace, she has been brought to him who can truly make her free. She feared the worst, but the compassionate presence of Jesus restored her freedom. She is free to go, no longer burdened by her past sin but redefined by encountering his freedom. This is not absolute autonomy. No, it is a life that was condemned to death and is restored to life because of a new encounter, an encounter with Jesus Christ.

The Christian understanding of freedom is the freedom to commit to Jesus Christ. Of course there are rules for this new life, a rule for the moral life, a rule for the societal life, and a rule for the spiritual life, but all of that comes from the first encounter with the freedom found in the Lord Jesus Christ.

An example we discussed in the previous chapter was Augustine. His early life begins with a false understanding of freedom. He is very intelligent but is consumed with the desire to express his sexuality and intelligence.[49] While at school, he expresses this sexual licentiousness, enjoying the experience of being free from his parents and no longer conforming to the Christianity of his mother. He expresses his new autonomy through bodily pleasure and pride in his reputation. His intelligence leads him to maximize these pleasures of mind and flesh. He focuses his energies on his career as a rhetorician and he achieves some of the highest honors for rhetoricians at this time. The emperor rewards him with an invitation to speak in front of his royal presence, one of the greatest honors for a professional rhetorician at that time.

His desire to perfect his craft leads him to the Christian orator and bishop, Ambrose of Milan. Ambrose's superior preaching impresses Augustine while also persuading him to read the Bible and reconsider the faith of Christianity. One of the new concepts he learns is that Christianity does not enslave. It sets free. Before baptism the intellect is captive to ignorance and the will is imprisoned by weakness. In baptism, one is clothed in a newness of life.[50] Baptism clothes the soul with freedom in Jesus Christ. All of Augustine's experiments with different philosophical

---

49 See Augustine, *Confessions*, trans. Henry Chadwick (New York: Oxford University Press, 1991), Book I.
50 This is his interpretation of the *tolle lege* moment of his conversion at the end of Book VIII.

schools—the Manichees, the Neoplatonists, and the academic skeptics—do not satisfy because theirs is but another system of man-made rules that bring death. For Augustine, Christianity is finally satisfying because here he sees that he could be brought up into the full glory of God's infinite being.[51]

Late, Augustine makes the discovery that our ultimate origin is in beauty and goodness, but because of the fall, human beings are now born wounded.[52] That natural freedom that Adam and Eve were given was corrupted, wounded, and needs healing. Augustine realizes that the only way out is by being healed by the only person not wounded by sin. Only the free one can save the enslaved one. Augustine realizes that he is free only in Jesus Christ. That knowledge changes everything for Augustine and the Christian tradition.[53]

In the West, this tradition of understanding freedom as being in relationship with Jesus Christ began to crumble during the Enlightenment. Modern thinking is rooted in the choice to determine through reason alone what is true, good, and beautiful. Reason is freedom. The upheavals of the Enlightenment and the French Revolution roiled Europe into a revolutionary state, which was often anti-clerical and even more so anti-ecclesial. The night before the storming of the Bastille, revolutionaries stormed the Vincentian Monastery, San Lazar. The revolutionaries wanted to secure San Lazar's grains and lands, but also to damage its prestige in the city. San Lazar was savior of Paris in many ways, especially spiritually because of the ministry of Vincent de Paul and the Lazarites (Vincentians). The mob destroyed the monastery, and killed the priests and the sisters. The first act of the French Revolution was not against the king, but against the Church. Before they tore down the Bastille, they torn down the steeple.

Freedom means commitment, commitment to hold on to someone. Love means suffering to protect this commitment. Love means falling in love with Jesus Christ and letting him take you wherever he wants you to go (Jn 21:18). God does not look at us from afar.

---

51 This is the best interpretation of his mystical experience with his mother Monica in Book IX.

52 Augustine, *On the Free Choice of the Will*, trans. Thomas White (Indianapolis, IN: Hackett Publishing Company, 1993), Bk. 3, sec. 19, pp. 107–8.

53 We could see some similarities in Thomas Aquinas's vision of freedom.

He enters into the midst of our relationships and forgives us there. He goes to the adulterous woman who meets him on her way to being stoned to death (Jn 8). Jesus Christ stands in the very real place of commitment to us. God is present to and within suffering to heal, transform, and redeem. He enters into suffering to its most extreme. His presence, his compassion reaches to the depths of hell. In the midst of the darkest of nights, he shines his brightest light.

Christianity's core perspective is that God is existentially and essentially above everything, but he chooses out of his love to enter deeply into everything that is human. He enters into humanity's rebellion and the consequences of that rebellion, even unto death, death on a cross—"For the wages of sin is death" (Rom 6:23). God so loves us that he undertakes this life-crushing debt. In Jesus Christ, the Son becomes disfigured beyond recognition (Is 52:14). His human soul is ripped from his human body. He enters into a real human death, a real separation of soul and body—a body in the grave, a soul in the underworld of hell.

Think about that. Jesus Christ experienced true human death, true separation of his human self. We need to meditate upon this mystery of Holy Saturday to know fully God's compassion for our suffering. We have that separation of body and soul in our suffering and death. And God takes that within himself.

As Christians, we must understand our God as the Trinity. God is Father, Son, and Holy Spirit. He is one God always and forever. He is Three Divine Persons always and forever. Jesus Christ has revealed this about his divine nature: he is Son and one with the Father and Holy Spirit. He is one with the Father in a complete union of nature in complete mutual love of the Holy Spirit. The Father loves the Son. The Son loves the Father. And the Holy Spirit is their mutual love. Because God is love, this love is a union of complete communion. On the Cross, we see revealed a new-to-us aspect of this triune love. Jesus Christ, the Son of God, on the Cross speaks the first verse of Psalm 22, "My God, my God, why have you forsaken me?" (Mk 15:34). He does not say, "My father, my father, why have you forsaken me?" but those distancing words, my God, my God. He is somehow unable to call God his Father as he experiences this real abandonment. In his preaching, Jesus had been calling God his Father and now on the Cross, it is as if he is lost: "God? Why have you forsaken me? Why have you abandoned me? Why are you letting me suffer this treachery? Why are you letting me be so horribly forsaken?"[54]

The depth of these words on the Cross—how can we capture their meaning? It is as if he is praying the *De Profundis*—"Out of the depths I cry to you, O Lord!" (Ps 130:1). Yes, Christians believe the Son, Father, and Holy Spirit are infinitely in union, but here we see, as it were, a kind of subjective perspective of the Son. He is feeling abandoned. "Why have you forsaken me?" The Son is existentially, not essentially, feeling forsaken by the Father. It's that moment in our prayer of suffering, "Where is God? How can there be a God here?"

Jesus on the Cross and in hell experiences the horror of separation from the Father. He is always in union with the Father but being separated to the utmost extent of that union hurts like an arm pulled to the point just before the shoulder dislocates.

We understand that this God is one, but now, because God has been stretched to the utmost extent—the Father, and the Son, with the Holy Spirit as their mutual love holding them together—we see all of them more distinctly. Holy Saturday, the day of remembering Jesus's descent, is the day of clearest revelation of the Trinitarian God. The fullest revelation of the Trinity happens in the death of the Son. We believe that because of this Trinitarian revelation we now can be inserted within these relations of the Father, Son, and Holy Spirit.

Wounds in our personal lives open up space for others. They make us need someone. They make room for others. When we see suffering in others, we can enter into those wounds to offer our healing presence.

By imitating Jesus Christ, by imitating his consoling presence to the deep wounds of others, we show we know him who is love (1 Jn 4:7-21).

You and I have been born into separation from God, but as we mature and accept God's offer of compassionate presence our separation is healed and a new life begins in the Father's unconditional love. We are also incorporated into his new people, the Church, who know and grow in this new freedom of love.

---

54 For a full treatment of this concept, especially as it can be found in Hans Urs von Balthasar and Adrienne von Speyr, see my book *Heaven Opens*, 147-88.

We are freed in the Sacrament of Baptism and participate in that continued sanctifying mercy in the Sacrament of Reconciliation. This sacrament makes us free again and again in the Lord's compassionate mercy. The rebirth to freedom in the Lord happens definitively in baptism and continues to be lived in through the Sacrament of Confession. Your sin is being cleansed, the chains of slavery are cut, the prison door is opened. After forgiveness, you are no longer autonomous. Autonomy is what got you into trouble in the first place. Now you're free to love in relationship with others and ultimately with God.

In Adrienne von Speyr's *Handmaid of the Lord*, we read a beautiful meditation on the assent of Mary.[55] The name of this first chapter is "The Light of Assent." For Speyr, the key to understanding Mary is not "ascent" but "assent." There is a strong stream in the history of Christian Spirituality celebrating, recommending, and developing ascent mysticism. The spirituality of John Climacus in his work *The Ladder of Divine Ascent* is an excellent example, and so is the work of Saint Teresa of Avila in *The Interior Castle*. For Speyr, Mary provides us with the best example of assent mysticism. All I need to do is say Yes definitively. All I need to do is say, "Thy will be done" in a complete and total way. God takes care of the rest.[56]

Speyr begins her important book on Mary by invoking the image of a sheaf of grain: "As a sheaf of grain is tied together in the middle and spreads out at either end, so Mary's life is bound together by her assent."[57] This is a beautiful first image of Mary as the one free to love. Mary's life is bound together, but by what? What is the cord tying the sheaf of her life together? Her assent. Her Yes. Where does Mary say Yes in the Gospels? In Chapter One of the Gospel of Luke, she speaks, "Behold, I am the handmaid of the Lord; let it be to me according to your word" (Lk 1:38). She does not just say, Yes. Her assent is of a different

55 Speyr, *Handmaid*, 7–17.
56 The little way of Saint Thérèse of Lisieux is a wonderful example of this assent mysticism. See Thérèse of Lisieux, *Story of a Soul: The Autobiography of St. Thérèse of Lisieux*, trans. John Clarke (Washington, DC: ICS Publications, 1996). See also Hans Urs von Balthasar, *Two Sisters in the Spirit: Thérèse of Lisieux and Elizabeth of the Trinity*, trans. Donald Nichols, Anne Englund Nash, and Dennis Martin (San Francisco: Ignatius Press, 1992).
57 Speyr, *Handmaid*, 7.

quality. When somebody asks you to do the dishes, you might say, "Yes." If you answer this request with the words, "Let it be done" there is something of a passivity to it. I cannot accomplish what you ask, but your power can accomplish what you say in me. That is her assent. Mary could say no. But she accepts with her assent, "Let it be done because I am a handmaid of the Lord." In a rich household, the handmaid was the lowest of the servants. Everything asked of a handmaid cannot be refused because of her position. Mary is not forced. She assents to seeing herself as the lowest servant in the Lord's kingdom. Mary could say, "No." Mary could say "Let me think about it." Or even, "Let me pray about it." She has been given this freedom, but she chooses immediate assent. Presented with the Father's will, she says "Let it be done." Here freedom chooses obedience.

Her surrender is a letting-happen what is in the heart of the Lord. When you encounter another, you are invited to give that person a "yes," a "let this relationship happen." And then you also become open to their suffering, their need. When you become aware of their suffering, you are invited to say "yes" again to this relationship. You are offering your loving presence in a new way when you become aware of their need for presence. As the relationship grows, there is a kind of letting-happen toward the other person.

In the annunciation, Mary is opening herself in freedom toward the angel. It's a freedom expressed toward the will of God who provided the encounter and also the meaning of the encounter, both leading up to the encounter as well as the future after the encounter.

The first sentence of Speyr's meditation states that Mary's whole life "is bound together by her assent."[58] Her assent binds all of her life together before the annunciation and after the annunciation so that her Yes gives meaning to her life beforehand as well as to her life afterward. Some assents are so fundamental that they become a defining moment for the whole of one's life. Now we come to Speyr's second sentence, "From this assent her life receives its meaning and form and unfolds toward past and future."[59] Mary's assent, is capturing what came before the annunciation and becomes definitively determinative of the rest of her

58 Ibid.   59 Ibid.

life. But, we must remember, she is saying yes to a life that is not known to her. No one else has been a mother in this way. She is going to be questioned by everyone, even her betrothed. At first, Joseph tries to find a way forward for Mary that is merciful, but ultimately this will be his life-defining moment of assent.

In the next moment of Speyr's reflection, she says, "This single, all-encompassing act accompanies her at every moment of her existence, illuminates every turning point of her life, bestows upon every situation its own particular meaning and in all situations gives Mary herself the grace of renewed understanding."[60] Her assent will sustain her in the most difficult seasons of her life. When she is at the foot of the Cross, she will need to come back to her assent. It will give her light on this darkest Friday and help her to call it good. She can lean on the fact that her assent was given according to the Lord's word. In all of the hidden moments that come with being a mother (Lk 2:51-52), she can come back to her assent. In all of the public moments like the pentecostal awakening of the Church (Acts 1:14, 2:1-4), she can come back to her assent.

Continuing further, Speyr writes: "Her assent gives full meaning to every breath, every movement, every prayer of the Mother of God."[61] Mary gives her assent to Jesus within her as her every prayer. In imitation, we need to learn from Mary to say Yes to Jesus Christ within us. The life of service according to the Marian way is letting the ways of God work within and through us. For Speyr, "This is the nature of an assent: it binds the one who gives it, yet it allows him complete freedom in shaping its expression."[62] Assent is a commitment to a vision that comes from the Lord, and this commitment depends on your freedom to express it in different ways. A love that is freely given is not a love loosely dispersed, but rather a love chosen, and intensely focused. Sure, we could say Solomon loved his seven hundred wives and three hundred concubines, but we would not compare that to a freely focused, sustaining, life-giving, concrete, and intense love for one spouse. Love dispersed becomes shallow if not meaningless. Love focused, and sustained with time and attention, becomes life-giving and meaningful.

In Speyr's opinion, the one who gives assent "fills his assent with his personality, giving it its weight and unique coloring."[63]

---

60 Ibid.   61 Ibid.   62 Ibid.   63 Ibid.

The Lord uses each person's gifts as he desires, but the person giving the assent fills this obedience with his own personality that is unique, freely given, and even surprising. One's different and surprising subjectivity is also offered to the Lord. Many are called to live a life of holiness in family life, but think of all the beautiful and varied ways in which that life of holiness is offered up to the Lord. Obedience to God is not outward, exterior conformity, but a deeply personal, unique expression of the self. Each person's assent to his mission has a unique color and it makes the Father delight in the various and colorful offerings of his children. Each star sparkles its own light that comes from the "Father of lights" (Jas 1:17).

Speyr continues, "But he himself is also molded, liberated and fulfilled by his assent. All freedom develops through surrender and through renunciation of liberty."[64] We see that freedom as autonomy is not enough. Freedom must be expressed through choosing, surrendering to a course of action. Here then freedom becomes actual. So Speyr concludes brilliantly, "And from this freedom within commitment there arises every sort of fruitfulness."[65] Freedom expressed through an absolute, ultimate letting go, a renunciation even of liberty, produces a dramatic fruitfulness.

In Scripture, fullfilled freedom means surrender. It's an imitation of Jesus whose mission was "not to be served but to serve" (Mk 10:45). For Christianity, the surrender is always a surrender to the one who has surrendered everything. When this free surrender opens itself to the Lord, he can work in miraculous and miniscule ways. Each small, daily surrender grows a habit of trusting the Holy Spirit to lead one in freedom, which is so true of Mary. She says Yes to the Lord at the annunciation. But it is also a Yes to the Lord for the rest of her life. She lives in a reaffirming Yes to the Lord as the child Jesus grows within her becoming more and more present to her and to Joseph. She says her Yes to the Lord when she meets Joseph and tries to explain her pregnancy. She says her Yes to the Lord when she acknowledges that her cousin Elizabeth's pregnancy is also a movement of the Lord's providence. She also says Yes as a renunciation of what perhaps she had planned for her life. She lives this saying of Jesus: "He who loses his life for my sake will find it" (Mt 10:39). She loses

---

64 Ibid.   65 Ibid.

her self and her plans, and say Yes in surrender to the Lord's plans for her. Mary's assent becomes more and more public, and therefore more and more difficult. And yet, she continues her surrendering Yes.

We must remember that Mary's Yes has those two parts. There is her surrendering of her will—"Let it be"—and then there is also as surrender of its meaning—"according to your word." God is going to accept her assent, but also guide her in the interpretation. Her understanding of her assent is not her word, but the power of God's word in her. We must learn to say Yes to requests from the Lord, but also to say Yes to the meaning of these requests. When one's freedom is given over to the Lord, there is also the giving over to the Lord of the meaning of it. Mary accepts her mission in the fullness of her freedom, giving complete, unreserved assent to the Lord. She has given over her freedom and is in an even more profound way, free to love.

8

Beauty

HANS URS VON BALTHASAR PROPOSED A THE-
ology of Holy Saturday—the day between Good Friday and Easter
on which the descent of Jesus to the dead is commemorated—
as essential to understanding the Christian view of God as the
God who suffered the worst of hell for and with us and thereby
redeemed human suffering. Within this theology of Holy Saturday, he has also constructed a radical theological aesthetics that
counterposes suffering as integral to understanding beauty. This
stands in contrast to traditional notions that posit beauty as an
abstraction characterized by qualities of timelessness and the
inability to change or suffer.

In this chapter, I will argue that Balthasar's theology of Holy Saturday is a credible account of the Christian view of beauty and that
it has decisive importance and relevance to the postmodern context.

What is Beauty?

I have become convinced that beauty is the glory of God manifesting itself through creation. God as Beauty itself converts us to
his truth and goodness through beauty. I have come to understand
what the twentieth-century Catholic theologian, Hans Urs von
Balthasar, wrote about beauty in his work *Love Alone is Credible*
when he said: "In the experiences of extraordinary beauty—whether
in nature or in art—we are able to grasp a phenomenon in its
distinctiveness that otherwise remains veiled. What we encounter
in such an experience is as overwhelming as a miracle, something
we will never get over."[1] In this passage, Balthasar suggests that
extraordinary beauty can overwhelm by its own power of being
beautiful. The miracle of beauty can leave a person permanently
awed by what he has just seen.

Hans Urs von Balthasar was called by Pope John Paul II "an
outstanding man of theology and of the arts, who deserves a

---

1 Hans Urs von Balthasar, *Love Alone is Credible*, trans. D. C. Schindler (San
Francisco: Ignatius Press, 2004), 52–53.

special place of honor in contemporary ecclesiastical and cultural life."[2] And Pope Benedict XVI, who worked with Balthasar on several projects including the journal *Communio*, said: "I consider that his theological reflection keeps its deep actuality intact to this day and still stirs many to penetrate ever further into the depths of the mystery of faith, holding the hand of this most authoritative guide."[3]

While it is impossible to summarize Balthasar's significance for twentieth-century theology (Catholic and Protestant), philosophy, literature (German and French), and drama, I would like to focus on his trilogy masterwork in fifteen volumes written from 1961 to 1987. The three transcendentals, Beauty, Goodness, and Truth, serve as the framework parts of his trilogy. With this masterwork, he wants to recover the relationship between the transcendentals and the analogy of being. Balthasar's interpretation of the analogy of being, which he received from the Jesuit philosopher Erich Przywara, is that God as Being itself is related to all created being not only because he created it but because he also destined created being to have its definitive end (telos) in Being itself. For Balthasar the analogy of being is connected to the Christian doctrine of participation. Created being is not just a static analogy of Being itself, but it is also interiorly directed toward an intimate sharing in divine life (see 2 Pet 1:4).

With his interpretation of the analogy of being, Balthasar now joins with it the Christian theological idea of the transcendentals. Since God is Being itself, he is also Beauty itself, Truth itself, and Goodness itself. Since God is the source of all Being, Beauty, Truth, and Goodness, anything that has created being, beauty, truth, or goodness necessarily participates in the intimate divine life of the Father, Son, and Holy Spirit. Within all created beauty, truth, and goodness, there is an interior missionary character directed toward its definitive end in God as Beauty itself, Truth itself, and Goodness itself.

---

2 John Paul II in a telegram at the death of Balthasar on June 30, 1988 in *Hans Urs von Balthasar: His Life and Work* (San Francisco: Ignatius Press, 1991), 289.
3 Benedict XVI, "Message," October 6, 2005; https://w2.vatican.va/content/benedict-xvi/en/messages/pont-messages/2005/documents/hf_ben-xvi_mes_20051006_von-balthasar.html.

With their definitive end in God, all the transcendentals are necessarily related to each other. Any time there is beauty, there is also goodness and truth. Any time there is goodness, there is also truth and beauty. Any time there is truth, there is also goodness and beauty. The three transcendentals are intimately connected because they have their origin and goal in God who is the source and telos of all created beauty, truth, and goodness.

The first part of the trilogy, called *The Glory of the Lord*, presents Balthasar's theological aesthetics, that is, his relating the transcendental of beauty to the analogy of being. It is an argument for recovering beauty as an entryway to man's encounter with God. When he looks for the first word for his fifteen-volume masterwork, he chooses the word beauty: "Beauty is the word that shall be our first."[4] In a retrospective statement on the first part of his trilogy on beauty, Balthasar said that he called it *The Glory of the Lord*

> because it is concerned, first, with learning to see God's revelation and because God can be known only in his Lordliness and sublimity (*Herr-heit* and *Hehr-heit*), in what Israel called *Kabod* and the New Testament *gloria*, something that can be recognized under all the incognitos of human nature and the Cross. This means that God does not come primarily as a teacher for us ("true"), as a useful "redeemer" for us ("good"), but to display and to radiate himself, the splendor of his eternal triune love in that "disinterestedness" that true love has in common with true beauty.[5]

Man's encounter with the revelation of God is known through God's radiating beauty, or what the biblical witness called glory. For example, it is the glory of the Lord manifested in the pillar of cloud by day and the pillar of fire by night that persuades Israel to persevere toward the promised land (Ex 13:17-22). It is the glory of the Lord that settles on Mount Sinai, manifesting the potent, fiery presence of the Lord who gives the Law to Israel through Moses (Ex 19:16-20). It is the glory of the Lord that comes upon the first temple built by Solomon revealing God's kingly dwelling in the Holy of Holies in Jerusalem (1 Kings 8:1-11). It is the

---

4 Balthasar, *The Glory of the Lord*, vol. 1, 18.   5 Balthasar, *My Work*, 80.

glory of the Lord that rushes upon Mary who conceives in her womb, by the power of the Holy Spirit, the Son of God incarnate (Lk 1:26–38). It is the glory of the Lord, represented by tongues of fire, that comes upon the apostles on the feast of Pentecost manifesting God's dwelling presence with his Church (Acts 2:1–13). For Balthasar, in the Old and New Testaments, it is the glory (beauty) of the Lord that manifests the Father's potent presence in the world through the Son and Holy Spirit, and reveals the goodness and truth about his love for the world. The Son of God did not come just to teach or to be useful; he came to reveal God's love.

According to Balthasar, any engagement with beauty necessitates a theory of vision, that is, a theory about the perception of beauty.[6] Beauty results from the intersection of *species* and *lumen* (form and splendor). At this intersection, beauty, so to speak, happens and there is a moment in the viewer of beholding and being enraptured.[7] It is truly an outpouring of the glory of the Lord through the Holy Spirit. To be enraptured by beauty, one must perceive the form. I say "perceive" in the sense of the German word *Wahr-nehmen*, "to take to be true"; not doing so is to pass over beauty or break it into tiny incomprehensible bits that make it devoid of truth and goodness and incapable of enrapturing the perceiver. When beauty is present, truth and goodness are equally present. Beauty is not a competitor to reason or the ethical, but the revelation of beauty is in harmonious relationship with the true and good because it is a revelation of God himself. When one sees truth or goodness, one sees beauty. At the intersection of form and splendor beauty, so to speak, happens and manifests truth and goodness.

Balthasar argues that the Christian can have a special kind of knowledge, a unique type of vision, one in which "the light of God which faith has sees the form as it is."[8] The spiritual eye can perceive the spiritual form and experience the awe of beholding beauty. This spiritual eye is that of both faith and knowledge. In

---

6 Balthasar, *Glory of the Lord* I, 125.

7 "The form as it appears to us is beautiful only because the delight that it arouses in us is founded upon the fact that in it, the truth and goodness of the depths of reality itself are manifested and bestowed, and this manifestation and bestowal reveal themselves to us as being something infinitely and inexhaustibly valuable and fascinating" (Balthasar, *Glory of the Lord* I, 118). 8 Ibid., 171–72.

the act of faith, knowledge does not disappear; rather it becomes truly possible and enlightened: "Faith is the foundation, *gnosis* [knowledge] is the edifice built upon it."[9] Instead of faith being criticized as myopic, faithfulness and knowledge of Jesus Christ gives the believer in Christ the ability to be more visually literate.

If a person wishes to see the whole of truth, goodness, and beauty, he must open himself to the revelation of the divinity of Christ. The first examination of beauty must begin with the Incarnation of the Son because it is, according to Balthasar, "the very apex and archetype of beauty in the world, whether men see it or not."[10] The hypostatic union of the personhood of the divine Son with the fullness of human nature is that of the greatest possible concreteness of an individual form and the greatest possible universality of the epiphany of Being itself. Jesus Christ is the most beautiful form and splendor because as God he is Beauty itself. The two polarities of form and splendor indissolubly intersect and give the definitive evidence that he is the most beautiful. By the act of faith given through grace, the Christian perceives the perfect beauty of the Incarnation and it will enrapture him. Faith-filled eyes, trained by viewing the perfect form, see that the beauty of life manifests the beautiful glory of God.

Through his theological aesthetics, Balthasar can conclude that when you behold beauty, you are actually beholding the glory of God and the glory is enrapturing you through its own evidential power of truth and goodness. The perfection of beauty and the full manifestation of the glory of the Lord is the revelation of Jesus Christ as the Son of God.

Balthasar will remind us that Jesus as the perfect form and splendor of beauty is also the one who experiences the sheer ugliness of death on the Cross. Perfect beauty has been made sin for us, that is, made ugly by us. In the death of Jesus Christ on the Cross, Beauty itself has been completely given away, nothing held back, all surrendered. Balthasar, influenced by the mystic Adrienne von Speyr, believes that since Jesus as the Son of God surrendered all, he revealed everything about himself and his Trinitarian relationship with the Father and the Holy Spirit, and that Christ's death on the Cross is the summit of revelation to us about who God is. The beautiful thing about the Cross is the

9 Ibid., 138.   10 Ibid., 69.

perfection of beauty and the glory of the Lord given away against the backdrop of the ugliness of death. Indeed, on many crucifixes in Eastern Orthodox churches, you will see the inscription "The Glory of the Lord." The fullness of beauty and glory of the Lord is manifested by the Son's truly perfect surrender of self on the Cross on Good Friday, followed by the unfathomable surrender to seeming abandoment in the underworld on Holy Saturday.

Holy Saturday and Beauty

Most of the debate about Holy Saturday revolves around "where was the soul of Christ on that day"? But actually there is a second side to the mystery: the body of Christ, lying in the tomb. If we are not docetists, then we have to ask this question about the location of the human soul of Jesus after his death on the Cross.

That body and soul are separated is a mystery that belong to the Passion more than it belongs to the Resurrection. Aristotle described the divorce between the soul-form and our body-matter caused by death as a "state of violence." So we could say that wherever the soul of Jesus is on that day, one thing we know for sure is that the person of Christ is in a state of violence. If we consider the body of Christ lying in the tomb, then we are invited to mourning, not to rejoicing. It does not seem that theology has been very concerned about this, but certainly iconographers and artist have been.

Russian iconography shows Jesus (with his body) raising up Adam and Eve and breaking open the gates of hell. Western iconography, on the other hand, puts the emphasis on the other side of the mystery; the *pietà* is our "Holy Saturday" icon. It focuses the mystery on the lifeless flesh of the incarnated Word.

Is there something of the Theology of Holy Saturday that can give Christian thinkers an entrée to postmodern art? And is there a way that this theology can make Christianity relevant to postmodern thought? The postmodern experience of the absence of God necessitates the Holy Saturday mystery. If there is any holy day that captures the postmodern moment and God's reply, it must be the mystery of Holy Saturday.

Sometimes Christian commentary on culture dismisses postmodern art. This cultural critique is based upon a valuation of art depending on how prominently the themes of redemption or judgment are present. True, postmodern artists often do not treat these themes, but the critique of these forms of art by Christians can be reductionistic and often fails to see the human experiences validly expressed in postmodern art.

In postmodernism, the concept of liminality is central. Liminality deals with those transitional moments in life which entirely remake the individual. Perseverance of personality, genetic material, and other factors keep you connected to your past identity, but an experience, a transition, a trauma, or a philosophical insight propel you through to a different (not necessarily better—that would be modernism) identity. The Holy Saturday Passion of Jesus Christ is an extreme liminality. In Trinitarian metaphysics, we must always say with faith that Jesus will always be the enfleshed Son of God. And yet, the passage through the underworld of the dead brings him to a new identity grasped by his human consciousness of the subjective abandonment by the Father as he experiences the Godforsakenness of hell.

Liminality is fundamental to drama. The actor on the stage has a liminality experience. He is becoming something more than he already was. This is achieved by mission. Mission in relation to the other actors changes the identities dramatically, to bring all into union with him completely.

The artist knows inspiration and trusts himself to it. We could use the word *mission*. It is the being-sent to which the artist has surrendered himself. This mission has a genealogy which others can also join. In my observations, the mature artist has a sense of collegiality with the generations of artists that preceeded him. Perhaps this is the Holy Spirit at work.

The artist Jesus has surrendered himself to being-sent and in the Holy Spirit, he accomplishes this. The compelling power of God is all.

The artist has surrendered to an inspiration that must be realized. This self-surrender entails certain strictures. There is for the artist a freedom within the strictures to invent something new. The actor does not concoct the play from nothing. Rather he accepts the script, the director, and even the audience. Within these strictures, he expresses his freedom to create.

As we think about the theology of Holy Saturday, we must remember that in the Christian view, God did not make death.

This is clear from the Book of Genesis and the Book of Wisdom. In the Book of Genesis, Adam and Eve somehow have an infinite existence in God, but only after the fall does death become a part of the human narrative. They are to live only for a time, "till you return to the ground, for out of it you were taken; you are dust, and to dust you shall return" (Gen 3:19). The Book of Wisdom is clear: "God did not make death, and he does not delight in the death of the living" (Wis 1:13). God has created us for life, "he created all things that they might exist" because "the dominion of Hades is not on earth" (Wis 1:14).

Still, God lets Jairus's daughter suffer death a little. He permits the widow of Naim's son to experience death briefly. God let his own Son remain in the tomb for three days. He did not create death, but he lets his people die. He lets his only-begotten Son die. This too must be a part of our reflection about the nature of God and our relationship with him.

The Book of Wisdom continues, "When it is extinguished, the body will turn to ashes, and the spirit will dissolve like empty air. Our name will be forgotten in time" (Wis 2:3–4a). "Let us crown ourselves with rosebuds before they wither" (Wis 2:8).

In the book *How Music Works*, David Byrne analyzes the history of music along the lines of venue theory.[11] He argues that the creation of music is the prerogative of genius, which would mean that music cannot be taught. Instead, the culturally relevant venues guide the creation of music such that, depending on the venues available, the music changes to suit that venue. He examines the wide open spaces of Sub-Saharan Africa that seem to call for deep explosively resonant drums, the long cavernous Gothic cathedrals that inspire simple polyphonies of Gregorian chant and organ, and the exquisitely intimate chateaus of the Renaissance that call for chamber music. Orchestra halls call for complex symphonies, and parades for marching bands. Making beautiful music is a constant, but the venue in which it manifests itself can change the expression of the beauty of music. It is as if there are ever new aspects of beautiful music that are uncovered as man invents new spaces in which to live and move.

What then is the venue of man at this stage of postmodern thought such that God can reveal his beauty and glory? We are

---

11 David Byrne, *How Music Works* (San Francisco: McSweeney's, 2012).

falling into the hell of our own making. He then reveals his glory in midst of death and absence and thus reveals his life and presence. The venue of man is centrifugal loneliness (a dispersing outward to go downward), the glory of God is centripetal presence (a gathering inward to go upward).

Beauty Saves

My friend Marian volunteered with the organization called Consolatio, a secular movement that serves the poorest of the poor in over twenty countries.[12] She was volunteering at the house in Brooklyn where they serve the elderly in a nursing home. While she was walking through the institutional halls, she heard from one of the rooms, "Help me!" She entered the room and saw an elderly woman contorted into a semicircle, with her neck misaligned, limbs limp, and face angry. When she knew someone else was in the room, she yelled, "I hate this! This stupid life. What the hell is the point? Just end this. My life stinks. Look at me. What am I doing here?" Full of disgust, contempt, despondency, she yelled one last time, "Help!"

"May I help you?" Marian asked softly. The woman swore at her vehemently and then, opening her eyes, she looked into Marian's face and started to say in a markedly different tone, "Oh. I'm sorry. I'm sorry." She reached for Marian's hand and then Marian asked if she could sit beside her on her bed. She was allowed to sit down, but the woman quickly retreated back into her dark cave of self-loathing.

"What are you doing here?" she bitterly asked.

"I heard you calling for help so I came to see if I could help you."

"Are you here alone?" the woman asked.

"Yes," and with a small smile, "Well, I got Jesus with me."

The woman would have none of that. "Ahh, Jesus. I don't believe in that." She pushed Marian's hand away and resumed swearing and yelling.

Then once again she subsided and her voice changed: "I'm sorry." She then started to tell Marian about how her legs hurt so terribly from never moving. Marian started to rearrange the pillows of her bed to help her feel better. She asked if she could massage

---

12 Adapted with permission from Marian West, "You'll Never Walk Alone," https://web.archive.org/web/20190609085829/http://landofcompassion. com/2012/03/16/youll-never-walk-alone/.

her legs. Marian had been a massage therapist before she was a volunteer. "Oh, that feels good," the elderly woman responded.

Marian offered a little bit of food and water that was at the woman's bedside. They sat together. Marian saw a sliver of sun coming through the shaded window. "Would you like to see outside?" Marian asked. Marian opened the curtains to where both of them could see over the Brooklyn brownstone rooftops warmed by a late winter sunset.

"Isn't it beautiful?" Marian asked. The woman was beginning to be warmed too.

"What's your name?" Marian asked. "Ira," the woman responded without a smile.

"I'm Marian. I'm glad to meet you."

"Oh, stop with that nonsense," the woman snapped. Marian laughed a little here, and Ira couldn't help but smile a bit too. Marian saw an opening and started to ask about her life. Ira answered that she grew up in Brooklyn, had been a beautiful lady with a good figure, and tried to be a model, but went to Brooklyn College to study English literature instead.

"Do you have a favorite poem?" Marian asked.

"No," Ira insisted.

"How about Robert Frost's 'Stopping by Woods on a Snowy Evening'?"

"Don't know it," Ira snapped, but Marian recited it anyway. "That is lovely. A beautiful poem," Ira realized. "I do have a favorite song."

"What is it?" Marian asked.

"'Someone to Watch Over Me.' Ooooh. I love that song," Ira revealed. Marian started to sing the refrain.

Ira melted, "Yes, that's the one." Marian started to rub Ira's hand. Marian sang the verse, "I'm a little lamb who's lost in the wood . . ." but forgot the rest. Ira continued to speak the words, "I know I could, always be good, to one who'll watch over me. Although he may not be the man some girls think of as handsome, to my heart he carries the key. Won't you tell him please to put on some speed, follow my lead, oh, how I need someone to watch over me."

"It's a nice song," Ira insisted. "But the words. The words really make it meaningful."

They sang more songs together. "Somewhere Over the Rainbow." "If I Loved You." "You'll Never Walk Alone" from Rodgers and

Hammerstein's *Carousel.* "When you walk through a storm, hold your head up high, and don't be afraid of the dark." Ira started to speak the words, "At the end of the road is a golden sky and the sweet silver song of a lark. Walk on through the wind, walk on through the rain, though your dreams be tossed and blown. Walk on, walk on, with hope in your heart, and you'll never walk alone. You'll never walk alone." They began to cry with each other. Marian smiled and thanked Ira. Marian kissed her hand.

"I'll never wash it," Ira chuckled.

Ira took Marian's hand and kissed it. She closed her eyes and began to rest deeply in her pillows. She finally went to sleep with a serene face.

It was compassion, walking into the suffering of another, that carried this lost lamb from screaming "Help" and obscenities to singing "You'll Never Walk Alone." From screaming to singing— here is the beauty of compassion. Indeed, beauty saves.

9
Eternity

IS IT TRUE THAT TIME HEALS ALL WOUNDS?
This is a common proverb in English. The idea is also present
in other languages. Behind it is the notion that the passage of
time by itself heals. As Macbeth says, "Come what come may,
time and the hour runs through the roughest day."[1] The trau-
matic impact of suffering, just like the effect of a rock hitting
a pool of water, will be met with restorative equilibrium. Time
will heal and restore the disturbed psychic pool and bring it
back to placidity.

"Time heals all wounds" offers a meta-narrative about the meaning of suffering. Quite frankly, in my view, it is not true. Instead,
I will present a different meta-narrative about the meaning of
suffering as it relates to time and how eternity, as the fulfillment
(not the negation) of time, is the overcoming of suffering. In this
way, this chapter can be placed in the sub-discipline of Christian
theology called eschatology, the study of the end of time.

This chapter will focus on the mysticism and spiritual writings
of Adrienne von Speyr as a development in Christian thought on
the meaning of time, suffering, and eternity. Above all, my intent
is that we will see her understanding of eternity not as outside
of time, but as fulfilled time. Suffering experienced in time will
be seen not as caused or cured by time but as participating in
the sanctifying and fulfilling effects of the Resurrection of Jesus
Christ, the Alpha and Omega, the Lord of Time, and therefore
the Meaning of Time.

The main strands of Christian eschatology emerged from Second Temple Jewish Apocalyptic literature and found its normative
expression in the book of Revelation.[2] Certainly, we see in the
book of Revelation the view that the end of time will heal all

---

1 *Macbeth*, Act 1, Scene 3, line 145-49.
2 See the Book of Ezekiel and the second half of the Book of Daniel, but
also First and Second Enoch. For an overview on this fascinating collection
of literature, see John Collins, *The Apocalyptic Imagination: An Introduction to
Jewish Apocalyptic Literature* (Grand Rapids, MI: Eerdmans, 2010).

wounds.[3] The Lord of all time will transform the present suffering of persecuted Christians through an eventual resurrection that will cause them to join the eschatological, eternal event of the heavenly liturgy, praising and adoring the Lamb that was slain (Rev 5:11–14).

Important to Western Christianity, the early Church theologian, Augustine, in his *Confessions,* developed a theory of time in which he conceived of time as a distention in the soul, a kind of extended suffering within the mind. This definition has definitely influenced the Christian assessment of *time as suffering.*[4] Roland Teske, a prominent scholar of Augustine, writes that Augustine "insists that time is a creature of God and that before God created anything there was no time. Hence, there was no time when God made nothing."[5] Whereas the Manichee position seemed to subject God to time, Augustine subjected time to God.[6] Since time is a creation, it too bore the consequences of original sin. Time also fell from its proper relationship with its Creator. Time had been created for God's glory, but after the fall, time became an arena of suffering.

Too briefly and maybe too strongly, we could say that in Western thought, Augustine's concept of time has been the dominant perspective in Christian Eschatology. However, Western perspectives on time changed dramatically during the Renaissance, with its ideas of the past as perfect and the future as corruption. Of course this overstatement of the past's perfection couldn't hold. The overreaction was clear and lasting. The Enlightenment's assessment of time obliterated these previous visions. Now, after the Enlightenment, time is viewed as always progressively better. I'm thinking of Hegel, but there are others. Indeed, the Enlightenment breeds the idea "time heals all wounds." Being on the "right side of

---

3 Rev 21:3–4: "I heard a great voice from the throne saying, 'Behold, the dwelling of God is with men. He will dwell with them, and they shall be his people, and God himself will be with them; he will wipe away every tear from their eyes, and death shall be no more, neither shall there be mourning nor crying nor pain any more, for the former things have passed away.'"
4 See Augustine, *Confessions*, XI, 14, 17.
5 Roland J. Teske, *Paradoxes of Time in Saint Augustine* (Milwaukee WI: Marquette University Press, 1996), 15.
6 This is also the position of many theologians who are critical of process or open theologies. The Lord is the Lord of time. Time is not the lord of the Lord.

history" is the moral judgment of the times. Add class consciousness and the evaluation of suffering of the proletariat and Marx stands close by to tell us that time marches socially and inevitably toward destructive reconstruction. Much in modern philosophy tends now toward the positive reading of time. It has been only with the advent of postmodern thought that time theory has been removed from value-meaning judgments of the always better future. We are now provided with a needed critique of modern thought's over-indulgence about the always better progressing future. Still, the common idea of the improving future remains in many cultures such that we uncritically say that development, progress, and time will heal all wounds.

In the era of postmodernism, Christian theologians have turned to many avenues to articulate the meaning of suffering and its relation to time and eternity.[7] One avenue worth exploring is Christian mysticism, so let's turn again to Speyr and her reflections on time, suffering, and eternity.[8]

In a sentence, Speyr's view of time, suffering, and eternity would be that time is separation and distraction, which means suffering in non-relational, monadic reality. Eternity is concentration and union, which means love in relational, Trinitarian reality.

Let me unpack this idea by looking at her image of perfection—the triune nature of God. The original image of triune love exists in eternity and eternity itself exists as triune love. Being is Trinitarian.[9] According to Speyr, eternity manifests triune love and triune love manifests eternity. Love has an interior drive toward eternity, such that one can best form a concept of the eternity of God on the basis of the concept of love. The lover wants to love the beloved forever and the beloved wants to receive and give back this love forever. The perfection of love finds eternal fulfillment in "the love between Father and Son in the Holy

---

7 In recent history, several modern Christian theologians have incorporated time as understood by modern physics into their theology (e.g., Jürgen Moltmann) by trying to include the theory of entropy together with the theory of evolution.

8 For an introduction to Speyr, see my *Heaven Opens*. Her most important work is her four-volume detailed commentary on the Gospel of John.

9 See one of the most important theological works on the communion of the Trinity, John D. Zizioulas, *Being as Communion: Studies in Personhood and the Church* (Crestwood, NY: St. Vladimir's Seminary Press, 1985).

Spirit, which from the beginning was always the same divine love, which determines the entire relationship between the Persons and illuminates and influences the entire atmosphere in which they live."[10] The essence of Trinitarian eternity is explained above all by the "fidelity and permanence of love."[11] True love would like to throw off the confines of space and time such that it can only be completely manifested in eternity. Triune love has this quality of eternal constancy. In the relations of the Divine Persons, there is a constancy grounded in the Father, communicated to the Son and the Spirit, and guaranteed in the relation of each Person. Self-giving love needs eternity to give its irrevocable constancy that will never disavow the other. Perfect love is between the Divine Persons who perfectly manifest their love in the timelessness (or better fulfilled time) of their perfect eternity.

Eternity is beyond measuring (beyond empiricism) and is simple unity (beyond relativism). True love cannot be quantified because love desires the immeasurable span of eternity. True love also cannot be composite, relativistic reality because love converges toward simple relational unity. Triune love is necessarily simple since it is perfect, fulfilled love.[12]

Eternity is not monotony but fullness, not solitude but the Kingdom of God. If one collects all the mystical visions of the Trinity, then one would see certain recurrent characteristics, in an ever-new and non-repetitive quality because eternity is not monotony but the true fullness of life. Often philosophers think about God alone as simple, unified, and at rest, as if God were content being an isolated monad. The belief of Christians is that God is love and this must mean that God is Trinity and not a divine monad. Monad means monotony; God as love means eternal, triune fullness. God is love and his eternal life must be full of loving relation. Since eternity is filled with triune love, the divine is an inexhaustible fruitfulness of life. Eternal life is the eschatological infolding of all time into triune love.[13]

---

10 Adrienne von Speyr, *The Gates of Eternal Life*, trans. Corona Sharp (San Francisco: Ignatius Press, 1983), 16.

11 Ibid, 17.

12 On divine being as absolutely simple, see Thomas, *Summa Theologiae*, I, 3, 1–8.

13 I also see this idea in Alexander Schmemann: "Eternity is not the negation of time, but time's absolute wholeness, gathering and restoration.

The fullness of eternity can be understood, however, as a resting in the beloved. The seventh day rest after creation is a revelation of the eternity of the Trinity. The rest of contemplation on the seventh day is the Father's rest in the Son and Holy Spirit.[14] Eternity as the seventh day is a repose in the Father's love of his Son and the Holy Spirit as that love.

The seventh day shows that there is a *diastasis* (distance) between transient and eternal time. With the first and fourth days of creation, the eternal God creates with his own divine powers outside his eternal duration a new, contingent duration.[15] He has filled his creation with the demarcation of time with "the greater light to rule the day, and the lesser light to rule the night" (Gen 1:16). Before the Fall of Adam and Eve, transient time had a fitting place in God's plan for creation which he contemplates on the seventh day. The distance between eternal and transient time was a distinction (*Unterscheidung*) but not yet a separation (*Scheidung*).[16] After the fall, there is now the separating distance between eternal and transient time. God had originally created transient time with a seventh day in order to be an invitation to his eternity. We should be asking ourselves, "What does this mean from the standpoint of eternity?"[17] Because of the Fall of Adam and Eve, creaturely life will need to find its meaning from the sphere of eternity and it will be the Son who will provide the bridge from the bounded time of the world to the boundless eternity of triune love.

Speyr's love theology of the Trinity is linked with her interpretation of time and eternity. God creates the world in the middle of his eternity. The new beginning of the world is a new inauguration of the realm of number and numeration. Day and night are separated in rhythmic succession. But at the beginning, the realm of number, rhythm, and finitude is not closed in on itself. It remains open to the wider areas of the inifinite, eternal life.

Eternal life is not what begins after temporal life; it is the eternal presence of the totality of life" (Alexander Schmemann, *The Journals of Father Alexander Schmemann 1973–1983* [Crestwood, NY: St. Vladimir's Seminary Press, 2002], 11).

14 Adrienne von Speyr, *The Boundless God*, trans. Helena Tomko (San Francisco: Ignatius Press, 2004), 9–20.

15 Adrienne von Speyr, *The Countenance of the Father*, trans. David Kipp (San Francisco: Ignatius Press, 1997) 7–29.   16 Speyr, *Gates of Eternal Life*, 7.

17 We should remember the important phrase from the life of Saint Aloysius Gonzaga: "*Quid est ad aeternitatem?*"

When we are told that the Father is in communion with the Son and with the Spirit from eternity, we also experience that he is a God of love who begets the Son as his image and likeness, who pours out the Spirit, and who lets them both participate in the same eternity and infinity while receiving from them this very same eternity and infinity. Love thus knows no bounds; it proceeds from and to the eternal God.[18]

Speyr maintains that God created time and also called it "very good" (Gen 1:31). The infinite God created finitude within his infinitude. In this original unity numeration was not closed from him. It participated in the eternal life. Numeration did not contain ending.[19]

However, Speyr does think that, because man's sins make him unworthy of God's love, God creates a punishment while also creating—as a new testimony of love—time which alone can be identified as the experience of finitude in the actual sense: he creates death. Through death, God puts an end to the creature who has chosen sin so that the condition of being in sin does not continue without bounds.[20]

Because of sin, an original disobedience rejecting God's love, relational rupture occurs and time now takes on a new quality of finite suffering, a decrescendo to death. The creature has chosen sin so God mercifully puts the creature to death. God uses the finitude of time to bind sin and gives it an ending, a finality that will be definitive.

From a Christian perspective, this judgment is not the end. God sends himself to heal his creation.[21] It is God who also takes this binding death sentence upon himself in the offering of his Son. In this way, humanity's finitude becomes graced, becomes an event of love within God's own being. God has released the punitive character of death upon himself to make it a portal to his eternity. Thus, God re-purposes finitude back toward his infinitude.

The suffering that comes with being finite has been taken into the peaceful realm of the eternal triune God. What seems

---

18 Speyr, *Boundless God*, 21.
19 The move from 1 to 2 does not need to negate 1 because the 2 contains the 1.   20 Speyr, *Boundless God*, 22.
21 For more on this, see Speyr, *Boundless God*, 22–23.

meaningless, now has meaning not because man decides it does, but because it has been taken into God's meaning-making. As cited earlier, "Things have meaning only to the extent that they lead to God, come from him and can be placed at his service."[22] Without God there is no meaning, there is only the temporary fooling of oneself. And this is really important for some kind of definitive statement about making sense of suffering: "All meaning resides in God. Without him everything would literally be meaningless."[23]

Eternity is not just outside of time, it is all times present—suffering and ecstasy, cross and redemption. Eternity is eras in a moment and epochs in a point.

One day of the year the Church withholds the Eucharist from the faithful and this day is Holy Saturday. During this funeral service for the Lord Jesus Christ, one may be able to receive the Sacrament in an emergency, but there will be no Mass and no consecration.[24] Ratzinger in his book, *Pilgrim Fellowship of Faith*, meditates on this fact as an opportunity for Christians to gain a deeper understanding of the Lord's love for them.[25] According to Ratzinger, on this day of mourning, the absence of the Eucharist can help us feel first-hand the devastation of abandonment.

Eternity, Eucharist, Ecclesia

The *Mystagogia*, a great work by the early Church theologian Maximus the Confessor (c. 580–662), captures many of the themes developed in this chapter, especially relevant for those now entering the Church, souls who are really entering a new cosmic experience of time in God.[26]

As one becomes more taken into the grace of the Lord, as one is made more united with the Trinity, one is also made more united

---

22 Speyr, *Mystery of Death*, 47.   23 Ibid., 48.

24 Traditionally, prior to 1955, Holy Communion was also not given on Good Friday; only the celebrant of the Mass of the Presanctified received the Host (and without the Precious Blood). The sacramental "deprivation" was meant as a way of entering into the Passion.

25 Joseph Ratzinger, "Communion: Eucharist—Fellowship—Mission," trans. Henry Taylor, in *Pilgrim Fellowship of Faith*, eds. Stephan Otto Horn and Vinzenz Pfnür (San Francisco: Ignatius Press, 2005), 60–89.

26 Maximus, "The Church's Mystagogy: In Which Are Explained the Symbolism of Certain Rites Performed in the Divine Synaxis," in *Maximus Confessor: Selected Writings*, trans. and ed. George Berthold (New York: Paulist Press, 1985).

with the Church (*ecclesia*), both here and always, both in time and eternity. According to Maximus, one enters the Church and is unified with others in order that one may enter the Trinity and be unified with the Trinity forever.

The Church becomes one's entrance into eternity, and for eternity we will sing of all God has done. The Church, according to Maximus, is the focal point of the convergence of many separate lines of individual Christians, and in the Pauline sense, the many members function in unity by the power of the Holy Spirit with Christ as the Head. In order to arrive at this theme, I will proceed to the convergence point through the other main themes and explicate the central theme of the text to which they lead. I will begin by examining Maximus's historical context and his life, then I will address, first, reading the spiritual sense of the Church, second, Maximus's anthropology, third, the Eucharistic life, and finally, the theme of being made one with the Trinity by being made one with the Church.

Maximus the Confessor is characterized by a majority of scholars as a theologian in whom the two lines of East and West converge. Hans Urs von Balthasar names Maximus the philosophical-theological thinker between East and West.[27] The East and West are more than Constantinople and Rome. The East and West, Balthasar contends, are Asia and the whole of the West. The influence of the East takes shape in Maximus's mysticism and explication of the liturgy. The influence of the West is apparent in Maximus's unwavering defense of Rome during the Lateran Synod (649).[28] Even Maximus's Christology is a theology of convergence. The two wills of Christ, one human and one divine, unite in volitional synergy by the human will's obedience to the divine will without division, without confusion.[29]

Maximus emerges at a critical crossroads when the Church has not yet separated decisively into East and West. The time is

---

27 See Hans Urs von Balthasar, *Cosmic Liturgy: The Universe According to Maximus the Confessor*, trans. Brian E. Daley (San Francisco: Ignatius Press, 2003).
28 Andrew Louth, "Postpatristic Byzantine Theologians," in *The Medieval Theologians*, ed. G. R. Evans (Oxford: Blackwell Publishers, 2001), 42.
29 G. W. H. Lampe, "Christian Theology in the Patristic Period," in *A History of Christian Doctrine*, ed. Hubert Cunliffe-Jones (Edinburgh: T&T Clark, 1978), 144–48.

ripe for a reunion and Maximus will be one to help both Eastern and Western Christianity.[30] In the time of Maximus, the Roman Empire was still enjoying the exceptional achievemnts of the august Justinian, who died fifteen years before Maximus's birth. Under Justinian, the Empire once again tasted its earlier splendor in both the East and West. The Church also benefited in this era. For example, Justinian sponsored the building of the brilliant Hagia Sophia in Constantinople. On the other hand, at the time of Maximus's death, the East had lost Syria, Palestine, and Egypt to the expanding Arab and Persian Empires. The Slav and Avar conquest of the Balkan region further split the East and West. The West received constant and malicious threats from rogue tribes. Maximus sensed the growing split between East and West, and yet, at his trial when he was asked the question, "Why do you love the Romans and hate the Greeks?" he answered that, "We have a precept, not to hate anyone: I love the Romans as sharing the same faith, and the Greeks as sharing the same language."[31]

We can see a pair of convergent paths in Maximus. The first path led him from the political to the ecclesial, starting as the Imperial Chancellor under Emperor Heraclius and ending as a monk and abbot in Chrysopolis.[32] Maximus's life began among the imperial elite then followed an unlikely path to an intense monastic life.

The second path led from the spiritual to the theological. The twenty-five year span of Maximus's writing (624–649) began with spiritual concerns. His early writings are letters or treatises like the *Centuries on Love* and *Centuries on Knowledge* that focus on his development of the monastic and spiritual life.[33] However, his later writings become more theological and polemical like the *Mystagogia*, *Ambigua*, and *Quaestiones ad Thalassium*. This shift can be traced to his participation in the Monothelite controversy and his defense of Jesus Christ's two energies and two wills.

3 0 Cyril O'Regan, "Von Balthasar and Thick Retrieval: Post-Chalcedonian Symphonic Theology," *Gregorianum* 77 (1996): 229.

3 1 George Berthold, trans. and ed., "The Trial of Maximus," in *Maximus Confessor: Selected Writings* (New York: Paulist Press, 1985), 26.

3 2 Jaroslav Pelikan, "Introduction," in *Maximus Confessor: Selected Writings* (New York: Paulist Press, 1985), 3–4.

3 3 Andrew Louth, "St. Maximus the Confessor between East and West," *Studia Patristica* 32 (1997): 342.

Let us look at his fascinating work, *Mystagogia*, because we will see in it four themes that help us see the connections of eternity, Eucharist, and *ecclesia*. The first theme is reading the spiritual sense of the Church.

In the *Mystagogia*, Maximus adheres to the understanding from Christian theology that a proper interpretation of Scripture requires both a literal and spiritual reading.[34] In their reading of Sacred Scripture, early Church theologians developed what is often called the fourfold interpretation of Scripture.[35] The first is called the literal sense, meaning the words and ideas chosen by the author in their plain sense. The next are the allegorical, topological, and anagogical senses grouped together and called the spiritual sense. The literal sense must be the starting point for the spiritual sense. Maximus uses these senses of reading Scripture and applies them to reading the Church (*ecclesia*). Maximus proposes that the literal sense of the Church is its earthly structure, but in a spiritual reading, the liturgy (Eucharist) should be seen as the spiritual interpretation of the Church. As with Scripture and so with the Church, the spiritual sense graced by the Holy Spirit will remove the veil of the literal.[36]

Maximus is not the first to engage in a spiritual reading of the Church and its liturgy. He acknowledges his deep indebtedness to Dionysius the Areopagite and his *Ecclesiastical Hierarchy*.[37] His intent is not to supersede or to comment on Dionysius's work, but to address subjects not yet discussed there.[38] The apophatic character in the text can be linked to Dionysius, but, to use a Balthasarian phrase, the Christian optic is more evident in Maximus's Neoplatonic appropriation.[39] In this sense, if Dionysius in the *Ecclesiastical Hierarchy* is engaged in cosmic theology, then

---

34 One example of many would be Augustine, *On Christian Teaching*, trans. R. P. H. Green (New York: Oxford University Press, 1997).

35 A nice history of this way of reading is Jaroslav Pelikan, *Whose Bible Is It? A Short History of the Scriptures* (New York: Penguin, 2005). See also the classic, Henri de Lubac, *Medieval Exegesis: The Four Senses of Scripture*, 4 vols., trans. Mark Sebanc (Grand Rapids, MI: Eerdmans, 1998).

36 Maximus, *Church's Mystagogy*, 197.

37 Dionysius, "Ecclesiastical Hierarchy," in *Pseudo-Dionysius: The Complete Works*, ed. and trans. Paul Rorem and Colm Luibheid (New York: Paulist Press, 1987). 38 Maximus, *Church's Mystagogy*, 184.

39 O'Regan, "Von Balthasar and Thick Retrieval," 323, 237.

Maximus is engaged in ecclesial mysticism.[40] If we were able to ask Maximus, he probably would not notice the difference between the two because ecclesial mysticism would necessarily imply a cosmic perspective. However, there is a marked difference. Whereas the optic in Dionysius is the Church reflecting the cosmos, the optic in Maximus is the Church reflecting the Trinity and the cosmos reflecting the Church.

The spiritual reading starts with the Church seen as an image and figure of God. It is in this context that we catch a glimpse of what I argue is the main theme of the *Mystagogia*. Since the Church was created by God, the Church shares and works the same effects as God; thus, Maximus can write, "In accordance with faith it [the Church] gives to all a single, simple, whole, and indivisible condition," and he continues, "It is through it that absolutely no one at all is in himself separated from the community since everyone converges with all the rest and joins together with them by the one, simple, and indivisible grace and power of faith."[41] In this context, Maximus uses Saint Paul's spiritual reading of Church as a head with many members who are united into the Mystical Body of Christ. For Maximus, in as much as the Church is unified, it is unified with God because the Church "realizes the same union of the faithful with God," and "as different as they are by language, places, and customs, they are made one by it through faith."[42] This particular comment seems to touch on the idea that the outpouring of the Holy Spirit at Pentecost did not cause all the witnesses to comprehend the same language. The Holy Spirit did not inspire all to speak Esperanto. The disciples proclaimed the Good News in their native tongue, yet the onlookers seemed to hear them in their own divers foreign languages. The Holy Spirit gave them the unity of faith constituting them as a Church; a Church where the disciples were made one with each other and with God.

The first and second chapters of the *Mystagogia* set up the spiritual reading of the Church as an image and figure of God. We see the central theme already coming through. Remembering that each of these themes converges on the central theme of being

---

40 Denys Rutledge, *Cosmic Theology: The Ecclesiastical Hierarchy of Pseudo-Denys: An Introduction* (Staten Island: Alba House, 1964), 3-4, 13.
41 Maximus, *Church's Mystagogy*, 187.   42 Ibid., 188.

made one with the Trinity by being made one in the Church, I focus in on the second theme, namely Maximus's anthropology.

In the anthropology of Maximus, we see two paths within the human soul converging upon the oneness of truth and goodness. Using the nave and sanctuary of the Church, Maximus sees the human soul as made of vital, active powers and intellectual, contemplative powers that lead indirectly or directly to God respectively. He further divides the intellectual powers into the nave and sanctuary of the Church, representing reason and mind. Reason leads to prudence that leads to action that leads to virtue that leads to faith that ultimately converges in goodness, which is God.[43] Mind leads to wisdom that leads to contemplation that leads to knowledge that leads to enduring knowledge (memory) that ultimately converges in truth, which is God. As reason stands to mind, so does prudence to wisdom, action to contemplation, virtue to knowledge, and faith to enduring knowledge—as one advances toward goodness and truth. These ten attributes are likened to the ten-stringed lyre of the Psalmist on which the songs of God's praises are sung.[44] As reason and mind advance toward truth and goodness, a unity is made, "of that intrinsic decade... once this unity is achieved, the soul becomes one, not only within itself but with its God: the true, the good, the one and the only God."[45]

Even in the midst of Maximus's anthropology, we come into the main theme of being made one with the Trinity by being made one with the Church. The paragraph above, if taken on its own, could suggest a rather individual and non-ecclesial deification, that the Church is not necessary for union with God. We could easily be lead to that conclusion, if it were not for the context surrounding Maximus's anthropology.[46] The perfection of the

---

43 Ibid., 191.
44 "I will sing a new song to you, O God; upon a ten-stringed harp I will play to you" (Ps 144:9). Maximus, *Church's Mystagogy*, 191–92: "the ten divine strings of the spiritual lyre of the soul which includes the reason resounding in harmony with the spirit through another blessed series of ten, the commandments, which spiritually renders perfect, harmonious, and melodious sounds in praise of God."
45 Julian Stead, *The Church, the Liturgy and the Soul of Man: The* Mystagogia of *St. Maximus the Confessor* (Still River, MA: St. Bede's Publications, 1982), 52.
46 Andrew Louth argues against this seemingly perceived individualism

"ten strings" of the human soul lead one to peace and to the holy embrace of God: "It is in this blessed and most holy embrace that is accomplished this awesome mystery of a union . . . by which God becomes one flesh and one spirit with the Church and thus with the soul, and the soul with God."[47] God becomes one with the Church that he may become one with the soul. This is a union of wedlock and it is in this context that Maximus quotes Paul's "the two shall become one flesh" (Eph 5:31; cf. Gen 2:24; Mt 19:5).[48] God's embrace is so crushingly compassionate that it unifies the soul with other souls in the Church and thus God with the Church. We have with Maximus a theology of deification that happens by, if I may use such a word, Churchification.

Knowing that the Church is the necessary arena for deification, Maximus discusses the nature of the Church as centered on the Eucharistic life and, therefore, we come to the third theme as we narrow the focus of the text.

The second section of the *Mystagogia* details each action of the liturgy and its spiritual interpretation. It is not pertinent here to review each part of the synaxis. Yet, it is necessary to comment on the centrality of the liturgy as the *raison d'être* for the Church because at the liturgy's pinnacle is the reception of the Eucharist, which is "the climax of everything."[49] The reception is the "causal good by grace and participation" in which the Christian is adopted through grace and is deified.[50] One transcends reason and mind to perfection in God through the Church by the reception of the Eucharist. The divisions within one's self and the divisions between others are overcome.[51] This overcoming of division happens in the Eucharistic liturgy that is "a corporate, ecclesial encounter with God that draws each participant towards the attainment of the reality that it sets forth."[52] Unification occurs in the Church because the Eucha-

---

in "Apophatic Theology and the Liturgy in St. Maximos the Confessor," in *Wisdom of the Byzantine Church: Evagrios of Pontos and Maximos the Confessor; Four Lectures*, ed. J. Raitt (Columbia, MO: Dept. of Religious Studies, University of Missouri, 1997).

47 Maximus, *Church's Mystagogy*, 194. Emphasis added.

48 Ibid. 49 Ibid., 203. 50 Ibid.

51 Louth, "Apophatic Theology," 5: "This overcoming of division is the focus of the liturgical celebration that takes place in the church."

52 Ibid., 6.

rist is the presence of the one and only God who is good and true. Unification with the Church leads to deification by God.[53]

Maximus expounds the Eucharistic liturgy because it is in this liturgy that the Christian is made most perfectly one with the Church, and therefore, made one with the Trinity. Thus, we have narrowed down the main theme upon which all the other themes converge: being made one with the Trinity by being made one with the Church.

Through the participation in and reception of the Eucharist, individual Christians are united with God. All the various members celebrate the liturgy in the Church while "the greeting, the Creed, the thrice-holy hymn, and the Lord's Prayer reflect, and effect, rising degrees of unity with God."[54] God enlightens each member through each aspect of the liturgy raising each one toward the reception of the Eucharist during which the faithful who worthily receive are united with God.[55] Maximus maintains that this unity with God necessarily implies unity with the other faithful because God effects through the Church "an unconfused unity from the various essences of beings, attaching them to himself as a creator at their highest point, and this operates according to the grace of faith for the faithful, joining them all to each other in one form."[56]

By being made one in the Church, the Christian soul is led to the ultimate union with the one God, of one nature and three

---

53 Ibid., 8: In the heart of the Eucharistic liturgy "is an encounter with God himself: an encounter that constitutes a human community—*the* human community—as the Church of God, called together to celebrate the glory of God, and to be transfigured into that glory."

54 Stead, *The Church*, 19.

55 However, the danger is to assume that the coming together of the members brings about the unity. A town meeting with a hearty exchange and agreement of ideas is not the ecclesial mysticism Maximus intends. Perhaps it is the modern problem; that is, the idea that the members draw from themselves the organic unity that brings about the presence of God in the congregation. For Maximus, the unity of the Church is vital; however, the process happens differently from this modern interpretation. The origin of the unity is in God. God consecrates the Eucharist with his presence as opposed to the coming together of the congregation consecrating the Eucharist. The unity of the members in the Church happens because of God's action, not the Church's action. Maximus does not allow for the possibility of this modern and theologically flawed interpretation of Eucharistic consecration.

56 Maximus, *Church's Mystagogy*, 208.

persons. The separate paths of individual Christians converge into the Church to be unified with each other, but they do not end there.[57] The paths converge into unity with the Trinity. The soul is lead in the Holy Spirit by Christ the Word of the Father to "such wisdom that it will comprehend the one God, one nature and three Persons, unity of essence in three persons and consubstantial Trinity of persons; Trinity in unity and unity in Trinity."[58] The triune God is the end.

At the summit of union, Maximus's mysticism is confessional. He speaks his mysticism with the language of the Creeds almost as if the Creeds of the Church provide the tangibility of saying something about the apophatic journey toward union with the Trinity.[59] Maximus even in his mysticism is theologically precise in his understanding of the union with God who is "one, single, undivided, unconfused, simple, undiminished, and unchangeable divinity, completely one in essence and completely three in persons, and sole ray shining in the single form of one triple-splendored light."[60]

Having gone through the Church, the Christian is made one with others and ultimately made one with the triune God. Thus, we have seen how the convergent paths end in the triune God through the Church. We began this discussion by examining convergent paths in Maximus's historical context and life. The East-West, the political-ecclesial, and the spiritual-theological paths meet in Maximus. Advancing into the *Mystagogia*, I examined the surrounding themes in order to focus in upon what I have argued is the main theological theme of the text. Beginning with reading the Church's spiritual sense, I moved into Maximus's anthropology and then to the Eucharistic life as the center of the ecclesial life. All of these themes converge on this one point: the Christian is made one with the Trinity by being made one with the Church.

---

57 In one sense, the convergence into the Church is preparatory; in another sense, the Church is the arena in which the paths converge into the Trinity.
58 Maximus, *Church's Mystagogy*, 205.
59 Louth, "Apophatic Theology," 8.
60 Maximus, *Church's Mystagogy*, 206.

10

Scripture

HOW DO WE COME TO HEAR THE COMPASSION-
ate voice of the Lord in Scripture? How are we to ponder this
voice with all our heart like Mary (Lk 2:19)?

In an important article, Rev. J. Michael Joncas asks if the propositional prose of theological monographs and articles is the only
place for authentic exegesis (interpretation) of Christian theology
and Scripture.[1] Are not other exegetical "texts" just as valid in
authentic exegesis of the truths of Christianity? Are not paint-
ings, statues, icons, liturgies, and ecclesial and mystical writings
appropriately functional as theological and exegetical texts? In my
view, propositional prose dominated by modern scientific argumentation cannot be the sole method of authentic interpretation
of Scripture. Christians believe Scripture should be viewed as
unique among all other writings and will require its own unique
methods of interpretation. The method must fit the object studied.
If the Church is right about the theo-dramatic event witnessed to
by Scripture, this revelatory Scripture must be interpreted with
the eyes of faith. As Hans Urs von Balthasar has written, if this
theo-dramatic "event truly is what the Church believes, then it
can be mastered through no methodology."[2] He means that a
man-created methodology will not be adequate for understanding
the God-initiated event of the redemption of humanity. If the
Church is right that Scripture was inspired by the Holy Spirit,
then Scripture must be read with the same Holy Spirit. In that
case I would also add that the mystic—not just any mystic, but
only one who reads Scripture in the heart of the Spirit and the
Church—should be viewed as an authentic exegete.

This chapter argues that propositional prose should not have a
monopoly on exegesis. I propose instead that the ecclesial mystic is
also an authentic exegete of Scripture. I will offer the writings of

---

1 Jan Michael Joncas, "Image of the Invisible God: Visual Artworks as
Theological Texts," *Logos* 7 (2004): 30–53.
2 Balthasar, *The Glory of the Lord*, vol. 7, 10.

the laywoman and mystic, Adrienne von Speyr, as I have throughout this book, as an exemplary *theo*-logical exegete, specifically by
analyzing her interpretations of John 21:1–8, the epilogue story
of the Gospel of John in which Jesus appears to Saint Peter and
a few other disciples and instructs them to cast out into the deep
to catch more fish.

My central presupposition is that God the Holy Spirit is the
real and active inspiration of both the writer of Scripture and
the mystic whose life is lived in the Holy Spirit: "All Scripture is
inspired by God" (2 Tim 3:16).[3] If the Holy Spirit is allowed to be
who the Holy Spirit is, then the argument can proceed. However,
if this is not allowed, then the following argument will be viewed
as, at best, quaint or, at worst, outdated. Still, throughout the ages
of Christianity, the ecclesial mystic (the mystic within the Church)
has been viewed as a valid source for understanding the Word of
God. It is time to listen again.

Ecclesial Mystic as Exegete

To carry this forward, I must build upon the discussion in
the previous chapter on the relationship between the letter and
spirit or the literal and spiritual senses of Scripture. Following
Avery Dulles, the first observation must begin with Scripture.[4]
According to the Gospel of John, the interpretation of the word
is *the* Word. For John, the Logos is *the* exegesis of God, "No one
has ever seen God; the only-begotten Son, who is in the bosom
of the Father, he has made him known" (Jn 1:18). Moreover, the
Risen Christ "interpreted to them in all the Scriptures the things
concerning himself" (Lk 24:27). Research in early Church exegesis
will find that above all, the early Christians assumed that Jesus
himself is *the* hermeneutical principle of Scripture.[5] Only in him
is Scripture interpreted properly and gracefully.

---

3 See previously, chapters 4 and 5 on the Holy Spirit.
4 For an example of his theological style of turning to Scripture first, see
Avery Dulles, "Who Can be Saved?" *First Things*, February 2008; website:
https://www.firstthings.com/article/2008/02/who-can-be-saved, accessed on
January 10, 2012.
5 Sandra M. Schneiders, "Scripture and Spirituality," in *Christian Spirituality:
Origins to the Twelfth Century*, ed. Bernard McGinn and John Meyendorff (New
York: Crossroad, 1985), vol. 1, 6–7. See also Johnson and Kurz, *The Future of
Catholic Biblical Scholarship*.

From Paul's Letter to the Romans, we learn that we must "walk not according to the flesh but according to the Spirit" (8:4). The Holy Spirit helps "us in our weakness" and intercedes for us (8:26) as the love of God "poured into our hearts" (5:5). From Paul's First Letter to the Corinthians, we also learn that "God has revealed to us through the Spirit" (2:10a) and that "no one comprehends the thoughts of God except the Spirit of God" (2:11). Only the "Spirit which is from God" (2:12), which is given to the "spiritual man" (2:15), is able to interpret the "spiritual truths" revealed by God (2:13). The "unspiritual man does not receive the gifts of the Spirit of God" and, therefore, "is not able to understand them because they are spiritually discerned" (2:14). The Christian must realize that his "body is a temple of the Holy Spirit" that is from God (6:19). If one thinks he is "spiritual," he "should acknowledge" (14:37) that what Paul, the "apostle of Christ Jesus" (1:1), is writing, "is a command of the Lord" (14:37), that is, the "spiritual" one finds his center in the Church.

From Paul's distinction between the "living according to the flesh" / "unspiritual man" and the "living according to the spirit" / "spiritual man," the tradition worked out a deeper understanding of letter and spirit specifically as they apply to Scripture.

Let us look next at Origen (c. 184–254), the great early Church theologian, especially significant for his interpretation of Scripture.[6] The different senses of Scripture, as I had spoken about in a previous chapter, are directly tied to Origen's anthropology, which comes from the Pauline distinction discussed above.[7] The literal and spiritual senses of Scripture correspond to the "outer" and "inner" man, respectively. Careful to avoid Gnosticism here, Origen believes that to see the spiritual meaning of Scripture in every passage one must view it with the eyes of the inner man. He says that training to see with this spiritual sense means abiding in the whole structure of the apostolic *kerygma* (authoritative teaching), which is vivified by the abiding of the Holy Spirit. With the eyes of the Church, which

---

6 Hans Urs von Balthasar, ed., *Origen: Spirit and Fire: A Thematic Anthology of His Writings*, trans. Robert Daly (Washington D. C.: Catholic University of America, 1984).

7 Brian E. Daley, "Origen's *De Principiis*: A Guide to the Principles of Christian Scriptural Interpretation," in *Nova & Vetera: Patristic Studies in Honor of Thomas Patrick Halton*, ed. John Petruccione (Washington, D. C.: Catholic University of America Press, 1998), 12.

is the locus of the Holy Spirit's activity in the world, one can see the real spiritual significance of every word of Scripture. The inner man must be transformed by the Holy Spirit to see spiritually.[8] According to the important patristic scholar, Peter Brown, Origen requires a Spirit-given asceticism for authentic exegesis:

> It had been Origen's life's labor, as an exegete and guide of souls, to make the "spiritual senses" of his charges come alive again in their original intensity. By withdrawing from the dull anesthesia of common, physical sensation, the soul of the "spiritual" person might recapture the sharp delights of another, more intensely joyful world. The believer's spirit would stand totally exposed before the Bridegroom, stripped of all sensual joys, to receive a "naked" sensibility to the exquisite touch of His darts.[9]

From this spiritual sense, arrived at through grace-filled asceticism, one comes to the heart of revelation, the Lord as "the Spirit" (2 Cor 3:17). Only then will the exegete experience the ecstatic joy of knowing the Bridegroom.

Origen is not alone in developing Paul's emphasis on spiritual interpretation. In his little work, *On Christian Teaching*, Augustine added that the matrix of love must be the guide for authentic interpretation of Scripture.[10] The sign (*signum*) points to the thing (*res*) and it is the thing that must be received in love (*amor*) through the sign. The Christian must learn to receive and cleave to the teaching of Scripture in love. If received in love, the interpretation will serve to build up love. According to Augustine, the loving interpretation cannot be a bad one.[11] If it is true love, the interpretation must have had its source in the "God who is love" (see 1 Jn 4:8). For Augustine, the spiritual interpretation must be found within the matrix of love.

In the Middle Ages, the spiritual sense of Scripture allowed for a more mystical and intuitive experience of God.[12] For example,

---

8 Peter Brown, *The Body and Society: Men, Women, and Sexual Renunciation in Early Christianity* (New York: Columbia University Press, 1988), 160–77.
9 Ibid., 172.
10 Augustine, *On Christian Teaching*, trans. R. P. H. Green (New York: Oxford University Press, 1997).
11 Ibid., I.2.2, I.23.22–23, I.35.39–40.44, especially I.36.40.
12 Balthasar, *The Glory of the Lord*, vol. 1, 371.

Bonaventure defines the spiritual sense as an interior act of the will and intellect that has been grasped by God in contemplation. [13] This interior act is a movement of love as *ekstasis* that is grace-given. [14] Unfortunately, the later interpreters of Bonaventure lost the necessary connection between the spiritual sense and the literal sense, which caused the extreme spiritual sense interpretations of Scripture to be discounted outright. It is quite clear that for the early Church, the literal sense is absolutely essential. Like Bonaventure, Thomas Aquinas also has a properly inclusive view of the letter and spirit that is in line with Origen and Augustine and that avoids a disconnected spiritual sense. One need only look at Thomas's Scripture commentaries or even the *Summa Theologiae* to see how soberly he takes the literal sense of each verse even though he is also interested in the spiritual sense. [15]

Ignatius of Loyola provides the next significant development in understanding the spiritual sense. In the *Spiritual Exercises*, which can be understood as a guided spiritual commentary on Scripture, one must "apply the five senses" to the biblical mystery. [16] According to Hans Urs von Balthasar who commented on the *Exercises*, two things come from this application of the corporeal senses. [17] First, the meditation is not with the senses but *on* the senses. One must use the five senses to receive the insight of the passage rather than doing away with the senses in order to achieve a mystical, spiritual flight. Second, the act of applying the senses affects the "mental representation of place" for its salvific merit. [18] While meditating on the passage, one finds one's affections are attuned to the moment of salvation now being made present. The application of the senses and the self-attunement of the affections determine

---

13 Ibid., 372–73.

14 See Bonaventure, "The Soul's Journey Into God," in *Bonaventure*, trans. Ewert Cousins (New York: Paulist Press, 1978).

15 Thomas Aquinas, *Summa Theologica*, trans. Fathers of the English Dominican Province (New York: Benziger, 1948), I.1.10. See also his *Commentary on the Gospel of St. John*, 2 vols., trans. James Weisheipl and Fabian Larcher (Albany, NY: Magi Books, 1998). See also *Reading John with St. Thomas Aquinas: Theological Exegesis and Speculative Theology*, ed. Michael Dauphinais and Matthew Levering (Washington, D. C.: Catholic University of America Press, 2005).

16 Ignatius, *Spiritual Exercises*, 121.

17 Balthasar, *The Glory of the Lord*, vol. 1, 375.

18 Ignatius, *Spiritual Exercises*, 47.

the theological meaning.[19] The implication is quite clear—the spiritual sense is not received without the five senses. Moreover, the ways in which these senses are applied determine the spiritual fruit received. Finally, for Ignatius, the application of the senses is always done in meditation and contemplation that must of necessity be obedient to the thinking of the Church: "For it is by the same Spirit and Lord who gave the Ten Commandments that our holy Mother Church is ruled and governed."[20] The guide for literal and spiritual interpretation must be the Church.

In my view, the analysis of Scripture and Tradition present us with four points. First, God is his own exegete.[21] And only in Jesus Christ, who is the exegesis of God, is Scripture understood. Second, Scripture must be experienced in the Holy Spirit who is the source of the inspiration. It is the Holy Spirit who attunes the spiritual man to spiritual things. Third, Scripture encounters man in a completely human way that presupposes devout bodily and spiritual senses. Fourth, since Scripture is written in the Church, the exegesis must necessarily be ecclesial. Scripture and Tradition lead us to conclude that there is a proper place for spiritual exegesis. Soon I will identify this spiritual exegesis with the ecclesial mystic but before I take that step, two matters must be addressed: I need to make more explicit the theological anthropology implied in this discussion, and I must define what is meant by an ecclesial mystic.

The theological anthropology advocated in this discussion has many aspects to it. I will address just those points pertinent to the argument. First, both the body and soul are involved in experiencing the world and, consequently, the divine.[22] The isolated soul abstracted from the body cannot attain spiritual insight into God any more than an isolated body abstracted from the soul can attain scientific insight into God. Both body and soul are present together as the human person and cannot be bracketed apart from each other in *any* human activity, especially exegesis. To do so is inhuman.

Second, God encounters man in the sphere of the senses.[23] The God who fills heaven and earth (Jer 23:24) can be mistaken for a gardener (Jn 20:15). If man is to avoid any docetic tendencies, then

---

19 Balthasar, *The Glory of the Lord*, vol. 1, 375.
20 Ignatius, *Spiritual Exercises*, 365.
21 Hans Urs von Balthasar, "God is His Own Exegete," *Communio* 4 (1986): 280–87.   22 Balthasar, *The Glory of the Lord*, vol. 1, 406.   23 Ibid.

he must look within the sphere of the senses to see God. In the Incarnation, "flesh speaks to flesh."[24] Any encounter with God is an encounter with him whom we can see, touch, hear, smell, and taste Eucharistically.[25] This calls for an anthropology that makes man bow before God. It is a doxological anthropology like that of Augustine's *Confessions* or Ignatius's "First Principle and Foundation": "Man is created to praise, reverence, and serve God our Lord, and by this means to save his soul."[26]

Third, the encounter with God is an encounter with his self-emptying. The Word is comprehensible only because he kenotically became flesh, which I explored in chapter three. With our senses, we perceive God, who kenotically radiates his glory. It is only possible for Mary Magdalene to mistake the risen Christ for a gardener because the Word kenotically condescended. Of course, we must interpret this kenosis as love (1 Jn 4:8-9). The condescension finds its motivation in love.[27] Only within the matrix of love—God's self-giving love—can man understand God. Only love can perceive and receive love.[28]

The second matter that still needs to be addressed is the definition of an ecclesial mystic. I will deal with the noun first and the adjective second. The term "mystic" has a complex history of meanings and connotations. As I have indicated earlier, I define a mystic as one who has had a super-sensual experience of God. By super-sensual, I mean both the bodily and spiritual senses are involved. As in any mystic experience, there is a great knowing/experiencing of God as well as a degree that is hidden in God.[29]

---

24 Ibid.

25 "Late have I loved you, beauty so old and so new: late have I loved you.... You called and cried out loud and shattered my deafness. You were radiant and resplendent, you put to flight my blindness. You were fragrant, and I drew in my breath and now pant after you. I tasted you, and I feel but hunger and thirst for you. You touched me, and I am set on fire to attain the peace which is yours" (Augustine, *Confessions*, trans. Henry Chadwick [New York: Oxford University Press, 1991], X.xxvii.38).

26 See Augustine's *Confessions*, I.i.1 and Ignatius, *Spiritual Exercises*, 23.

27 Balthasar, *The Glory of the Lord*, vol. 1, 407.

28 For more on this interpretation of love, see Balthasar, *Love Alone is Credible*.

29 Balthasar, *The Glory of the Lord*, vol. 1, 412-13: "in 'mysticism' every deeper experience (*Erfahrung*) of God will be a deeper entering into (*Einfahren*) the 'non-experience' of faith, into the loving renunciation of experience, all the way into the depths of the 'Dark Nights' of John of the Cross."

The mystic feels himself experiencing something very *real*, but it is a realness that surpasses what he would ordinarily call "real." Bernini's famous sculpture of *The Ecstasy of St. Teresa* captures the moment of the mystical experience with an allusion to the statuary tradition of Cupid and Psyche. Bernini presents this mystical experience as a very real, bodily piercing by God's consuming love, but Teresa's ecstatic face also captures how "unreal" it all is.[30] Some scholars of mysticism like Evelyn Underhill or Steven Fanning would call the mystic one who has had a "direct" experience of God.[31] We must be metaphysically careful here.[32] If we are speaking of an authentically Christian mysticism it is necessarily mediated—and in that way indirect—through the bodily and spiritual senses. "Direct" experience of God as a Neoplatonic mystical journey must be rejected if it does not submit to the metaphysically revelatory event of the Incarnation.

Another way to understand the mystic explores the common distinction between meditation and contemplation. Meditation can be thought of as an exercise of the human will engaging one's own faculties (e.g., one's imagination and memory) and applying it to the biblical mystery at hand. Contemplation can be thought of as an exercise of God's free will giving a gift—his presence, grace, infused knowledge, a visionary encounter with a saint or angel, et cetera. Meditation comes from one's own initiative; contemplation comes from God's initiative. While there is no doubt that it requires the mystic's own cooperation, contemplation finds its origin in the deep intentions of the Trinity to overtake the world in love. With this distinction in mind, we see that the mystic receives the contemplative, super-sensual experience through God's initiative.

The question arises then about how to discern between meditation and contemplation, between an act of exegesis initiated by

---

30 See Teresa of Avila, "Book of Her Life," in *The Collected Works of St. Teresa of Avila*, trans. Kieran Kavanaugh and Otilio Rodriguez, vol. 1 (Washington, D. C.: ICS Publications, 1976). Teresa of Avila's experience on mysticism is much more spiritual and complex than this statue, of course. See the nice interpretive work of Ruth Burrows, *Interior Castle Explored: St. Teresa's Teaching on the Life of Deep Union with God* (Mahwah, NJ: Hidden Spring, 2007).
31 Steven Fanning, *Mystics of the Christian Tradition* (New York: Routledge, 2001), 1–3; Evelyn Underhill, *The Mystics of the Church* (Cambridge: J. Clarke & Co., 1925), 9.
32 For an in-depth discussion of my interpretation of mystics and mysticism, see chapters two and three of my book, *Heaven Opens*.

man's will and an act of exegesis initiated by God's will. There are many rules for discernment. We could invoke the rules found in Ignatius's *Spiritual Exercises* as an exemplary list. I wish to focus only on one essential key to the discernment of an authentic exegesis given by a mystic. The key is the Church. The people of God, who have received the Word in the Spirit, are able to recognize among themselves the ecclesial mystics.

The authentic mystic exegete must be centered in the heart of the Church. Mysticism without the Church will degenerate into a private affair that is contrary and perhaps not complementary to public revelation. We must hold that the Word has already revealed all that is pertinent to salvation. Christians are not Gnostics and mysticism must not degenerate into Gnosticism either in its soft or hard varieties. The first two millennia of Christianity witnessed the mystic having an ecclesial responsibility and function.[33] Just as we hold firmly to the once-for-all revelation of the Word become flesh and the descent of the Holy Spirit at Pentecost, we must similarly hold firmly that the world has been raised to a "final trinitarian potency."[34] Moreover, the theologian Balthasar makes clear:

> There is no reason why the Church's participation in the fullness of revelation, as it took shape in the Biblical period, should not also be a participation in the prophetic and charismatic experiences of Biblical man ... this [Holy] Spirit is free to make use also of the Biblical modes of archetypal experience in order to demonstrate in the Church of all centuries the continual reality of revelation—not as something past, but as something present.[35]

The Church should expect nothing less from the Trinity than the continual giving of the mystical charism to certain members. Consequently, it should not surprise the mystic that his obedience to the Church is necessary. The charismatic/mystical member of the Church must "make his special mission known and accepted in the church precisely in the measure that he does not stand opposed to the church."[36] He must rather demonstrate "that he is vitally

---

33 The canonization and elevation to Doctor of the Church of Hildegard von Bingen provides evidence of the Church's desire to learn from her as an ecclesial mystic.   34 Balthasar, *The Glory of the Lord*, vol. 1, 408.
35 Ibid., 408–9.   36 Ibid., 410.

integrated into the communion of love of all the members."[37] We have a testimony of this in the tradition with Ignatius's *Spiritual Exercises*.[38] A more recent example of a mystic accepting ecclesial discernment, Saint Maria Faustina Kowalska wrote in her diary that during one of her many mystical visions of Jesus she said to him,

> O Eternal Truth, Word Incarnate, who most faithfully fulfilled Your Father's will, today I am becoming a martyr of Your inspirations, since I cannot carry them out because I have no will of my own, though interiorly I see Your will clearly. I submit in everything to the will of my superiors and my confessor. I will follow Your will insofar as you will permit me to do so through Your representative. O my Jesus, it cannot be helped, but I give priority to the voice of the Church over the voice with which You speak to me.[39]

Notice that she is deeply convinced of the reality and exigency of these visions. She wants to die as a martyr for them. Notice also that although she is convinced about the reality of the visions she submits herself in total obedience to the offices of the Church as representatives of the Lord. She recognizes her fallibility in being able to communicate the visions of the Lord, but she does not question either the concreteness of them or the discerning wisdom of the Church. Faustina is an exemplary model of an *ecclesial* mystic.

Having agreed on the authenticity of the ecclesial mystic as an exegete, the encounter with one becomes urgent. The point is this: when encountering the Lord in Scripture, "only the innermost love" is able to understand him.[40] We can hear "what the Spirit says to the churches" (Rev 2:11), but perhaps we must open ourselves to the ecclesial mystic. Let us consider the mystical experience of Adrienne von Speyr and her commentary on John 21:1–8, where we encounter the resurrected Jesus by the Sea of Tiberius.

---

37 Ibid.

38 See his "Rules for Thinking with the Church," in Ignatius, *Spiritual Exercises*, 352–70: "If we wish to proceed securely in all things, we must hold fast to the following principle: What seems to me white, I will believe black if the hierarchical Church so defines. For I must be convinced that in Christ our Lord, the Bridegroom, and in His spouse the Church, only one Spirit holds sway, which governs and rules for the salvation of souls" (365).

39 Maria Faustina Kowalska, *Diary: Divine Mercy in My Soul* (Stockbridge, MA: Marians of the Immaculate Conception, 2002), 497.

40 Speyr, *John*, vol. 4, 301.

Adrienne von Speyr as Exemplar and Exegete

Encountering Adrienne von Speyr is at once both astonishing and joyful as we have explored in previous chapters and also in my book *Heaven Opens*. From an early age Speyr experienced visions of Mary, Ignatius, her guardian angel, and the saints, and her intense contemplation of the triune life conflicted with her upbringing in the independent Reformed Church.[41] In 1940, her search eventually brought her to a meeting with Hans Urs von Balthasar. After a short period of catechesis, Speyr entered the Catholic Church on All Saint's Day in 1940, fittingly for her theology, and began experiencing a waterfall of mystical experiences.

The greater part of Balthasar's work "is a translation of what is present in more immediate, less technical fashion in the powerful work of Adrienne von Speyr."[42] When all of her works are published and carefully read, Balthasar thinks, the "richness contained there will only be recognized in more mature times."[43]

Speyr does not specifically engage with modern theologians or the intricacies of the theological tradition in the mode of a professional theologian. Balthasar provides that engagement, but Speyr's importance continues beyond Balthasar's examination of her work. It is significant that, soon after Speyr's death, Pope John Paul II asked Balthasar to arrange a conference on Speyr and her ecclesial mission. The Holy Father then attended this conference and presented his affirmation of Speyr's contribution.[44] One way

---

41 Hans Urs von Balthasar, *First Glance at Adrienne von Speyr*, trans. Antje Lawry and Sergia Englund, O. C. D. (San Francisco: Ignatius Press, 1981) and *Our Task: A Report and a Plan*, trans. John Saward (San Francisco: Ignatius Press, 1994).

42 Balthasar, *My Work*, 105.   43 Ibid., 106.

44 John Paul II, "Allocution du Saint-Père aux Participants," in *La Mission Ecclésiale d'Adrienne von Speyr: Actes du Colloque Romain 27-29 Septembre 1985*, ed. Hans Urs von Balthasar, Georges Chantraine, and Angelo Scola (2nd International Colloquial on Christian Thought Organized by ISTRA [Istituto di Studi per la Transizione]; Paris: Éditions Lethielleux, 1986), 197-98: "Finally, I am delighted because the Church always has need to propose by example laymen of faith very rooted in their social-professional vocation and immersed in God. Is it not Eckhart who teaches to his disciples, 'All that God asks you in the most urgent way, is to come out of one's self... and to let God be God in you' (cf. *Treatises and Sermons*)? One could think that in parting with creatures, the mystic neglects the brotherhood of man. The same Eckhart affirms that, on the contrary, he is marvelously present at the only level where he can truly reach them, that is to say in God" [my translation].

that Speyr has served the Church is through her almost seventy volumes, most of which were dictated in the state of mystical prayer to Balthasar. Her writings include several scriptural commentaries, thematic works, books on saints, an autobiography, a few medical works, her diaries, and letters. There is a great need to examine Speyr's thought theologically.

Her commentary on the Gospel of John is her longest and most important work.[45] She offers an intense verse-by-verse meditation that demands a slow reading. It is quite clear that it is composed during continuous, deep contemplative prayer.[46] The exegesis is always in the spirit of the gospel writer, John, and so her commentary is not academic-scientific exegesis. Balthasar commented: "Adrienne never, even from a distance, looked into an exegetical work.... Adrienne, however, listened to the Word in the center of the Church's heart, where the self-revealing triune God communicates his eternal mystery of love to the beloved Bride of the Son, the Church."[47] Her exegetical method is to listen to the Word in the heart of the Church indwelt by the Spirit.

With this brief introduction to Speyr and her commentary on John, I can now turn to her exegesis of John 21:1-8, the story of casting out into the deep, which is found in the fourth volume, *The Birth of the Church*.[48] I should just briefly note that I chose this passage of Speyr's exegesis because it at once reveals both how approachable and how fruitful mystical exegesis can be. Speyr avoids two pitfalls. She does not give in to a mystical/speculative flight or tack a philosophical/ideological spin onto every passage. If anything, it is quite like a circling around the passage, drawing closer and closer to a settled idea about its meaning.

In reference to John 21:1, Speyr remarks that this "epilogue" of sorts comes from John's desire to reveal all he knows just as a lover might continue to ramble on about his beloved. The story is filled with detail because "Whoever loves someone is interested in the smallest details of that person's life ... everything becomes

---

45 Adrienne von Speyr, *John*, trans. Lucia Wiedenhöver, Alexander Dru, Brian McNeil, E. A. Nelson, and David Kipp, 4 vols. (San Francisco: Ignatius Press, 1994).

46 Her commentary on John 21:1-8, the focus of this section, occupies forty-six pages in the English translation: Speyr, *John*, vol. 4, 269–315.

47 Hans Urs von Balthasar, *First Glance*, 100–101.

48 Speyr, *John*, vol. 4. The following numbers in parentheses refer to this text.

significant to us" (269). The visionary appearance of Jesus shows how he will appear in the Church: "After this Jesus revealed himself again" (Jn 21:1). He shows that he continues to oversee the fledgling Church. His love is expressed to us by depriving us of the ability or the space to do anything fruitfully without him. The resulting renunciation of self-reliance demands patience and trust born of an authentic Christian asceticism (272).

Of the disciples who "were together" (Jn 21:2), Peter is named first, which gives him precedence as the head of the apostles. The named ones, though they have denied Christ in their own way, are the support for the nameless—for the "two others" that were with Peter, Nathanael, and the sons of Zebedee. Together, they form the one redeemed Church as they have all been redeemed after their denials of the Crucified Lord.

Something new begins in John 21:3. As the head, Peter initiates, "I am going fishing" (Jn 21:3). He is thinking of fish, but John, describing the scene, already has in mind the real catch. Peter does not invite or suggest, rather they all know that they must go along at his command. Speyr remarks that, "Whatever the Church does in general must also be done by the individual" (273). They all stand in obedience to Peter in whom they feel obedient to the Lord: "They know that the ties uniting them to Peter are the same that bind them to the Lord.... They are like children who were never disobedient because it never entered their heads to be so. That is true freedom" (272–273). Even today, Speyr writes, we are called to a childlike naïveté of obedience to the Lord. Together the disciples turn to something new as "they went out and got into the boat" (Jn 21:3). They join the expedition of the Church. This is the new, first voyage of the Church: "the period of schooling is over; theory is transferred into practice" (276). They are like a newlywed Bride adapted to the Bridegroom. In the Church's first excursion, they catch nothing, at least nothing visible. This is a really important ecclesiological principle. The first catch of the Church's initiative is a failure. It is night. They begin to do theology. They begin to speak of the Lord as they wait in the boat in the night and "at night, God acts" (282). God is forging their unity through their shared failure.

In John 21:4, "just as day was breaking," the fulfillment is Jesus standing on the beach. On their first excursion, they are about to learn that only the Lord can lead the Church, but at this stage "they are still not open enough to recognize him in every situation" (286). They will learn the ascetical principle of accepting failure as an invitation to accept the Lord even when there is no consolation. This ascetical failure will provide "a new possibility of entry into eternal life" (286).

The Lord speaks: "Children, have you any fish?" (Jn 21:5). He addresses them as children. He shows them how to contact others, that is, as simply as possible. The Lord, the male, presents himself in love, and desires for the Church, the female, to receive his love with love, in self-surrender and availability to his love: "Love wants only love" (287). Jesus says to them, "have you any fish?" The Church answers him in simple humility/humiliation, "No" (Jn 21:5). To the Lord their No sounds like a Yes because they have to admit to him their failure and even their inability: "In their No is contained that which they have humanly comprehended; in the yes that the Lord hears is contained that which his grace will make of their failure" (290).

The Lord gives a clear directive, "Cast the net on the right side of the boat" (Jn 21:6). When the disciples are at their strength's end, they are given a tiny penance after an infinite absolution. The Lord gives them a command to go and cast again. He gives to them a promise that they will catch some fish. The disciples think in their human way of knowing. They have done all they can, but they possess a "naïve movement of the good toward the good" (293). They obey the even greater expectation of the Lord. Called to the asceticism of obedience, they cast the net again. They are tired and dejected at their previous night's failure, but their asceticism leads them to obey even though their total emptiness stands in clear contrast to their future superabundance. The Lord will show them that his love is incomprehensible and superabundant lavishness. Obediently, they cast out into the deep. The Lord will fulfill *wholly* all that he promised them: "It was not until, in their obedience, the Lord had lent them his strength that they caught something" (298). They caught so much they "were not able to haul it in, for the quantity of fish" (Jn 21:6). The disparity between their human initiated efforts and the divine initiated effort is absolutely clear. They caught nothing by themselves and more than enough by the Lord.

John, the disciple whom Jesus loved, says, "It is the Lord" (Jn 21:7). The disciples only recognize the Lord because of the love of John (301). Love is the catalyst for belief and knowledge. Only in love can one interpret love. John, the one who loves, sees the Lord and shows this to Peter, the one who officiates. Here is where we find the mystery of the Eucharist. The one in love will recognize the Lord and point to him, but this love ties itself up with the official order of the Sacrament. No one can claim himself so personally united in love to the Lord not to need office and the sacraments. There is a unity of love for the Lord and the love for the Church, which John makes apparent. Office and love come together in the synthesis of the Lord: "When John says, *it is the Lord*, he utters, as it were, the first '*Hoc est corpus meum*'" (308). Peter goes out to the Lord, clothing himself first, to show the dignity of his office (311). In all of this, he chooses the quickest way, "He sprang into the sea" (Jn 21:7).

At the conclusion of the passage, the disciples are "dragging the net full of fish" (Jn 21:8), and Speyr ends with the observation that the Church is able to do nothing by herself. But since "the Lord was able to do everything" (312), the Church is able to do everything in the Lord. The Church made herself available to the Lord and he accomplished everything he desired for her. All has become abundance for the Church, as represented by these disciples, with more than enough fish for all of them. The Lord has provided this superabundance after their failure. We see quite a difference between how things started and how they ended (312).

In my analysis of this passage, three themes emerge—asceticism, obedience, and abundance. The first excursion for the Church was *asceticism*. In this voyage, they learned the failure of their own powers. They come back to land having no fish. They are sent out again in *obedience* to the Lord's command to cast their net once again. Only after this obedience to the Lord, having been prepared through the first excursion's asceticism, do the disciples receive the Lord's *abundance* on this second excursion. The three themes interlock with each other in a tightly woven trinity of meaning. Though many scholarly commentaries dismiss this passage as epilogue, through Speyr's spiritual exegesis, we can savor its rich theological content.

Having examined Speyr's interpretation of these verses, I would like to make a few observations about how Speyr brings the three themes of asceticism, obedience, and abundance to her teaching on how to read Scripture, which can be found in her thematic work, *They Followed His Call: Vocation and Asceticism.*[49]

The Christian's ascetical attitude is an urgent demand of Scripture because it is the same attitude as that of Jesus, the Incarnate Word of God. The Gospels contain many stories in which the Lord is tired and, yet, he welcomes the crowds who give him no rest. There is the story at the Mount of Olives in which the Lord admonishes the disciples to watch and pray with him (Lk 22:39–46). Similarly, in the passage of John 21:1–8 he teaches the disciples to go out fishing again in spite of their bodily weariness. Speyr is making the same point as Origen's, which I mentioned earlier. Scripture teaches us how to read Scripture. The Word has a total claim also to demand asceticism in our reading of Scripture (96). Asceticism involves man exerting and disciplining himself because Scripture is always calling for "more"—more reading, more exegesis, and more contemplation. No doubt, God's own strength intervenes, but only if one has already given oneself wholly over to the Word. When one has labored all night over the meaning of a passage and has caught no fish, the Lord will surely say, "Cast the net again." The disciples in John 21:1–8 needed to practice asceticism in order for the Lord to teach them that everything depends on the Lord. They had to tame "their impatience, put a rein on their impulse to question and on their thirst for instruction, in order to accept step by step, day by day, what was offered to them" (104). Speyr outlines the ascetical attitude required of any disciple who would study the Scriptures:

> He knows they are inspired, and he suspects the great correspondences they contain, the presence in them of the most profound truths and the abundance of their Christian teachings. In many places he sees heaven stand open and send down an enticing ray of its glory. But a human being cannot live in continual ecstasy or think constantly of eternity. The substance of contemplation

---

49 Adrienne von Speyr, *They Followed His Call: Vocation and Asceticism*, trans. Erasmo Leiva-Merikakis (San Francisco: Ignatius Press, 1986), 96–106. The following numbers in parentheses refer to this text.

must include the terrestrial and the present in a kind of analogy to the Incarnation. It must be content with what is small even when something great could practically be grasped, and it must also be able to detach itself even from what is small when this is demanded, thus remaining open for both extremes and everything in between (104–5).[50]

Reading Scripture calls for the attitude of asceticism. The attitude is needed to look into even the tiniest of words for a long time. It will always yield more as the Lord demands more.

Once God gives the insight, the exegete must respond in obedience. The exegete "must subordinate his 'knowing better' to the Lord's truly better wisdom" (100). Nevertheless, they surrender their "knowing better" to the Lord. They obey. The same attitude of obedience must accompany the interpreter of Scripture. The inspiration from God cannot be denied when it is given. It must be carried out. The Christian is also called in obedience to read the Scripture ecclesially because "Scripture was entrusted by the Lord to his Bride, the Church" (97). The exegete must be obedient to the mediating role of the Church.

Since obedience is demanded, abundance will come from it alone. This abundance will be always more than expected. Just as the disciples did not expect to catch any fish that morning—because they had caught none that night—the exegete will not expect the fruit that will come to him from the Lord. The Word offers more than one can expect. It is the Word who knows our needs and only the Word can care for them in his own "abundant manner" (104). The Lord is the one who provides through the Scriptures what the exegete needs and will provide abundantly.

These last remarks have juxtaposed the concept of the ecclesial mystic as exegete and Speyr's commentary on John 21:1–8. Certainly, I am using the form of propositional prose to critique propositional prose's monopoly on scriptural exegesis. Nevertheless, in my view, the exclusion of the ecclesial mystic's modes of commentary has meant that academic theology has been doing a disservice to the Church today. The ecclesial mystic should be seen

---

50 Here we also see Speyr's way of understanding how contemplation is informed by the literal and spiritual senses.

as an authentic exegete of Scripture. The theological fruitfulness of accepting the ecclesial mystic's exegesis can be seen in Speyr's commentary on John 21:1–8. The ways of the Lord call for the ascetical, obedient, and abundant reading of his Word. The ecclesial mystic provides this essential role from within the heart of the Church, the same heart of the Bride that beats with love for the Bridegroom, the same compassionate heart that ponders all the compassionate words of the Lord (Lk 2:19, 51).

Psalm 51: Miserere Mihi

HAVING MEDITATED ON THE IMPLICATIONS OF
Holy Saturday, I would like to conclude by turning to a critical
idea from an important book, Balthasar's slim volume *Love Alone
Is Credible*. He believed that the compassion of the Trinity is alone
credible. The previous theological models (cosmological or anthropological) are no longer compelling. However, love, he believed,
is authentically and exclusively credible. Love alone. Our journey
has been pursuing this mystical thought: the love of God alone
is credible in this age and all ages. He alone, out of complete
sacrificial love, has become alone to bring us out of our lonliness.
The following meditation on Psalm 51 will show us.

Meditation on Psalm 51

Psalm 51 is a penitential psalm (similar to Ps 6; 25; 32; 38; 130;
143). The title guides the interpretation: "To the choirmaster. A
Psalm of David, when Nathan the prophet came to him, after he
had gone in to Bathsheba." David composed this song after the
prophet Nathan confronted him about his adultery with Bathsheba
and his murder of Uriah, her husband (2 Sam 12). The psalm is a
personal prayer pleading for God's mercy, for God's compassionate
love. It demonstrates David's sincere repentance of his sins. In
this confession, we receive a revelation of the merciful nature of
God. This psalm instructs the congregation to seek God alone who
can heal and forgive (Ps 51:16-19) so that all in the community
can receive the compassion of the Lord's steadfast love. Like other
cries for mercy in Scripture, such as Moses's on Mount Sinai
(Ex 34:9), Psalm 51 dwells on the Lord, who desires only authentic
sacrifice—a heart that is humble and trusting.

Psalm 51:1. *"Have mercy on me, O God, according to your merciful love;
according to your abundant mercy blot out my transgressions."*

The mercy we are begging for is not a condescending mercy,
a sympathetic mercy, or a temporary mercy. The mercy we seek

from God is a mercy according to his steadfast love, according to his covenant love (*hesed* in Hebrew). He has already promised us that he will never leave us. We recall for him (more for us) that he has promised he will always be merciful. If Jesus teaches that we should be merciful seventy times seven times, think about the exponentially infinite multiplication of God's mercy toward us. Our transgressions, our sin, our lack of love has left us bloody. It has left the earth bloody. Just as you would take gauze to a profusely bleeding wound, the Lord lovingly applies his mercy to our wounding transgressions. For David, this compassion springs from the Lord's love alone; it is certainly not due to David's merit. While the terms "wash" and "cleanse" evoke the Levitical sacrifices of the temple worship, here they are all being performed not by the temple priesthood, but by God alone.

Psalm 51:2. *"Wash me thoroughly from my iniquity, and cleanse me from my sin!"*

The cleansing of the wound begins. The original mortal gash of David's iniquity has bled into everything else he has done. The sin is so damaging to every aspect of his life that the divine scrubbing must be as thorough. No sin, no iniquity can remain. The cleansing must be complete. When we look at David's life, we see so much good because there is so much of God in him. His heart is meant for God alone, but one afternoon while David's armies are fighting his battles, he notices the beautiful woman Bathsheba bathing on her roof. At the sight of her cleansing bath, David lusts to corrupt. The lust of his heart is realized in the adultery of their relationship. The sin of his heart desires another to partake of it if only to rationalize the initial disobedience. David's sin captures Bathsheba's innocence. David's sin grasps at Uriah's life, whose dignity David cannot destroy. For David and Bathsheba, their sin has soiled everything. The purification must be thorough. As a sign that the wages of sin is death, their child dies. For these two sinners, two innocents die. The mire of their hell necessitates the cleansing from heaven.

Psalm 51:3. *"For I know my transgressions, and my sin is ever before me."*

The guilt of David's sin will not depart from his vision of himself, the world, and his kingdom. He knows he is a sinner in the presence of his Lord. He knows well how this should make the Lord unapproachable. Much like the prophet Isaiah's vision of the Lord in the temple (Is 6), David is saying in a sense, "Woe is me! For I am lost; for I am a man of unclean lips, and I dwell in the midst of a people of unclean lips; for my eyes have seen the King, the LORD of hosts!" (Is 6:5). God is not to blame. David knows that it is his own fault. God is free not to forgive, not to have mercy, not to have compassion. For David, his sin is always before him as he interprets his standing before the all-knowing God. But David reveals a deep trust in the compassionate nature of God. He knows how wretched are his wounds and he offers them to the One alone who can heal him. David does not hide the transgression from his mind or his prayer. He knows it has occurred. He knows he is the one responsible. But he also knows the One alone who can heal him.

Psalm 51:4. *"Against you, you only, have I sinned, and done that which is evil in your sight, so that you are justified in your sentence and blameless in your judgment."*

Not only does David know he has crossed the boundary of sin, he also knows he has transgressed against the love of the Lord. And really this is true of all sin. He met the love of the Lord with his own lack of love. David's sin was a failure to love, a failure to love Bathsheba (by not honoring her marriage vow), a failure to love Uriah (by not honoring his marriage vow, his military service, and the dignity inherent in his personhood), and a failure to love the Lord (by not living according to God's eternal love, nature, and power). David perhaps thought initially he was only offending Bathsheba (rationalized by his power and her fear of his power), but quickly his sin destroys many others, including Uriah, their child, and the whole kingdom's stability. David in this verse becomes aware that the Lord will always be just in his sentences. God is not in the dock; David is. As David represents all of us estranged ones, God is not on trial; we are. The measure of our lives will not be our family, our friends, our nation's culture, or our ancestors. The Lord alone is the measure of our lives and his ruling measure cannot be doubted or tested for verification. In this moment, David exposes the truth that in sinning against Bathsheba and Uriah he sinned against the Lord who is love. David knows now that there is no private sin. Every action is connected and so every action touches the justice of the Lord who alone may judge, who alone can redeem.

Psalm 51:5. *"Behold, I was brought forth in iniquity, and in sin did my mother conceive me."*

The history of David's sin does not begin with him. The roots of his iniquity are in his family's ultimate genealogy. It does not begin with his father, his grandfather, or any intermediate ancestor. The iniquity beats from the hearts of Adam and Eve. As a human, David was brought forth into the disobedient iniquity of his first ancestors. He offers this realization not as a rationalization but as a diagnosis. His wounded nature needs a healing outside of his unchaste, murdering heart. His heart beats Adam's lustful and Cain's murderous blood. His healing will be through a transfusion from the Sacred Heart alone.

Psalm 51:6. *"Behold, you desire truth in the inward being; therefore teach me wisdom in my secret heart."*

The blood of the Sacred Heart alone is the Lord's truth beating within David's inward being. In the next verses, David turns to God's restorative presence manifested in God's truth (6), face (9), and Holy Spirit (11). In this verse, David appeals to God alone who is Truth itself. He desires this truth in his deepest interior. His secret heart invites now only what God alone declares about his own heart.[1] He invites the compassionate presence of God alone to speak to him the truth of his authentic identity. He opens all boundaries to the Lord's invasion of truth. He allows heart to speak unto heart (*cor ad cor loquitur*).

Psalm 51:7. *"Purge me with hyssop, and I shall be clean; wash me, and I shall be whiter than snow."*

These branches of hyssop act as an astringent. When dipped in water or blood, they are good for sprinkling, and were used in Levitical cleansing ceremonies (Lev 14:6; Num 19:6). At the Cross, we read about the hyssop branch dipped in sour wine offered to the dying Jesus (Jn 19:29). The verse in John connects

---

1 Balthasar explored this idea in his mystical work, *Heart of the World*, trans. Erasmo S. Leiva-Merikakis (San Francisco: Ignatius Press, 1979).

to Psalm 69:21 (see also Mt 27:34, 48). The sour wine could be only a moistening of Jesus's throat to proclaim, "It is finished" (Jn 19:30), but could it not also and more significantly (and John would be the one to do it) connect this moment to the Passover ceremony in which blood is sprinkled on the door posts using a hyssop branch (Ex 12:22)? If so, John is connecting the original Passover to the Crucifixion of Jesus Christ and David provides the link, as it were, to the hyssop branch being used for the cleansing of his sin. We are made clean by this same hyssop branch that was offered to Jesus on the Cross. He tasted the astringent hyssop that we can now taste. He became sin for us, so that we can be made clean. Only with this blood-soaked hyssop branch can we be washed more luminescent than snow. David longs for a complete cleansing. He desires not an arbitrary justification, but a true, transformative sanctification. He wants to be thoroughly cleansed and not just covered. He wants to become again light.

Psalm 51:8. *"Make me hear joy and gladness; let the bones which you have broken rejoice."*
    David believes the Lord is the source of joy and gladness. Joy is not a man-made effort or choice, but a supernatural virtue. David longs for the joy that comes from truth, purging, cleansing, that is, from the compassion of the Lord. Yet David is also clear about who crushed him. The Lord crushed him so he can rejoice once again. God permits David to feel crushed under the weight of his sins. His broken bones will rejoice in the new life of forgiveness. God's compassion will bring him joy through judgment and justification. David is clear that God's presence does mean judgment, but this judgment is not the end of his life. God's compassionate, steadfast love will break David to release joy. God's mastery over our bones (as in Ps 38:3) has wonderful canonical parallels, such as Ezekiel's vision of the dry bones rising to new life (Ezek 37). David prays in faith to the Lord who can make these dry bones rejoice again.

Psalm 51:9. *"Hide your face from my sins, and blot out all my iniquities."*
    David explores in this verse the relationship between hiding and blotting. Both actions are active on God's part. God's honor would be preserved as he turns his face away, while also performing the

cleansing. David wants the purity of the Lord to be honored, but he is also aware that his impurity needs the Lord's purification. God does not think this way, as he offers his presence. He will never be made impure by his involvement with the world of sin, just as darkness cannot destroy light. David acknowledges how much he does need the Lord even as he feels so far from him. Feeling helpless, he calls for help.

Psalm 51:10. *"Create in me a clean heart, O God, and put a new and right spirit within me."*

David's prayer has become my prayer. A recreated, clean heart (Ps 51:10) means a "heart of flesh" (Ezek 36:26) beating with enlivening blood. But the heart must work with the spirit. A cleansed heart is a right (steadfast) spirit. Being formed into a new creation requires that God transform David's spirit to reflect God's Holy Spirit.

Psalm 51:11. *"Cast me not away from your presence, and take not your holy Spirit from me."*

David's prayer begs for the Lord not to take away the Spirit that anointed and empowered his kingship (1 Sam 16:13–14), but perhaps something more is happening here. David could be praying for the cleansing, enlivening power of God's Holy Spirit to shape his heart rightly, not according to God's just judgment, but according to his compassionate mercy. Even as David confronts his sin, he presses into God's presence as his only path. As Jesus will reveal in the beatitudes, David knows that he is "poor in spirit" and realizes that the only remedy for this poverty is the Kingdom of Heaven, and the presence of God. The chaotic waters of David's stirred up conscience are being calmed by the Lord's wisdom. The Spirit, through the prophet Nathan, has made a hurricane of the waters, only to create a new heart in David.

Psalm 51:12. *"Restore to me the joy of your salvation, and uphold me with a willing spirit."*

David is asking that his spirit of kingly dignity, his identity and mission in the Lord be restored to him; that the dignity of dancing with joy before the presence of the Lord be restored. He had known that he was chosen and saved by the Lord; he asks for his knowledge that God had chosen to be with him to be restored. Perhaps he knows he can be saved, but here he is praying for the *joy* of being saved—he wishes to have again this experience of the joy of the Lord being his strength. When someone is alone, perhaps he could articulate that he will be alright at some point, yet the joy is missing. I may be saved, but do I know the joy of what that means that I am saved?

Psalm 51:13. *"Then I will teach transgressors your ways, and sinners will return to you."*
David now realizes that the pain he has caused his people and his God will be used for good. He is learning so that he can teach others and more lost ones will be found. Paul speaks about this (2 Cor 1:4). In God's way, the lonely will come to know his compassionate presence and then will be able to share that compassionate presence with others. We have to remember it was Nathan who reached out to David, yes, convicting him, but also instructing him about repentance. The psalmist David is now giving the same instruction to the congregation. From these sins of David and this psalm, how many have been restored? What great good has come from the words of this psalm through the ages?

Psalm 51:14. *"Deliver me from bloodguilt, O God, O God of my salvation, and my tongue will sing aloud of your deliverance."*
As Jesus taught us to pray, Deliver us from evil (Mt 6:13). These verses turn the private prayer of David into corporate worship. When God is guiding the healing, he transforms suffering isolation into connected worship. Through God's compassion, my pain in isolated suffering becomes our joy in communal worshiping. Jesus tells us that the heavens rejoice more over the return of one sinner than the ninety-nine righteous (Lk 15:7). And indeed who better to declare God's righteousness than one who has been forgiven such a great sin? Like Cain (Gen 4:11-16), David, who is guilty because of taking the blood of Uriah (2 Sam 11:17; 12:9), prays to the Lord that he be spared the just revenge. And indeed, God is not interested in revenge (although it is the prerogative of God alone to take revenge—Deut. 32:35, cf. Rom 12:19; "I, the LORD, love justice" Is 61:8). Our God is not the God of revenge, but of salvation. He desires not destructive vengeance, but healing restoration.

Psalm 51:15. *"O Lord, open my lips, and my mouth shall show forth your praise."*

All those who pray the Liturgy of the Hours begin by reciting this verse while also crossing their lips. "O Lord, open my lips." It presumes everything that has gone before—confession, humility, and a new affirmation to live this day in the Lord. David shows us that our prayer is not our own. It is the Lord's word in us. Our subjective word is overtaken into God's objective Word.[2] My mouth cries out, "Am I alone!" But then my mouth is filled with the words of praise: "I am not alone!" The Lord is near. And this prayer indicates that David has received a cleansed heart that can now speak praise—for from the heart, the mouth speaks (Mt 15:18; Lk 6:45).

Psalm 51:16. *"For you take no delight in sacrifice; were I to give a burnt offering, you would not be pleased."*

The follower of the Lord must delight in what the Lord delights in. God's joys become my joys. The whole economy of sacrifice established in the Torah has one central goal that is captured in the next verse. It is the teaching of Jesus Christ and becomes the central argument of the Letter to the Hebrews. The early story of David was one of Samuel learning to see as God sees, looking for the next one to anoint not based upon birth or stature, but on a heart for the Lord. While David's actions do not justify him in the sight of the Lord, the disposition of David's heart toward the Lord changes everything. God desires the "living sacrifice" (Rom 12:1).

Psalm 51:17. *"The sacrifice acceptable to God is a broken spirit; a broken and contrite heart, O God, you will not despise."*

Why does the Lord now require a broken spirit? To all who are lonely and broken hearted: "The LORD is near to the brokenhearted, and saves the crushed in spirit" (Ps 34:18). A heart broken is a heart ready for healing and growth. The grain of wheat must fall and die to bear fruit (Jn 12:24). The Lord can reveal his power to a heart contrite and repentant. The whole of Paul's teaching to the Corinthians and the Philippians is contained in verses which declare that the weakness of men reveals the strength of God

---

2 Sutton, *Heaven Opens*, 49–60.

(2 Cor 12:9-10; Phil 2:1-11). The psalmist David prompts the congregation to realize that God embraces the broken. Though men are prone to despise the broken (Jesus's story of the Good Samaritan captures this trait—Lk 10:25-37), the Lord draws near because of his mercy and compassion.

Psalm 51:18. *"Do good to Zion in your good pleasure; rebuild the walls of Jerusalem."*

David now has the congregation pray for the whole of Zion (see Ps 69:35; 122:6), for the entirety of God's people. This song of personal contrition is also a plea for a blessing upon the whole people, to deliver *us* from evil by building strong protective walls. These walls will be built of God's compassion for David's brokenness, and founded on God's covenant promise to all his people. In a real sense the whole community is a forgiven, being-healed people. They have all fallen short of the glory of God (Rom 3:23). When they all return to the Lord with a broken, contrite heart, the Lord will build up the walls of Jerusalem, walls that protect his people's intimate relationship with the Lord.

Psalm 51:19. *"Then will you delight in right sacrifices, in burnt offerings and whole burnt offerings; then bulls will be offered on your altar."*

God's delight is first in a humble contrite heart and only then in a whole burnt offering (Deut 33:10), according to the proper rites (Ps 4:5), that is in keeping with the righteousness of the Lord (Mal 3:3). The response to receiving forgiveness is worship. The response to a broken spirit is worship. The response to restoration is worship. Do not miss this point. The whole of Psalm 51 is worship, beginning with the knowledge of one's sin, through prayer for mercy, to finally accepting forgiveness. The whole of the way of salvation is worship, a sacrifice of praise from a contrite or restored heart. It is all worship of the Lord, from the brokenhearted in whom the Lord delights.

We can come to understand David and his brokenness ("I can count all my bones," Ps 22:17), while acknowledging that he freely walked into his own tragedy. He chose these sins, these hells. However, he also chose to repent with a humble and contrite heart and this graced choice makes all the difference. The Lord approaches this brokenness with restoration. To those who do not choose the sins and yet live in these hells, the Lord also comes. To all whose bones are broken, the Lord reaches out. The Lord comes close to all who are in the pit.

In the aftermath of the September 11, 2001 attacks on the World Trade Center, pages from the Gospel of Matthew were found fused to one of the collapsed steel beams.[3] This fascinating artifact of the horrendous tragedy, which can be seen at the 9/11 Memorial Museum, reveals in one of many ways God's presence in this hellish event. The message was fused in the depths of this hell. The Word of God spoke in this pit and spoke again Jesus's words on the Sermon on the Mount, "Ye have heard that it hath been said, An eye for an eye, and a tooth for a tooth: But I say unto you, That ye resist not evil: but whosoever shall smite thee on thy right cheek, turn to him the other also" (Mt 5:38–48, KJV).

This generation is the most fatherless—suicidal, addicted, betrayed, forgotten. But this is the generation that will be found. This is the generation to which the Father's merciful love will be revealed on a scale never seen before. This is the generation whose stormy loneliness will be calmed by the peace of the compassionate presence of God.

From Pain to Paint

We are now drawing to the end of our theological meditations on compassion. Let us remember that there are two Holy Saturdays (sabbaths).

The First Holy Saturday is the seventh day in the Book of Genesis (2:1–3). God beholds his creation and having declared it "very good," he dwells with his creation, with his people through his resting presence. The Second Holy Saturday is the day between Good Friday and Easter Sunday, which has been the focus of our discussion. These two Holy Saturdays belong together. The first is about creation. The second is about redemption. But they are both about God's compassionate presence, God alone present.

What happens on the second Holy Saturday in the Son's descent to hell? God is rescuing his creation, that creation that he saw in the beginning and declared very good. He's also saying that on

---

3 David Dunlap, "At 9/11 Memorial, an Enduring Message of Forgiveness," *New York Times*, September 25, 2015, http://www.nytimes.com/live/pope-visit-2015/an-enduring-message-of-forgiveness/.

this second Holy Saturday, and every Holy Saturday in our lives too. But with this second Saturday, it is very good because he is making it new—"Behold, I make all things new" (Rev 21:5). That's what we should ponder in our hearts.

Scripture opens us to the Lord. I love the verse, Romans 8:28. It is all about expectancy—"We know that in everything God works for good with those who love him, who are called according to his purpose." It is a beautiful word that teaches Christians that they need to know that God is working in everything. God is working in everything for those that love him, for his purposes. Not for our purposes but for *his* purposes. Expect God to be present; that is foundational in the Christian life.

Now, later in the same chapter in Romans, Paul writes, "For I am sure that neither death, nor life, nor angels, nor principalities, nor things present, nor things to come, nor powers, nor height, nor depth, nor anything else in all creation, will be able to separate us from the love of God in Christ Jesus our Lord" (Rom 8:38–39). It is a beautiful phrase that reemphasizes that nothing can separate us from God's love. Nothing can separate us. Notice how this verse begins: "Neither death, nor life" (Rom 3:38). In life, we can understand that God is present because he is the source of life. But the verse says he is also present in death. In death, we expect absence. When we see a body that was alive, presence is missing. But nothing can separate us from the love of God, not even death, "even death on a cross" (Phil 2:8). And as we think of death, we will also have to think about Sheol, after death. Bearing in mind the lesson of Romans 8:38, we should also go to Psalm 139:7–9: "Where shall I go from your Spirit? Or where shall I flee from your presence? If I ascend to heaven, you are there! If I make my bed in Sheol, you are there!"

To delve into this word deeply, let's consider three points: Joseph, Mary, and why we should not be afraid.

When we think about Joseph in Scripture, I want us to remember all three Josephs: Joseph the son of Jacob, Joseph the husband of Mary, and Joseph of Arimathea. These three Josephs belong together because all of them had a Holy Saturday moment. What do I mean by a Holy Saturday moment? I mean feeling abandoned by man and God. The first Joseph, Joseph son of Jacob, has a dream that all of his brothers are going to bow to him. He tells this to his brothers. Even though his father, Jacob, loves Joseph very much, the brothers rebel in hatred. As when we read the story of Cain and Abel, we read again of a brother's hatred. Like Cain, Joseph's brothers ask, "Am I my brother's keeper?" (Gen 4:9). They contemplate killing Joseph. Rueben persuades the others to have Joseph enslaved instead—at least that way they will get paid. They lower Joseph into a pit. It is only the beginning of Joseph's Holy Saturday experience. It will get worse. While the brothers wait for someone to sell Joseph to, Joseph, suffering in this underworld, must have wondered, "Why have my brothers put me here? What's going to happen to me? Am I going to perish in these depths?"

Joseph is sold into slavery and lives much of his life enslaved in Egypt. Initially, he becomes a servant in the house of Potiphar, captain of the guard. When it seems Joseph's faithfulness has earned him some success, Potiphar's wife takes a liking to him, and propositions him. Joseph resists her, and she gets her revenge by having him jailed on a false charge of rape. Once again, he is imprisoned and thrown into a dungeon.

If you've been counting, that is two trips underground for Joseph so far. Here in this pit, he is abandoned again. He has been good and faithful to God's ways and yet everything fell apart. It does not make sense. This was not because of anything he did. He did not deserve to be sold into slavery. He does not deserve to be punished for rape. Though innocent, he is abandoned and forgotten.

Due to Joseph's faithfulness, the Lord guides him out of the depths to the heights of kingdom. The Spirit speaks through the dreams of Pharaoh's cup bearer and rescues Joseph.

These experiences of abandonment place Joseph in a position to lead Egypt, his family, and the world through the depths of a famine.

In the last chapter of Genesis, Joseph's brothers are gathered around him after the death of their father. His brothers wonder if Joseph will abandon them now that their father has passed away. In this moment of anxiety, Joseph speaks one the most beautiful lines in all of the Bible.

Joseph says to his brothers, "As for you, you meant evil against me; but God meant it for good" (Gen 50:20). He is clear about the evil of his brothers trafficking him. But he is even more clear about the goodness of the Lord. The evil of man is transfigured by the goodness of God: "By his stripes, we are healed" (Is 53:5).

Let's explore the next Joseph in Scripture: Joseph, the husband of Mary and the foster father of Jesus. Joseph knows disappointment. In his mind, he had made the many plans any engaged man might. He had imagined the beauty of family life with his soon-to-be wife. He had made plans, as a carpenter would, of a home full of love and warmth. But God has other plans. The betrothed Mary is pregnant.

On that day's annunciation, Joseph must have felt the deepest abandonment. All he planned is destroyed. He is in his Holy Saturday. He is another Joseph in another pit of abandonment. All of his plans for his life are undone. Yet he tries to remain faithful to his love for Mary and to protect her. He seeks to hide her from the shame (Mt 1:19). He tries to find a way to be good to her even though he mistakenly thinks that evil has been done to him. But God means it for good.

I like Joseph. He is like so many of us, trying to figure out the right thing to do in what feels like a horrible situation. Joseph has not yet given up on trying to imitate the goodness of God, but he does not yet understand the goodness of God. To this dreaming Joseph, God shows that his plans for his family will be transfigured into the plan for the redemption of the family of man. His disrupted life in Nazareth will be used to reveal the goodness of the God of Nazareth. His age of disappointment will bring forth the joy of the ages.

The first two Josephs did not understand the reason for the pit, but they remained faithful. Their descent made them able to see the descent of God in their lives. Their pain led them into a new way to praise. The same is true of the third Joseph of Scripture, Joseph of Arimathea, the patron saint of Holy Saturday. As I write this chapter on Holy Saturday, I think of all that changed for Joseph during these days. As a rich man, he had planned his retirement, including his burial place. He owned a man-made cave meant for him, but on this day, he will come to see that the cave was God-made for the Son of Man.

We think of Joseph of Arimathea as a distinguished leader in the Jewish community in Jerusalem. He was a member of the Sanhedrin, the very council which, in a clandestine trial, declared

Jesus worthy of destruction. The secret Sanhedrin destroys all of Joseph's plans overnight. And Joseph chooses to walk the dead Jesus to his burial place.

Joseph was placed here on Holy Saturday by the Father to accompany the Son in his darkest days. The Son of God looked to the Father and cried, "My God, my God, why have you forsaken me?" The Father prepared Joseph to bring his son's body to rest for three days in that rich man's grave. Already the Father is bringing his hidden but deeply intimate goodness to his Son, by appointing a Joseph to accompany him into the underworld. And there Joseph meets God as God meets Joseph.

All three Josephs in Scripture journeyed through Holy Saturdays. They each saw their plans completely destroyed and yet they trusted in the goodness of God. As these Josephs felt the sorrow of abandonment, so did the Son. The first Joseph, the second Joseph, and the third Joseph walked into the dark cave of darkened dreams. And so too did the Son walk into this den of death. In this darkness of despair, we must ask, who turned out the lights?

At the end of this meditation on the Holy Saturday of God, let's ask the most important questions: Who turned out the lights? Who allowed this to happen? Yes, sometimes hells come from our families, work, nations, and the world. But, what about the hells that are permitted by God?

In the end, we turn to Mary. One of my favorite images of her was painted by Sassoferrato in the mid-seventeenth century. Mary is bowed in prayer, gently receiving wisdom from the Lord as she treasures these revelations in her heart. Covering her is an intensely blue cloak from which eminate overwhelming waves of blue, bringing to mind an ocean tempest.

In the seventeenth century, this particular blue was difficult to achieve. It required lapis lazuli, a mineral more costly than gold. Producing this tint was so expensive that it came to be used for only one purpose—painting Mary's mantle.

To make the paint, the precious lapis lazuli stone had to be crushed. What about the geological history of this stone? In geological terms, Sassoferrato's paint has a millennial history. We could say that God formed that rare gem deep in the underworld knowing that in millennia it would be given to his Handmaid. God sees everything, knows everything, is present to everything. To put it too simply but still profoundly, God prepared this precious stone ages before there was a Sassoferrato or a Mary. Before stone, Sassoferrato, Mary, and we who view it, God had a plan for these transformational encounters.

I want you to think about the disappointment that you have had in your life, the being crushed, the being pulverized that you have known in your life and have seen in the lives of others. We have to see as God sees. He sees futures of transformational encounters that we cannot possibly imagine. Think of that lapis lazuli. It was refined in crushing heat and pressure in the depths of the earth. If I feel the crushing pressure of being in the depths, I must steadfastly hope in the future God is preparing me for. All is darkness in this underground cavern of refinement, until the Lord mines me, and transforms me into a color in the divine artist's portrait of redemption. For those ages below ground, I may not know that I am beautiful. And in that darkness who could see it but the Lord alone? He knows I am precious even as I dwell in the sunless depths. He knows that when I'm pulverized into a paint and the sun illuminates me, my beauty will radiate.

We have this promise spoken over us. Our pain will be used to paint a beautiful image, an image that will radiate glorious triumph. Let us praise the Lord even in the pit, rejoicing in the one who turned out the lights, so that we can be refined, crushed, pulverized, into a radiant ultramarine blue.

On Holy Saturday, Mary could not yet see that her Son, in the depths of the earth, crushed by hell, would rise to be the light to the nations. But she believed that God the Father would bring her Son in the Holy Spirit back to her. Her faith was the one Easter light that continued to burn even on Holy Saturday. She believed that her son's pain in the depths would be transformed into the beauty that restores humanity back into the intimate union with the Father by the compassionate love of the Holy Spirit.

When our three Josephs and now our mother Mary experienced their Holy Saturday, when they asked that question, "who turned out the lights?" the song they sang was of praise to the Lord in their abandonment—to trust in him even in depths of hell. They sang Psalm 139: "Where shall I go from your Spirit? Or where shall I flee from your presence? If I ascend to heaven, you are there! If I make my bed in Sheol, you are there!"

When we worship together surrounded by amazing people singing beautiful psalms, we are storing up in preparation for the time of famine. We are ascending into heaven in our worship together, delighting in God's presence so that when we're in Sheol, when we are in hell, when we are in loneliness and tragedy, we can still sing of the Lord's compassionate presence, "Then my soul shall rejoice in the LORD, exulting in his deliverance" (Ps 35:9). We will offer that last worship as we give up our last breath.

Why Are You Afraid?

There are many wonderful stories in Matthew 8, but let's just look at Matthew 8:23–27, the calming of the sea: "When he got into the boat, his disciples followed him. And behold, there arose a great storm on the sea, so that the boat was being swamped by the waves; but he was asleep. And they went and woke him, saying, 'Save us, Lord; we are perishing!' And he said to them, 'Why are you afraid, O men of little faith?' Then he rose and rebuked the winds and the sea; and there was great calm. And the men marveled saying, 'What sort of a man is this, that even winds and sea obey Him?'"

What a beautiful passage to mediate on when you are in a Holy Saturday of loneliness! Jesus and the apostles got into the boat, they set sail, the storm started, and Jesus slept. Historical studies concerning the Sea of Galilee at this time suggest that this boat may have had some sort of room below decks. Did Jesus descend to this lower room? Did he go down into the bowels of the boat and fall asleep? It had been a long day of preaching and healing. He is exhausted. His mind is not on the storm but on rest.

The apostles, however, have their mind on the storm. In our storms of pain and disappointment, our mind is buffeted by wind and waves. The disciples frantically seek out the Lord. Their fear breaks their courage, but they present their fear to the Lord and worship. When the storms are raging around them, they do not curse the storm. They worship Jesus: "Save us, Lord; we are perishing."

Dear reader, I do not know where you are on your journey. Maybe you are on this same boat with the wild winds and storming sea. Maybe you are in a kind of Holy Saturday. If so, then pray with the apostles, and with me, "Save us, Lord; we are perishing."

As you pray that prayer, please hear what Jesus says in response: "Why are you afraid?" He does not rebuke his disciples for their lack of faith. He encourages them. Why are you afraid?

It is as if he is saying, "Yes, there is a storm raging around you. You have done the right thing by coming to me. Do not be afraid." Then he rebukes the winds and sea. Calm returns and so does faith and wonder. He turns pain into paint. He turns fear into faith. Our declarations of disappointment, our stories of storms are going to be used by the Lord for generations to paint a beautiful picture of his glorious faithful presence. He is here—why am I afraid?

He who is the Lord of the winds and seas, who possesses the keys of Death and Hades, speaks his compassionate presence in every storm, death, and hell. He is here; where can we go from his compassionate presence?

BIBLIOGRAPHY

Allen, Woody. *Without Feathers*. New York: Ballantine Books, 1986.

Alter, Robert. *The World of Biblical Literature*. New York: Basic Books, 1992.

———. *The Art of Biblical Narrative*. New York: Basic Books, 2011.

Anselm. *Proslogian, with the Replies of Gaunilo and Anselm*. Translated by Thomas Williams. Indianapolis: Hackett Publishing, 1995.

Apostoloi, Andrew. *Fatima for Today: The Urgent Marian Message of Hope*. San Francisco: Ignatius Press, 2012.

Aquinas, Thomas. *Summa Theologica*. Translated by Fathers of the English Dominican Province. 4 vols. New York: Benziger, 1948.

———. *Commentary on the Gospel of St. John*. Translated by James Weisheipel and Fabian Larcher. 2 vols. Albany: Magi Books, 1998.

Augustine. *On Faith and Works*. Translated by Gregory J. Loubardo. New York: Newman Press, 1988.

———. *Confessions*. Translated by Henry Chadwick. New York: Oxford University Press, 1991.

———. *On the Free Choice of the Will*. Translated by Thomas White. Indianapolis: Hackett Publishing Company, 1993.

———. *On Christian Teaching*. Translated by R.P.H. Green. New York: Oxford University Press, 1997.

———. *The Trinity*. Fathers of the Church Patristic Series, Vol. 45. Translated by Stephen McKenna. Washington, D.C.: Catholic University of America Press, 2002.

Bacovcin, Elen, translator. *The Way of the Pilgrim and the Pilgrim Continues His Way*. New York: Doubleday, 1978.

Balthasar, Hans Urs von. *The Moment of Christian Witness*. Translated by Richard Beckley. Glen Rock, NJ: Newman, 1969.

———. *Elucidations*. Translated by John Riches. San Francisco: Ignatius Press, 1975.

———. *Heart of the World*. Translated by Erasmo Leiva-Merikakis. San Francisco: Ignatius Press, 1980.

———. *First Glance at Adrienne von Speyr*. Translated by Antje Lawry and Sergia Englund, O.C.D. San Francisco: Ignatius Press, 1981.

———. *The Glory of the Lord: A Theological Aesthetics*. Edited by Joseph Fessio, S.J., and John Riches. 7 vols. San Francisco: Ignatius Press, 1982–1989.

———. *The Christian State of Life*. Translated by Mary Frances McCarthy. San Francisco: Ignatius Press, 1983.

———. *Origen: Spirit and Fire: A Thematic Anthology of His Writings*. Translated by Robert Daly. Washington, D.C.: Catholic University of America Press, 1984.

——. *New Elucidations*. Translated by Mary Theresilde Skerry. San Francisco: Ignatius Press, 1986.

——. "God Is His Own Exegete." *Communio: International Catholic Review* 4 (1986): 280–87.

——. *Prayer*. Translated by Graham Harrison. San Francisco: Ignatius Press, 1986.

——. *Truth Is Symphonic: Aspects of Christian Pluralism*. Translated by Graham Harrison. San Francisco: Ignatius Press, 1987.

——. *Theo-Drama*. Translated by Graham Harrison. 5 vols. San Francisco: Ignatius Press, 1988–98.

——. *Test Everything: Hold Fast to What Is Good: An Interview with Hans Urs von Balthasar by Angelo Scola*. Translated by Maria Shrady. San Francisco: Ignatius Press, 1989.

——. "Theology and Sanctity." Translated by A.V. Littledale and Alexander Dru. In *Explorations in Theology*, 181–209. San Francisco: Ignatius Press, 1989.

——. *Unless You Become Like This Child*. Translated by Erasmo Leiva-Merikakis. San Francisco: Ignatius Press, 1991.

——. *Two Sisters in the Spirit: Thérèse of Lisieux and Elizabeth of the Trinity*. Translated by Donald Nichols, Anne Englund Nash, and Dennis Martin. San Francisco: Ignatius Press, 1992.

——. "Patristics, Scholastics, and Us." Translated by Edward Oakes. *Communio* 24 (1997): 347–96.

——. *Paul Struggles with His Congregation: The Pastoral Message of the Letters to the Corinthians*. Translated by Brigitte Bojarska. San Francisco: Ignatius Press, 1992.

——. *My Work: In Retrospect*. Translated by Brian McNeil, Kenneth Batinovich, John Saward, and Kelly Hamilton. San Francisco: Ignatius Press, 1993.

——. *Our Task: A Report and a Plan*. Translated by John Saward. San Francisco: Ignatius Press, 1994.

——. *The Grain of Wheat: Aphorisms*. Translated by Erasmo Leiva-Merikakis. San Francisco: Ignatius Press, 1995.

——. *Mysterium Paschale: The Mystery of Easter*. Translated by Aidan Nichols. San Francisco: Ignatius Press, 2000.

——. *The Christian and Anxiety*. Translated by Dennis Martin and Michael Miller. San Francisco: Ignatius Press, 2000.

——. *Theo-Logic: Theological Logical Theory*. 3 vols. San Francisco: Ignatius Press, 2000–2005.

——. *Cosmic Liturgy: The Universe According to Maximus the Confessor*. Translated by Brian E. Daley. San Francisco: Ignatius Press, 2003.

——. *Epilogue*. Translated by Edward Oakes. San Francisco: Ignatius Press, 2004.

——. *Love Alone Is Credible.* Translated by D. C. Schindler. San Francisco: Ignatius Press, 2004.

——. *Dare We Hope "That All Men Be Saved?": With a Short Discourse on Hell.* Translated by David Kipp and Lothar Krauth. Second edition. San Francisco: Ignatius Press, 2014.

Basil. *On the Holy Spirit.* Translated by Blondfield Jackson. Crestwood, NY: St. Vladimir's Seminary Press, 1980.

——. *Basil of Caesarea: Christian, Humanist, Ascetic: A Sixteen-Hundredth Anniversary Symposium.* 2 vols. Toronto: Pontifical Institute of Medieval Studies, 1981.

Benedict XVI. "Message." https://w2.vatican.va/content/benedict-xvi/en/messages/pont-messages/2005/documents/hf_ben-xvi_mes_20051006_von-balthasar.html.

——. "Homily at Esplanade of the Shrine of Our Lady of Fátima." https://w2.vatican.va/content/benedict-xvi/en/homilies/2010/documents/hf_ben-xvi_hom_20100513_fatima.html.

Berthold, George, editor and translator. "The Trial of Maximus." In *Maximus Confessor: Selected Writings.* New York: Paulist Press, 1985.

Bonaventure. *The Soul's Journey Into God.* In *Bonaventure.* Translated by Ewert Cousins. New York: Paulist Press, 1978.

Brown, Peter. *The Body and Society: Men, Women, and Sexual Renunciation in Early Christianity.* New York: Columbia University Press, 1988.

——. *Augustine of Hippo: A Biography.* Revised Edition. Berkeley: University of California Press, 2000.

Burrows, Ruth. *Interior Castle Explored: St. Teresa's Teaching on the Life of Deep Union with God.* Mahwah, NJ: Hidden Spring, 2007.

Byrne, David. *How Music Works.* San Francisco: McSweeney's, 2012.

Carey, Patrick, editor. "The Creed of Nicaea," vol. 1 of *Marquette History of Theology: From the Primitive Church to 1350.* (n.p.n.d.)

Clément, Olivier. *The Roots of Christian Mysticism.* Translated by Theodore Berkeley. Second edition. Hyde Park, NY: New City Press, 1995.

Coffey, David. *Grace: The Gift of the Holy Spirit.* Sydney, Australia: Catholic Institute of Sydney, 1979.

——. *Deus Trinitas: The Doctrine of the Triune God.* New York: Oxford University Press, 1999.

Collins, John. *The Apocalyptic Imagination: An Introduction to Jewish Apocalyptic Literature.* Grand Rapids, MI: Eerdmans, 2010.

Con-solatio Missionaries. *Come Abide: Con-solatio, a Ministry of Presence.* Brooklyn, NY: Angelico Press, 2021.

Cossec, Igumen Symeon. "The Search for God in the Hesychast Tradition." *Sourozh: A Journal of Orthodox Life and Thought* 73 (1998): 30–36.

Costas, Orlando. *Christ Outside the Gate: Mission Beyond Christendom.* Maryknoll, NY: Orbis Books, 1982.

Crouch, Andy. *Culture Making: Recovering Our Creative Calling.* Downers Grove, IL: IVP Books, 2008.

D'Arcy, M. C. *St. Thomas Aquinas.* Westminster, MD: Newman, 1954.

Daley, Brian E. "Origen's *De Principiis*: A Guide to the Principles of Christian Scriptural Interpretation." In *Nova et Vetera: Patristic Studies in Honor of Thomas Patrick Halton*, edited by John Petruccione. Washington, D.C.: Catholic University of America Press, 1998.

Dauphinais, Michael and Matthew Levering. *Reading John with St. Thomas Aquinas: Theological Exegesis and Speculative Theology.* Washington, D.C.: Catholic University of America Press, 2005.

Del Colle, Ralph. *Christ and the Spirit: Spirit-Christology in Trinitarian Perspective.* New York: Oxford University Press, 1994.

———. "Holy Spirit: Presence, Power, Person." *Theological Studies* 62 (2001): 322–40.

Delio, Illia. "Bonaventure's Metaphysics of the Good." *Theological Studies* 60 (1999): 228–46.

Dempsey, Michael, editor. *Trinity and Election in Contemporary Theology.* Grand Rapids, MI: Eerdmans, 2011.

Denzinger, Heinrich. *Enchiridion Symbolorum: A Compendium of Creeds, Definitions, and Declarations of the Catholic Church.* San Francisco: Ignatius Press, 2012.

de Paul, Vincent and Louise de Marillac. *Rules, Conferences, and Writings.* Edited by Frances Ryan and John Rybolt. New York: Paulist, 1995.

Dionysius. *Pseudo-Dionysius: The Complete Works.* Edited and translated by Paul Rorem and Colm Luibhéid. New York: Paulist Press, 1987.

Dobbie-Bateman, A. F. "St. Seraphim of Sarov." In *A Treasury of Russian Spirituality*, edited by G. P. Fedotov. New York: Sheed and Ward, 1948.

Dulles, Avery. "Who Can Be Saved?" *First Things*, February 2008.

Dunlap, David. "At 9/11 Memorial, an Enduring Message of Forgiveness." *New York Times*, September 25, 2015.

Dupuis, Jaques, and J. Neuner, editors. *The Christian Faith: In the Doctrinal Documents of the Catholic Church*, Seventh Edition. New York: Alba House, 2001.

Eliot, T. S. *Collected Poems 1909–1962.* New York: Harcourt Brace & Company, 1991.

Emery, Gilles. *The Trinitarian Theology of Thomas Aquinas.* Translated by Francesa Aran Murphy. Oxford: Oxford University Press, 2010.

Fanning, Steven. *Mystics of the Christian Tradition.* New York: Routledge, 2001.

Flannery, Austin, editor. *Dei verbum*, in vol. 1 of *Vatican Council II, New Revised Edition.* Northport, NY: Costello Publishing Company, 1996.

Donal Anthony Foley. *Medjugorje Complete: The Definitive Account of the Visions and Visionaries.* Brooklyn: Angelico, 2021.

Forster, E. M. *Aspects of the Novel.* New York: Harcourt, Brace & World, 1927.

Friedman, Russell L. "Divergent Traditions in Later-Medieval Trinitarian Theology: Relations, Emanations, and the Use of Philosophical Psychology, 1250–1325." *Studia Theologica* 53 (1999): 13–25.

Funchion, John. *Novel Nostalgias: The Aesthetics of Antagonism in Nineteenth Century U.S. Literature*. Columbus, OH: Ohio State University Press, 2015.

Garvey, James. "Characterization in Narrative." *Poetics* 7 (1978): 63–78.

Göbbeler, Hans-Peter. *Existenz als Sendung: Zum Verständnis der Nachfolge Christi in der Theologie Hans Urs von Balthasars: unter besonderer Berücksightigung der Gestalt des Priestertums und von Ehe und Familie*. St. Ottilien: EOS-Verlag, 1997.

Graef, Hilda, and Thomas Thompson, S.M. *Mary: A History of Doctrine and Devotion*. Notre Dame, IN: Ave Maria Press, 2009.

Greiner, Maximilian. "The Community of St. John: A Conversation with Cornelia Capol and Martha Gisi." Translated by Michael Waldstein. In *Hans Urs von Balthasar: His Life and Work*, edited by David L. Schindler. San Francisco: Ignatius Press, 1991.

Gregory of Nyssa. *Gregor Von Nazianz: Orationes Theologicae—Theologische Reden*. Translated by Hermann Josef Sieben. Fontes Christiani. Freiburg im Breisgau: Herder, 1996.

———. *The Life of Saint Macrina*. Translated by Kevin Corrigan. Toronto: Peregrina, 1998.

Haight, Roger. *The Experience and Language of Grace*. New York: Paulist Press, 1979.

———. *Jesus Symbol of God*. Maryknoll, NY: Orbis Books, 2000.

Heller, Nathan. "Why Are So Many Americans Living by Themselves." *The New Yorker*, April 16, 2012 .

Henrici, Peter. "Hans Urs von Balthasar: A Sketch of His Life." Translated by John Saward. In *Hans Urs von Balthasar: His Life and Work*, edited by David L. Schindler, 7–43. San Francisco: Ignatius Press, 1991.

Hildebrand, Stephen. *The Trinitarian Theology of Basil of Caesarea: A Synthesis of Greek Thought and Biblical Truth*. Washington, D.C.: Catholic University of America Press, 2007.

Hinerman, Nate, and Matthew Lewis Sutton, editors. *On Suffering: An Inter-Disciplinary Dialogue on Narrative and the Meaning of Suffering*. Oxford: Inter-Disciplinary Press, 2012.

Hochman, Baruch. *Character in Literature*. Ithaca: Cornell University Press, 1985.

Hur, Ju. "A Dynamic Reading of the Holy Spirit in Luke-Acts." *Journal for the Study of the New Testament*, Supplement Series, 211. Sheffield, England: Sheffield Academic Press, 2001.

Ignatius of Loyola. *The Spiritual Exercises of St. Ignatius: Based on Studies in the Language of the Autograph*. Translated by Louis J. Puhl. Chicago: Loyola, 1951.

Ilibagiza, Immaculée. *Our Lady of Kibeho: Mary Speaks to the World from the Heart of Africa*. Carlsbad, CA: Hay House, 2008.

John Paul II. *Dives in misericordia*. Vatican: Libreria Editrice Vaticana, 1980.

——. "Message of Mary's Maternal Love." http://w2.vatican.va/content/john-paul-ii/it/homilies/1982/documents/hf_jp-ii_hom_19820513_fatima.html.

——. *Dominum et vivificantem*. Vatican: Libreria Editrice Vaticana, 1986.

——. *Man and Woman He Created Them: A Theology of the Body*. Translated by Michael Waldstein. New York: Pauline Books, 2006.

Jenkins, Philip. *The Next Christendom: The Coming of Global Christianity*. Third Edition. New York: Oxford University Press, 2011.

Johnson, Luke Timothy, and William Kurz. *The Future of Catholic Biblical Scholarship: A Constructive Conversation*. Grand Rapids, MI: Eerdmans, 2002.

Joncas, Jan Michael. "Image of the Invisible God: Visual Artworks as Theological Texts." *Logos* 7 (2004): 30–53.

Kant, Immanuel. *Religion within the Limits of Reason Alone*. Translated by Theodore M. Greene and Hoyt H. Hudson. New York: Harper, 1960.

——. *Conflict of the Faculties*. Translated by Mary J. Gregor. New York: Abrabis Books, 1979.

Keane, Kevin. "Why Creation? Bonaventure and Thomas Aquinas on God as Creative Good." *Downside Review* 93 (1975): 100–21.

Kilgannon, Corey. "Nestled in the Projects and Nourishing Souls." *New York Times*, Sep. 28, 2012.

Klinenberg, Eric. *Going Solo: The Extraordinary Rise and Surprising Appeal of Living Alone*. New York: Penguin, 2012.

Kowalska, Maria Faustina. *Diary: Divine Mercy in My Soul*. Stockbridge, MA: Marians of the Immaculate Conception, 2002.

Kristeva, Julia. *Strangers to Ourselves*. Translated by Leon S. Roudiez. New York: Columbia University Press, 1991.

Küng, Hans. *On Being Christian*. Translated by Edward Quinn. Garden City, NY: Doubleday, 1976.

Kurz, William. *Reading the Bible as God's Own Story: A Catholic Approach for Bringing Scripture to Life*. Ijamsville, MD: Word Among Us Press, 2007.

Laeuchli, Samuel. *Power and Sexuality: The Emergence of Canon Law at the Synod of Elvira*. Philadelphia: Temple University Press, 1974.

Lampe, G. W. H. "Christian Theology in the Patristic Period." In *A History of Christian Doctrine*, edited by Hubert Cunliffe-Jones. Edinburgh: T&T Clark, 1978.

Leo XIII. *Divinum illud munus*. Vatican: Libreria Editrice Vaticana, 1897.

Lewis, C. S. *Till We Have Faces: A Myth Retold*. New York: Mariner, 1984.

Lohfink, Gerhard. *Does God Need the Church?: Toward a Theology of the People of God*. Translated by Linda M. Maloney. Collegeville, MN: Liturgical Press, 1999.

———. *Jesus of Nazareth: What He Wanted, Who He Was.* Translated by Linda M. Maloney. Collegevill, MN: Liturgical Press, 2012.

Louth, Andrew. "St. Maximus the Confessor between East and West." *Studia Patristica* 32 (1997): 332–45.

———. "Apophatic Theology and the Liturgy in St. Maximos the Confessor." In *Wisdom of the Byzantine Church: Evagrios of Pontos and Maximos the Confessor; Four Lectures.* Edited by J. Raitt. Columbia, MO: Dept. of Religious Studies, University of Missouri, 1997.

———. "Postpatristic Byzantine Theologians." In *The Medieval Theologians.* Edited by G. R. Evans. Oxford: Blackwell Publishers, 2001.

Lubac, Henri de. *Medieval Exegesis: The Four Senses of Scripture.* Translated by Mark Sebanc. 4 vols. Grand Rapids, MI: Eerdmans, 1998.

Luckman, Harriet A. "Pneumatology and Asceticism in Basil of Caesarea: Roots and Influence to 381." Dissertation, Marquette University, 2001.

Mason, Daniel. *The Sabbath of History: William Congdon: With Meditations on Holy Week by Joseph Ratzinger.* New Haven: Knights of Columbus Museum, 2012.

Maximus. *The Church's Mystagogy: In Which Are Explained the Symbolism of Certain Rites Performed in the Divine Synaxis.* In *Maximus Confessor: Selected Writings.* Translated and edited by George Berthold. New York: Paulist Press, 1985.

McCormack, Bruce. *Karl Barth's Critically Realistic Dialectical Theology: Its Genesis and Development 1909–1936.* New York: Oxford University Press, 1995.

McGuckin, John Anthony. "The Vision of God in St. Gregory Nazianzen." *Studia Patristica* 32 (1992): 145–52.

McIntosh, Mark A. *Christology from Within: Spirituality and the Incarnation in Hans Urs von Balthasar.* South Bend, IN: University of Notre Dame Press, 1996.

McLynn, Neil. "A Self-Made Holy Man: The Case of Gregory Nazianzen." *Journal of Early Christian Studies* 6 (1998): 463–83.

Meredith, Anthony. "The Pneumatology of the Cappadocian Fathers and the Creed of Constantinople." *Irish Theological Quarterly* 48 (1981): 196–211.

Merton, Thomas. *The Seven Storey Mountain: An Autobiography of Faith.* New York: Harvest, 1948.

Molnar, Paul. *Incarnation and Resurrection: Toward a Contemporary Understanding.* Grand Rapids, MI: Eerdmans, 2007.

———. *Thomas F. Torrance: Theologian of the Trinity.* Surrey, England: Ashgate, 2009.

Moore, Stephen D. "Afterword: Things Not Written in This Book." In *Anatomies of Narrative Criticism: The Past, Present, and Futures of the Fourth Gospel as Literature.* Edited by Tom Thatcher and Stephen D. Moore. Atlanta: Society of Biblical Literature, 2008.

Nichols, Robert L. "The Friends of God: Nicholas II and Alexandra at the Canonization of Serafim of Sarov, July 1903." In *Religious and Secular Forces in Late Tsarist Russia: Essays in Honor of Donald W. Treadgold*, edited by Charles E. Timberlake, 207–29. Seattle: University of Washington Press, 1992.

Norris, Frederick. *Faith Gives Fullness to Reasoning: The Five Theological Orations of Gregory Nazianzen*. Translated by Lionel Wickham and Frederick Williams. Vol. 13 of *Supplements to Vigiliae Christianae*. Leiden, Netherlands: E. J. Brill, 1991.

——. "Gregory the Theologian." *Pro Ecclesia* 2 (1993): 473–84.

Novatian. "De Spectaculis." In *The Trinity, The Spectacles, Jewish Foods, In Praise of Purity, Letters*. Translated by Russell J. DeSimone. *The Fathers of the Church*. Washington D.C.: Catholic University of America, 1974.

O'Donnell, Hugh. *Vincent De Paul: His Life and Way*. New York: Paulist Press, 1995.

O'Regan, Cyril. "Von Balthasar and Thick Retrieval: Post-Chalcedonian Symphonic Theology." *Gregorianum* 77 (1996): 227–60.

Oakes, Edward T. *Pattern of Redemption: The Theology of Hans Urs von Balthasar*. New York: Continuum, 1994.

Origen. *On First Principles*. Notre Dame, IN: Ave Maria Press, 2013.

Pelikan, Jaroslav. *Jesus through the Centuries: His Place in the History of Culture*. New Haven, CT: Yale University Press, 1985.

——. "Introduction." In *Maximus Confessor: Selected Writings*. New York: Paulist, 1985.

——. *Whose Bible Is It? A Short History of the Scriptures*. New York: Penguin, 2005.

Pius XII. *Mystici corporis*. Vatican: Libreria Editrice Vaticana, 1943.

Powell, Mark Allen. *What Is Narrative Criticism?* Minneapolis: Fortress Press, 1990.

Putnam, R. D. *Bowling Alone: The Collapse and Revival of American Community*. New York: Simon & Schuster, 2000.

Rahner, Karl. *The Trinity*. Translated by Joseph Donceel. New York: Crossroad, 1997.

Ramos, Alice. *Dynamic Transcendentals: Truth, Goodness, and Beauty from a Thomistic Perspective*. Washington, D.C.: Catholic University of America Press, 2012.

Ratzinger, Joseph. "Communion: Eucharist—Fellowship—Mission." Translated by Henry Taylor. In *Pilgrim Fellowship of Faith*. Edited by Stephan Otto Horn and Vinzenz Pfnür. San Francisco: Ignatius Press, 2005.

Rimmon-Kenan, Shlomith. *Narrative Fiction: Contemporary Poetics*. London: Routledge, 1983.

Rousseau, Philip. *Basil of Caesarea*. Berkeley: University of California Press, 1995.

Rutledge, Denys. *Cosmic Theology: The Ecclesiastical Hierarchy of Pseudo-Denys: An Introduction.* Staten Island: Alba House, 1964.

Saward, John. *The Mysteries of March: Hans Urs von Balthasar on the Incarnation and Easter.* New York: HarperCollins, 1990.

Schneiders, Sandra M. "Scripture and Spirituality." In *Christian Spirituality: Origins to the Twelfth Century.* Edited by Bernard McGinn and John Meyendorff. New York: Crossroad, 1985.

Schmemann, Alexander. *The Journals of Father Alexander Schmemann 1973-1983.* Crestwood, NY: St. Vladimir's Seminary Press, 2002.

Schmidt, William. "The Sacrament of Confession as Sequela Christi in the Writings of Adrienne von Speyr." Dissertation, Lateran Pontifical University, John Paul II Institute of Studies on Marriage and Family, 1999.

Schumacher, Michele M. "Ecclesial Existence: Person and Community in the Trinitarian Anthropology of Adrienne von Speyr." *Modern Theology* 24 (2008): 359-85.

———. *A Trinitarian Anthropology: Adrienne von Speyr and Hans Urs von Balthasar in Dialogue with Thomas Aquinas.* Washington, D.C.: Catholic University of America Press, 2014.

Seraphim of Sarov. "A Conversation of St. Seraphim of Sarov with Nicholas Motovilov Concerning the Aim of the Christian Life." In *A Treasury of Russian Spirituality.* Edited by G.P. Fedotov. New York: Sheed and Ward, 1948.

Shepherd Jr., William H. "The Narrative Function of the Holy Spirit as a Character in Luke-Acts." *Society of Biblical Literature Dissertation Series,* 147. Atlanta: Scholars Press, 1994.

Smith, Timothy. *Thomas Aquinas' Trinitarian Theology: A Study in Theological Method.* Washington, D.C.: Catholic University of America Press, 2010.

Speyr, Adrienne von. *Das Angesicht des Vaters.* Freiburg: Johannes Verlag Einsiedeln, 1955.

———. *Die Beichte.* Freiburg: Johannes Verlag Einsiedeln, 1960.

———. *Die Nachlasswerke.* 12 vols. Freiburg: Johannes Verlag Einsiedeln, 1966-1975.

———. *The Cross: Word and Sacrament.* Translated by Graham Harrison. San Francisco: Ignatius Press, 1983.

———. *The Gates of Eternal Life.* Translated by Corona Sharp. San Francisco: Ignatius Press, 1983.

———. *Handmaid of the Lord.* Translated by E.A. Nelson. Second edition. San Francisco: Ignatius Press, 1984.

———. *The World of Prayer.* Translated by Graham Harrison. San Francisco: Ignatius Press, 1985.

———. *They Followed His Call: Vocation and Asceticism.* Translated by Erasmo Leiva-Merikakis. San Francisco: Ignatius Press, 1986.

——. *Three Women and the Lord*. Translated by Graham Harrison. San Francisco: Ignatius Press, 1986.

——. *The Christian State of Life*. Translated by Mary Frances McCarthy. San Francisco: Ignatius Press, 1986.

——. *The Mystery of Death*. Translated by Graham Harrison. San Francisco: Ignatius Press, 1988.

——. *Elijah*. Translated by Brian McNeil. San Francisco: Ignatius Press, 1990.

——. *The Victory of Love: Meditation on Romans 8*. Translated by Lucia Wiedenhöver. San Francisco: Ignatius Press, 1990.

——. *John*. Translated by Alexander Dru, Lucia Wiedenhöver, E.A. Nelson, David Kipp, and Brian McNeil. Four volumes. San Francisco: Ignatius Press, 1994.

——. *My Early Years*. Translated by Mary Emily Hamilton and Dennis Martin. San Francisco: Ignatius Press, 1995.

——. *With God and with Men: Prayers*. Translated by Adrian Walker. San Francisco: Ignatius Press, 1995.

——. *The Letter to the Ephesians*. Translated by Adrian Walker. San Francisco: Ignatius Press, 1996.

——. *The Mission of the Prophets*. Translated by David Kipp. San Francisco: Ignatius Press, 1996.

——. *The Countenance of the Father*. Translated by David Kipp. San Francisco: Ignatius Press, 1997.

——. *The Letter to the Colossians*. Translated by Michael Miller. San Francisco: Ignatius Press, 1998.

——. *The Passion from Within*. Translated by Lucia Wiedenhöver. San Francisco: Ignatius Press, 1998.

——. *The Holy Mass*. Translated by Helena M. Saward. San Francisco: Ignatius Press, 1999.

——. *Mary in the Redemption*. Translated by Helena M. Tomko. San Francisco: Ignatius Press, 2003.

——. *The Boundless God*. Translated by Helena M. Tomko. San Francisco: Ignatius Press, 2004.

——. *Light and Images: Elements of Contemplation*. Translated by David Schindler, Jr. San Francisco: Ignatius Press, 2004.

——. *To the Heart of the Mystery of Redemption*. Second edition. San Francisco: Ignatius Press, 2005.

——. *Book of All Saints: Part One*. Translated by D.C. Schindler. San Francisco: Ignatius Press, 2008.

——. *Lumina and New Lumina*. Translated by Adrian Walker. San Francisco: Ignatius Press, 2008.

——. *Mark: Meditations on the Gospel of Mark*. Translated by Michelle K. Borras. San Francisco: Ignatius Press, 2012.

———. *Confession.* Translated by Douglas W. Stott. Second edition. San Francisco: Ignatius Press, 2017.

Stead, Julian. *The Church, the Liturgy and the Soul of Man: The* Mystagogia *of St. Maximus the Confessor.* Still River, MA: St. Bede's Publications, 1982.

Steiner, George. *Real Presences.* Chicago: University of Chicago Press, 1989.

Sutton, Matthew Lewis. "Mysterium Christi: The Christologies of Maurice De La Taille and Karl Rahner." *International Journal of Systematic Theology* 10, no. 4 (2008): 416–30.

———. "A Compelling Trinitarian Taxonomy: Hans Urs von Balthasar's Theology of the Trinitarian Inversion and Reversion." *International Journal of Systematic Theology* 14, no. 2 (2012): 161–76.

———. "Hans Urs von Balthasar and Adrienne von Speyr's Ecclesial Relationship." *New Blackfriars* 94 (2013): 50–63.

———. *Heaven Opens: The Trinitarian Mysticism of Adrienne von Speyr.* Minneapolis, MN: Fortress Press, 2014.

Sutton, Matthew Lewis, and William L. Portier, editors. *Handing on the Faith.* Maryknoll, NY: Orbis Books, 2014.

Tavernise, Sabrina. "U.S. Suicide Rate Surges to a 30-Year High." *New York Times,* April 22, 2016.

Teresa of Avila. "Book of Her Life." Translated by Kieran Kavanaugh and Otilio Rodriguez. In *The Collected Works of St. Teresa of Avila,* Volume 1. Washington, D.C.: ICS Publications, 1976.

Thérèse of Lisieux. *Story of a Soul: The Autobiography of St. Thérèse of Lisieux.* Translated by John Clarke. Washington, DC: ICS Publications, 1996.

Tertullian. "De Spectaculis." Translated by T.R. Glover. In *Apology, De Spectaculis.* Cambridge, MA: Harvard University Press, 1931.

Teske, Roland J. *Paradoxes of Time in Saint Augustine.* Milwaukee: Marquette University Press, 1996.

Tracy, David. "The Hidden God: The Divine Other of Liberation." *Cross Currents* 46 (1996): 5–7.

Turkle, Sherry. *Alone Together: Why We Expect More from Technology and Less from Each Other.* New York: Basic Books, 2011.

Underhill, Evelyn. *The Mystics of the Church.* Cambridge: J. Clarke & Co, 1925.

United States Conference of Catholic Bishops. *Roman Missal.* Washington D.C.: USCCB, 2011.

Ware, Kallistos. "The Spiritual Father in Orthodox Christianity." *Cross Currents* 24 (1974): 296–313.

Warth, Robert D. "Before Rasputin: Piety and the Occult at the Court of Nicholas II." *The Historian* 47 (1985): 323–37.

Weigel, George. *Witness to Hope: The Biography of Pope John Paul II.* New York: HarperCollins, 1999.

West, Marian. "You'll Never Walk Alone." https://web.archive.org/web/20190609085829/ http://landofcompassion.com/2012/03/16/

youll-never-walk-alone/

Yamamura, Kei. "The Development of the Doctrine of the Holy Spirit in Patristic Philosophy: St. Basil and St. Gregory of Nyssa." *St. Vladimir's Theological Quarterly* 18 (1971): 3–21.

Zizioulas, Jean. *Being as Communion: Studies in Personhood and the Church.* Crestwood, NY: St. Vladimir's Seminary Press, 1985.